A Simple Chess Opening Repertoire for White

Sam Collins

First published in the UK by Gambit Publications Ltd 2016

ISBN-13: 978-1-910093-82-5
ISBN-10: 1-910093-82-3

DISTRIBUTION:
Worldwide (except USA): Central Books Ltd, 99 Wallis Rd, London E9 5LN, England. Tel +44 (0)20 8986 4854 Fax +44 (0)20 8533 5821.
E-mail: orders@Centralbooks.com

Gambit Publications Ltd, 99 Wallis Rd, London E9 5LN, England.
E-mail: info@gambitbooks.com
Website (regularly updated): www.gambitbooks.com

Edited by Graham Burgess
Typeset by Petra Nunn
Cover image by Wolff Morrow
Printed in the USA by Bang Printing, Brainerd, Minnesota

10 9 8 7 6 5 4 3 2 1

Gambit Publications Ltd
Directors: Dr John Nunn GM, Murray Chandler GM, and Graham Burgess FM
German Editor: Petra Nunn WFM

Contents

Symbols

+	check
++	double check
x	captures
#	checkmate
!!	brilliant move
!	good move
!?	interesting move
?!	dubious move
?	bad move
??	blunder
0-0	castles kingside
0-0-0	castles queenside
+−	winning position for White
±	large advantage for White
⩲	slight advantage for White
=	equal position
∓	slight advantage for Black
∓	large advantage for Black
−+	winning position for Black
1-0	The game ends in a win for White
½-½	The game ends in a draw
0-1	The game ends in a win for Black
Ch	Championship
(*n*)	*n*th match game
(D)	see next diagram

Bibliography

Websites
chess24.com
chessbase.com
chesspublishing.com
davidsmerdon.com
youtube.com

Magazines
New in Chess
Chess Today

Books
J.Aagaard & N.Ntirlis, *Playing the French* (Quality Chess, 2013)
V.Bologan, *Bologan's Black Weapons* (New in Chess, 2014)
L.D'Costa, *The Panov-Botvinnik Attack Move by Move* (Everyman, 2014)
J.Emms, *Attacking with 1 e4* (Everyman, 2001)
M.Flores Rios, *Chess Structures: A Grandmaster Guide* (Quality Chess, 2015)
P.Negi, *Grandmaster Repertoire: 1 e4 vs The French, Caro-Kann & Philidor*
    (Quality Chess, 2014)
N.Vitiugov, *The French Defence: A Complete Black Repertoire*
    (Chess Stars, 2010)
D.Evseev, *Fighting the French: A New Concept* (Chess Stars, 2011)

Databases
Mega Database 2015 (ChessBase)

Engines
Houdini 3
Rybka 3
Komodo 9
Stockfish 7

Introduction

Choosing an opening repertoire (with either colour) is one of the most important decisions a player can make. When players start out, they tend to select trappy variations (of the 1 e4 e5 2 ♕h5 ♘c6 3 ♗c4 ♘f6?? 4 ♕xf7# variety), which tend to be discarded later.

As players gain more experience, the path splits somewhat. Often a choice will be made based on whether a line has a lot of theory (and, hence, requires a lot of time to learn) or is more of a sideline. Some players model their opening repertoires on their favourite players, which is quite a reasonable approach.

In my view, the best way to pick an opening is to think carefully about the typical middlegame positions (and, in particular, the typical structures) to which it leads. Since all mainstream openings are perfectly playable, by picking an opening you are really selecting a position after 10-15 moves which you need to be comfortable playing. For example, if you treasure space, then the Pirc (1 e4 d6 2 d4 ♘f6 3 ♘c3 g6) and the Modern (1 e4 g6) defences are obviously unsuitable, since Black immediately cedes central space to White.

The white repertoire I present in this book is aimed, in so far as reasonable, for a particular pawn-structure, namely the Isolated Queen's Pawn ('IQP'), together with the related structures of the Isolated Pawn Couple and Hanging Pawns. Of course White can't force Black into an IQP structure in every line. And in some lines, it isn't possible to obtain a decent version of the IQP (as we shall see, when the side with an IQP goes wrong, they can often be seriously worse). But the strong preference, throughout this repertoire, is for this structure.

This decision has been made for a number of reasons:

1. This group of related structures are amongst the most important in chess, since they arise from a wide range of openings. To mention just some of the most common (which are outside the present repertoire), IQP positions commonly arise from the Nimzo-Indian, Queen's Gambit Accepted, Slav, Queen's Gambit Declined and Tarrasch Defences, and the English Opening. Accordingly, rather than gaining experience in positions which will be useless as you progress to higher levels, experience with the IQP will serve you well at all stages of your chess career.

2. IQP positions promise rich chances for both sides. As we shall see, having an IQP gives a player more space and (typically) some initiative, while playing

against it offers a solid position with no weaknesses and, ultimately, a pleasant endgame. While there are some balanced positions in chess which you might not like to play with either colour (like the sharp positions with castling on opposite sides which arise in the main lines of the Najdorf or the Dragon, or the dry positions of the Exchange Variations of the French and Slav defences), IQP positions offer something for everyone. In addition, if you decide to play against the IQP in some openings, your experience with this repertoire should prove valuable since you will know the ideas you need to defend against.

3. Because they can arise so often (see point 1) and have their own attractions for Black (see point 2), IQP positions can be reached in a significant percentage of your games. Even when they arise from diverse openings, the same plans and themes apply, and sometimes a direct transposition to another opening is possible. Accordingly, it is possible to gain substantial experience in these positions quite rapidly, and this will make you all the more effective in handling them.

All lines in this repertoire feature the same basic philosophy of quick, active development and central control. It is largely based on my own repertoire and is quite sound, if not the most popular or theoretical repertoire available. I hope you enjoy the lines, and wish you every success in your own games.

Sam Collins
Dublin, April 2016

1 Introducing the IQP

To get things started, I have annotated some model IQP games. As emphasized in the Introduction, this is a structure of enormous richness and complexity and players should seek to continue learning about it throughout their chess careers. Both Alex Baburin and Ivan Sokolov have written outstanding books on the IQP and they are highly recommended reading for ambitious players.

Game 1
Ding Liren – Lu Shanglei
Danzhou 2015

I glanced at this game online at various intervals as it was played. The position after White's 17th move didn't make a huge impression on me – I thought it was equal, or marginally better for White. I was surprised to see the game end three moves later! This is a fantastic demonstration of the power that the d5 break can unleash in White's pieces. While White in this game is well known (not least for his fantastic performances in Olympiads and top tournaments like Wijk aan Zee, and as one of the world's top players, rated 2749 at the time of this game), it should be noted that Black is a 2595 GM.

1 d4 d5 2 c4 e6 3 ♘c3 ♘f6 4 ♗g5 dxc4

Not a line I was particularly familiar with, but one which Lu Shanglei has essayed on several occasions. We soon enter IQP channels.

5 e3 a6 6 a4

Lu's previous opponents played 6 ♗xc4, but after 6...b5 Black obtained reasonable counterplay.

6...h6

Black has tried various moves in this position. My preference is for straightforward play in the centre with 6...c5.

7 ♗h4 (D)

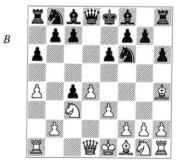

7...b6?!

This seems to be too ambitious. I much prefer the following development: 7...c5 8 ♗xc4 (White can take on c5 here or on the next move, but the resulting position looks close to equal) 8...♘c6 9 ♘f3 cxd4 10 exd4 (the first IQP of the book appears!) 10...♗e7 11 0-0 0-0 12 ♖e1. Here Black uses a development which was introduced by (or at least associated with) the first World Champion, Wilhelm Steinitz: 12...♗d7!? 13 ♘e5 (perhaps White should play for equality with 13 ♗xf6 ♗xf6 14 d5 exd5 15 ♘xd5 =) 13...♖c8 14 ♗b3 ♗e8! with a very solid position in D.Martinez-Sulava, Toscolano 1997.

8 ♗xc4 ♗b7 9 ♘f3 c5

The computer suggests that this move may be rather inaccurate since White could reply 10 ♗xf6 followed by d5 to good effect. But our principal interest in this game is in the IQP position that soon arises.

10 0-0 cxd4

Black elects to go into an IQP position, which is a risky decision. The following factors might have led to a more conservative move:

1. White is substantially ahead in development. All of his minor pieces are active and he has already castled.

2. Black has some weaknesses compared to a standard IQP – in particular, he has already committed to ...h6. This move can be useful but can also prove compromising, for instance by making sacrifices on e6 more attractive since the light squares around Black's king will be compromised.

However, it is not clear that Black had any good way to avoid the IQP. White can meet 10...♘c6 by 11 ♕e2!, when 11...cxd4 (otherwise White will

put a rook on d1 anyway, when the black queen could run short of squares after dxc5) 12 ♖ad1 ♗e7 13 exd4 0-0 transposes to the game.

11 exd4 ♗e7 (D)

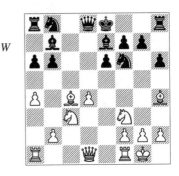

According to my database, this is already a new position! However, it seems like a very typical IQP battle.

12 ♕e2

Ding adopts a straightforward plan of bringing his rooks to the centre.

12...0-0 13 ♖ad1 ♘c6

I'm not sure about the merits of this development. 13...♘bd7 looks more compact, though Black struggles to free himself after 14 ♖fe1.

14 ♖fe1!

Calmly building his position. 14 ♗xe6!? is a typical sacrifice which was already possible here: 14...fxe6 15 ♕xe6+ ♖f7 (15...♔h7 or 15...♔h8 also drops material to 16 d5 when, if the knight moves, 17 d6 will catch the bishop on e7) 16 d5. Now if the knight moves, White has 17 ♘e5, when he will gain (at least) a rook and two pawns for two pieces, plus a strong initiative. Accordingly Black's best try is 16...♘xd5! 17 ♖xd5 ♕c8 18 ♕xc8+ ♖xc8 19 ♗xe7 ♘xe7 20 ♖d6 ♗xf3 21 gxf3 ♖b8 with good drawing chances since White's extra pawn isn't particularly felt.

We now return to 14 ♖fe1! *(D)*:

14...♘d5

It is possible that Black had intended 14...♘b4. If this knight reaches d5, Black's position will be considerably more secure. However, 15 d5! +− lands with decisive effect. Then Black loses material in all lines; for instance, 15...♘bxd5 16 ♘xd5 ♗xd5 17 ♗xd5 ♘xd5 18 ♗xe7 ♕xe7 19 ♖xd5 and White is a piece up.

14...♖e8 is directed against 15 d5, but White has other opportunities to exploit his perfect mobilization; for instance, 15 ♗xe6! (sharper than 15 ♘e5, which also leads to some advantage) 15...♗d6 (15...fxe6 16 ♕xe6+ is even better for White than the variation given in the note to his 14th move) 16 ♗xf7+! ♔xf7 17 ♕c4+ ♔f8 18 ♘e5 ±. White already has two pawns for the piece and a raging attack.

15 ♗xd5!

15 ♘xd5 gives nothing special after 15...♗xh4 =.

15...♗xh4 16 ♗e4 *(D)*

Black now has a move to prepare for d5, but nothing satisfactory is available.

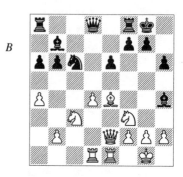

16...♖e8?

16...♗f6 is relatively best, but after 17 d5 exd5 18 ♘xd5! (here 18 ♖xd5 is less effective after 18...♕c7) 18...♖e8 19 ♕e3 ± Black is struggling to cover his weaknesses. The b6-pawn is particularly vulnerable.

17 d5! +−

Winning!

17...exd5 18 ♖xd5 ♕e7

After 18...♕f6 19 g3 ♗g5 20 h4 the bishop is trapped.

19 ♕d2 ♕f6 20 ♖d7! 1-0

A crisp finish. There is no way to deal with the threats (including ♖xb7 and ♘d5).

Game 2
Zviagintsev – R. Vasquez
Khanty-Mansiisk rapid 2013

1 c4 c6 2 e4

While IQP positions can arise from a range of openings, this is obviously one of the simplest direct transpositions to our proposed repertoire (which would have arisen after 1 e4 c6 2 c4).

2...d5 3 exd5 ♘f6 4 ♘c3 cxd5 5 cxd5 ♘xd5 6 ♘f3 e6 7 ♗c4 ♘c6 8 0-0 ♗e7 9 d4 0-0 10 ♖e1 ♘f6 11 a3 a6 12 ♗a2 *(D)*

12...b5?

A very common mistake, which has been played by several GMs. Flores Rios recommends 12...♕c7 13 ♗e3 ♖d8 14 ♕c2 followed by ♖ad1, limiting White to a slight advantage.

13 d5! exd5 14 ♘xd5 ♘xd5 15 ♕xd5!

The key move, since Black can't trade queens.

15...♗b7

15...♕xd5?? 16 ♗xd5 drops a piece.

16 ♕h5 ♕c7

Or:

a) Khenkin gives 16...g6 17 ♕h6 ♘d4 18 ♘g5 ♗xg5 19 ♗xg5 ♕b6 20 ♖ad1 ±.

b) 16...♕d6 ('?!' – Khenkin) 17 ♗g5 ♖ad8 18 ♗xe7 (following 18 h4?!

h6 Black had almost equalized and even went on to win in Razuvaev-Haba, Bundesliga 1990/1) 18...♘xe7 19 ♘g5 ♕g6 *(D)*.

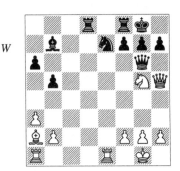

Now several GMs (including Aagaard, Benjamin and Gritsak) have been successful in the pawn-up endgame starting with 20 ♕xh7+, but the most incisive is 20 ♕xg6! ♘xg6 21 ♘xf7! (21 ♖ad1?! ♘e5 22 ♖xd8 ♖xd8 23 f4 ♘c4 24 ♗xc4 bxc4 25 ♘e4 ♗xe4 26 ♖xe4 was agreed drawn in Arlandi-Magem, European Team Ch, Batumi 1999) and now:

b1) 21...♖d2?! 22 ♖ed1! +− (really impressive precision by White, keeping the a2-bishop defended) 22...♖xb2 (after 22...♖xd1+ 23 ♖xd1 ♗c8 Khenkin gives 24 f3 as winning, though White has many other wins at this point, being a pawn up with a dominant position) 23 ♘d6+ ♔h8 24 ♘xb7 ♖fxf2 25 ♖d8+ ♘f8 26 ♗d5 g5 27 ♘c5 ♖bd2 28 ♘e6 ♖f5 29 ♖f1 1-0 Khenkin-V.Bagirov, Münster 1997. Admittedly inferior play by Black, but even so a very powerful display by Khenkin.

b2) Khenkin modestly assesses the line 21...♖xf7 22 ♖ad1 ♖xd1 23 ♖xd1 ♗c6 24 ♖d6 ♗e8 25 ♖xa6 ♔f8 26 ♗xf7 as ±. It will certainly be tough for Black to hold this endgame.

We now return to 16...♕c7 *(D)*:

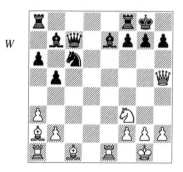

17 ♗g5!

17 ♘g5 is also strong; for instance, 17...♗xg5 18 ♗xg5 ♖ae8 and now Flores Rios suggests 19 ♗d2! ±, when the dark-squared bishop will be extremely strong on the long diagonal. Instead White gradually let his advantage slip after 19 ♖ad1 in de Toledo-Lima, Santos 2001.

17...♗xg5 18 ♘xg5 h6 19 ♖e3!

The rook-lift on the third rank is one of the characteristic manoeuvres in IQP positions, and here it works to perfection.

19...♘a5?

The final mistake, allowing a sweet finish. Flores Rios gives 19...♘e5 as the last chance, when White is a pawn up with an attack after 20 ♘e6! fxe6 21 ♖xe5 ±.

20 ♕g6!!

Beautifully played.

20...hxg5 21 ♖h3 ♖fc8

Flores Rios notes that 21...♖fe8 leads to mate after 22 ♖h7! ♕e5 23 ♕xf7+ ♔xh7 24 ♕h5#.

22 ♖e1!

Bringing in the last piece and cutting off the black king's escape-route.

1-0

Game 3
S.B. Hansen – Chuchelov
Bundesliga 2005/6

Apologies in advance for the depth of annotations to this game, but it is one of the most important for our repertoire. This is for two reasons. First, it is an outstanding illustration of the d5 break when used to generate slight positional pressure (rather than an immediate tactical breakthrough). Secondly, the position after move 11 is a very important one for our repertoire, since it can arise from several move-orders and Black can steer the game into this position. I believe the position is very promising for White but he needs to be accurate and Black has scored his share of wins here too.

1 e4 c5 2 ♘f3 ♘c6 3 c3

This is a common move-order to reach the c3 Sicilian. 2...♘c6 is a commitment which cuts out a few of Black's main systems, and this encourages White to change direction. Of course, nothing comes for free, and if you play 2 ♘f3 (as opposed to the immediate 2 c3) you have to be ready for many other moves, most importantly 2...d6, when there is no good way to get back to the c3 Sicilian since 3 c3 ♘f6!, while a playable line for both sides, leads to completely different positions.

3...d5 4 exd5 ♕xd5 5 d4 *(D)*

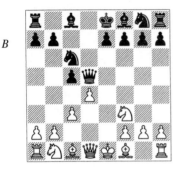

5...e6

Black can play 5...♘f6 followed by 6...e6 or use the move-order in the game. I'm not aware of a major difference between the two move-orders and they normally transpose.

6 ♗e3

With the knight on c6, I think this is a good move. As we shall see in Chapter 3 (Game 19 to be precise), in the analogous position with a knight on f6 (and no knight on c6) 6 ♗e3 used to be a very popular move to reach the position which arises in the game. However, Black then realized he had some good options, including 6...cxd4 7 cxd4 ♗b4+ 8 ♘c3 b6 (or 8...♗d7) followed by taking on c3 and trading bishops with ...♗a6 (or ...♗b5), or simply playing 6...♗e7, when the capture on c5 gives Black reasonable compensation in the endgame. However, with the knight already on c6, the plan

based on exchanging light-squared bishops is ruled out.

6...cxd4

6...♘f6 challenges White's commitment to taking on c5. Here 7 ♗e2 is popular (and White often continues to refrain from taking on c5 when Black refuses to play 7...cxd4). However, this is a slight concession compared to the main line, since White would prefer his bishop to be more actively placed on d3. Here I would recommend going for 7 dxc5 ♕xd1+ (the significance of ♗e3 is that 7...♗xc5?? drops a piece to 8 ♕xd5 exd5 9 ♗xc5) 8 ♔xd1 ♘g4 9 b4 *(D)*.

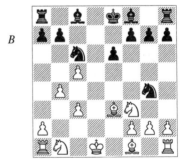

This is a position where computer engines tend to feel Black is fine (showing how far they have come, since Black is a pawn down for unclear-looking compensation!), but I think White's game is easier to play. A few examples:

a) 9...a5 10 ♗b5 and then:

a1) 10...♘xe3+ 11 fxe3 ♗d7 was played in Pavasović-Podlesnik, Slovenian Ch, Dobrna 2002, and now White played a typical consolidating manoeuvre which is well worth bearing in mind: 12 a3 ♗e7 13 ♖a2!. Black can't go for 13...axb4 14 cxb4 ♘xb4?? since White wins material by 15 ♗xd7+ ♔xd7 16 ♖d2+ ♘d5 17 e4. Accordingly he simply has to play for positional compensation. While the engines may well feel Black is still OK, I like White's position, since his extra pawn forms part of an extremely strong queenside pawn-chain that restricts the black pieces.

a2) 10...♗d7 11 ♘d4 ♘xd4 (the alternative 11...axb4 might be a better try, when 12 ♗xc6 ♗xc6 13 ♘xc6 b3! 14 ♘d2 b2 15 ♖b1 bxc6 leads to unclear play) 12 ♗xd7+ ♔xd7 13 ♗xd4 with the better game for White in Greet-Plaskett, Southend 2007.

b) 9...♘xe3+ 10 fxe3 g6 was played in a recent game between two 2400-rated players. 11 ♘d4 ♗d7 12 ♗b5 a5 13 ♗xc6 (this exchange is necessary at some point to reduce the pressure on the b4-pawn, which can't simply be held with a3 due to the pin down the a-file; generally speaking, the alternative is to push forward with b5, which has its attractions but makes it much easier for Black to win his pawn back since c5 becomes extremely weak) 13...♗xc6 14 ♘xc6 bxc6 15 a3! (White uses a mechanism we saw in Pavasović-Podlesnik in line 'a1' above) 15...♗g7 16 ♖a2! ♔e7 17 ♖d2 ♗e5 18 ♔e2, Bortnyk-Nedilko, Lutsk 2015. Black definitely has some compensation, but White has started to consolidate. He went on to win.

7 cxd4 ♘f6 8 ♘c3 *(D)*

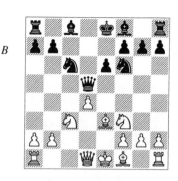

Black now has a choice of ways to meet the attack on his queen.

8...♕d6

This is by far the most popular move in this position. Generally speaking, d6 is a good square for the queen, since it is relatively active, off the back rank (so the rooks can be easily connected and come to the e- and d-files), and can retreat to b8 (once the queen's rook is developed) where it is out of harm's way. Other options:

a) 8...♗b4 develops a piece while dealing with the threat to the queen, but Black will ultimately have to lose time with the queen and/or the bishop (or take on c3, which will lead to a promising position for White with the Isolated Pawn Couple on c3 and d4). 9 ♕c2 0-0 10 ♗e2 ♕d8 11 0-0 ♗e7 12 a3 was a normal IQP position in Tkachev-Hulak, Croatian Team Ch, Rabac 2003.

b) 8...♕a5 looks tempting, keeping the queen active on the fifth rank. 9 a3 ♘d5 10 ♗d2 ♗e7 11 ♗d3 0-0 12 0-0 ♖d8 was Haznedaroglu-Fedorchuk, Kolkata 2014. Now White can exploit the position of the queen on a5 with

13 b4! ♘xc3 14 ♗xc3 ♕h5 15 b5 ♘b8 ±. Black has been pushed back and White's space advantage and initiative are substantial. The game might continue 16 ♗a5 ♖e8 (16...b6 17 ♗e4 collects the exchange) 17 ♖e1 ♘d7 18 ♕b3, when it is unclear how Black can complete his development, since 18...b6 19 ♗e4 ♖b8 20 ♗d2 leaves him with a chronic weakness on c6.

c) 8...♕d8 looks passive but was played by Nakamura and so is likely to become more popular. White has several promising set-ups but after 9 a3 (covering b4, in particular with a view to preventing ...♘b4-d5) 9...♗e7 10 ♗c4 0-0 11 0-0 *(D)* I prefer White's chances:

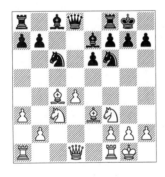

B

c1) 11...b6 12 ♕d3 ♗b7 13 ♗a2 ♘b8 (starting an interesting regrouping that doesn't quite equalize; Black doesn't have any easy answers here, while White can simply bring his rooks to d1 and e1 before looking for a breakthrough in the centre) 14 ♖fd1 (dealing with the incidental threat of 14...♗a6, which can now be easily met by moving the queen) 14...♘bd7

15 d5!? (White could also simply continue improve his position, but he is well placed for opening the centre) 15...exd5 was played in Gormally-Bosker, Groningen 2012. Now I like the simple 16 ♘xd5; for example, 16...♘xd5 17 ♗xd5 ♗xd5 18 ♕xd5. No easy path to equality is available for Black here, because 18...♘c5 19 ♕h5 leaves White with annoying pressure.

c2) 11...a6 12 d5 exd5 13 ♘xd5 ♘xd5 14 ♗xd5 ♗e6 15 ♗xe6 fxe6 gave White an enduring advantage based on his better structure in Solozhenkin-A.Vovk, Vaujany 2013.

9 ♗d3 ♗e7 10 0-0 0-0 *(D)*

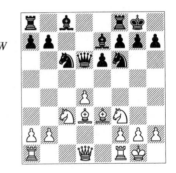

W

This is a highly typical IQP position. Black intends to complete his development – the bishop can go to b7 (after ...b6 or ...a6 and ...b5) or, perhaps, to d7 and e8 (once the king's rook is developed – the First World Champion Wilhelm Steinitz was particularly fond of this method of development) and the rooks can find useful work on the c-, d- and e-files. Black can also consider the manoeuvre ...♘b4-d5 to solidly blockade the d4-pawn (using the other knight on d5 would weaken the king's defences).

White has a number of ways to set up his game here. While play on the queenside was common during the early days of the development of IQP theory (for instance, Botvinnik played many model games with this plan), direct play in the centre and on the kingside is more to modern tastes.

11 a3!

I really like this move, which takes the b4-square under control and so prevents the ...♘b4-d5 manoeuvre while allowing White to consider a highly aggressive set-up with ♗c2 and ♕d3, aiming at the black kingside.

11...b6

Aiming to develop the bishop to b7. Black can also play for an extended fianchetto with 11...a6, intending to put his pawn on b5. White continues 12 ♕e2 and now Black has a number of options:

a) 12...♖d8 was convincingly dealt with in a couple of games by c3 Sicilian expert GM Duško Pavasović. 13 ♖ad1 *(D)* and then:

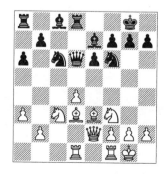

a1) After 13...♗d7 14 ♖fe1 ♕c7 15 ♗g5 ♗e8 16 ♗b1 h6 17 ♗h4 the danger for Black inherent in these positions is well illustrated by the following game: 17...♘d5? (other moves were preferable, but White retains a promising position regardless) 18 ♕c2 g6 19 ♘xd5 ♖xd5 (after 19...exd5? 20 ♖xe7 White wins a whole piece thanks to the pin on the c-file) 20 ♗xe7 ♕xe7. It looks like Black is surviving, but now 21 ♗a2! is decisive. Black should simply give up the exchange here, since 21...♖d6 22 d5! decisively opens the position. After 22...♘d8 23 ♕c5 b6 24 ♕e3 ♔g7 25 dxe6 ♖xd1 26 ♖xd1 ♘xe6 27 ♕xb6 Black resigned in Pavasović-Barle, Ljubljana 2007, which is a somewhat odd decision since this is the best position he's had for 5 moves! The sequence since move 22 wasn't the most precise but Pavasović's play in this game makes a powerful impression.

a2) 13...b5 14 ♘e4 ♘xe4 15 ♗xe4 f5 (it is necessary to push the bishop off the dominant e4-square – this is another typical device in IQP positions; now the bishop re-routes to the a2-g8 diagonal to target the weak e6-pawn; instead, 15...♗b7 16 d5! is promising for White) 16 ♗b1! ♗f6 17 ♗a2 ♘e7! (putting the knight on d5 is another standard idea, especially once Black has played ...f5; the knight is outstandingly placed on this square, blocking the d4-pawn and protecting the e6-pawn from attack by the bishop on a2) 18 ♗g5 ♘d5 19 ♖fe1 ♖a7 20 ♖c1 ♖e7, Pavasović-Gjuran, Nova Gorica 2009.

Black has played well, but I still prefer White after the simple 21 ♕d2, protecting the bishop and preparing to occupy e5 with the knight.

b) 12...b5 *(D)* represents the consistent choice.

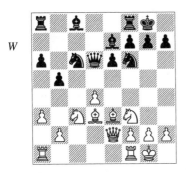

The weakening of the c-file suggests that White can consider playing on the queenside, and I like 13 ♘e4!? ♘xe4 14 ♗xe4 ♗b7 15 ♖ac1 ♖ac8 16 b4 f5 (Black should have preferred a more conservative approach, since he gets serious weaknesses on the e-file now) 17 ♗b1 ♘b8 (probably missing White's next move, although it is hard to offer Black particularly good advice here) 18 ♗f4! (taking on f4 would be met by ♕xe6+, with a rout) 18...♗xf3? (18...♕d7 was the only way to stay in the game, although after 19 ♗a2 ± Black's position is extremely unpleasant) 19 gxf3 ♕d7 20 ♗a2 (without his light-squared bishop, Black has nothing to oppose the awesome power of the a2-bishop on the a2-g8 diagonal) 20...♖f6 21 ♖xc8+ ♕xc8 22 ♖c1 ♖g6+ 23 ♔f1 ♕d7 24 ♗xb8 ♗g5 25 ♖c7 1-0 J.Horvath-Wegerle, Deizisau 2001.

12 ♕e2 ♗b7 13 ♖ad1 ♖ad8 *(D)*

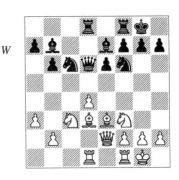

14 ♗b1

This is a typical regrouping. Now ♕c2 or ♕d3 would come with serious mating threats, and the rook is unleashed down the d-file, supporting the d5 break and making the black queen feel uncomfortable. In addition, the bishop can come to a2, supporting the d5 break and exerting pressure down the a2-g8 diagonal, while being immune from attack.

Another good example is Pavasović-G.Grigore, Bratto 2009 which continued 14 ♗g5 ♖d7 15 ♗b1 ♕b8 16 d5 exd5 17 ♗xf6 ♗xf6 18 ♘xd5 ♖d6. Here I like 19 ♘xf6+ ♖xf6 20 ♖fe1, when White's pieces are far more active with a completely open centre, which leaves Black with a very difficult defence.

14...♖fe8 15 ♖fe1 ♕b8

By far the most popular move here, getting the queen off the dangerous d-file.

White now has a wide choice. I like Hansen's move, which is a useful waiting move and cuts out ...♘g4 ideas.

16 h3 g6

Blocking the powerful bishop is sensible. Black also has ideas of ...♗f8-g7, defending his king and putting pressure on the d4-pawn.

17 ♗a2 (D)

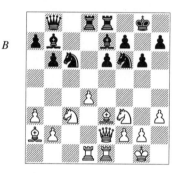

17...♗f8

Or:

a) 17...♕a8 (Pavasović-Kobaliya, European Team Ch, Batumi 1999) and now I like 18 ♗g5 with strong pressure.

b) 17...♘d5 18 ♘xd5 exd5 19 b4 leaves White with the more active pieces in a symmetrical structure.

c) 17...♔g7? 18 ♕d2 ♔g8 just loses time, and 19 ♗h6 led to a strong initiative for White in R.Ibrahimov-Batsanin, Moscow 1997.

18 d5

18 ♗g5 is also possible, as in Arenas-S.Sanchez, Bagre Antioquia 2014, but I prefer the immediate strike in the centre.

18...exd5 19 ♘xd5 ♘xd5 20 ♗xd5 (D)

GM Dorian Rogozenko gives a good summary of this position: "The

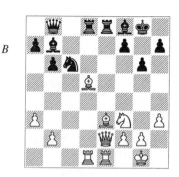

position simplified, but again, it is Black who must be very accurate. The problem is that Black does not have a clear way to equality – everywhere there are some problems. White has several unpleasant ideas, first of all ♕c4 and ♘g5. Sometimes even sacrifices on f7 are possible."

20...♘e7

Trying to exchange the powerful d5-bishop is a logical defence.

As Rogozenko notes, White was already threatening to take on f7; for instance, 20...♗g7? 21 ♗xf7+ ♔xf7 22 ♘g5+ ♔f8 and now the quickest mate is the elegant 23 ♗c5+ bxc5 24 ♕f3+ ♔g8 25 ♖xe8+ ♖xe8 26 ♕d5+ ♔h8 (or 26...♖e6 27 ♕xe6+ ♔h8 28 ♘f7+ ♔g8 29 ♘d8+, also with mate) 27 ♘f7+ ♔g8 28 ♘h6++ ♔h8 29 ♕g8+ ♖xg8 30 ♘f7#.

20...♖d6 is one of Black's soundest moves, but White retains a slight initiative after 21 ♘g5 ♘e5 22 ♘e4 ♗xd5 23 ♖xd5 ♖xd5 24 ♘f6+ ♔h8 25 ♘xd5.

21 ♗xb7 ♕xb7 22 ♗d4

Setting up dangerous threats on the long diagonal.

22...♕b8!

The best move, stopping ♕e5; obviously Black would love to exchange queens here.

23 ♗e5 ♕c8 24 ♖xd8 ♖xd8 25 ♕e4! *(D)*

Simple and powerful chess from the seven-time Danish Champion. White's army is beautifully centralized and Black's position is very unpleasant.

25...♕c6?

In such positions it is almost impossible for humans to avoid mistakes. 25...♘d5 would have kept up a tough defence in a tricky position.

26 ♕h4 ±

Now White has an overwhelming superiority in firepower on the kingside. His threats include ♘d4, when Black has great difficulty covering the f6-square (and so preventing a fatal queen and bishop alignment on the long dark-squared diagonal).

26...♖e8 27 ♕f6!

White had other good moves, but Sune goes for an 'eternal' pin on the e-file. It's not hard to see that Black will face decisive material loss.

27...♕xf6 28 ♗xf6 h6 29 h4 a6 30 a4 ♔h7 31 ♔f1 ♔g8 32 b3 ♔h7 33 ♖e3 ♔g8 34 g4 ♔h7 35 h5 b5 36 axb5 axb5 37 ♘g1!

Being careful not to put the knight on the d-file, when ...♖d8 might get out of trouble.

37...♔g8 38 ♘e2 ♔h7 39 ♘f4 1-0

White will win at least an exchange, so Chuchelov threw in the towel. A really nice, controlled performance by Hansen, and a game which amply repays deep study.

In the following game, I had an IQP and good attacking chances. However, I wanted to show the game to sound a note of caution. IQPs tend to lead to promising attacking opportunities, but these opportunities can be quite difficult to spot and assess correctly. In particular, in this game, my kingside attack was only good enough for a draw. In failing to acknowledge this (before this game I had had an excellent tournament and some prospects of playing for a GM norm) I erred and lost. Incidentally, after this reprieve, my opponent went on to win the tournament!

Game 4
Collins – Wirig
Vandoeuvres 2013

1 d4 d5 2 c4 dxc4 3 ♘f3 ♘f6 4 e3 e6 5 ♗xc4 c5 6 0-0 a6

The Queen's Gambit Accepted often leads to IQP positions.

7 ♗b3

Probably the modern main line. Kramnik and Anand in particular have played several heavyweight battles in the IQP positions arising from this move, and I strongly recommend you take a look at those games.

7...♘c6 (D)

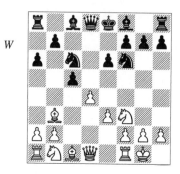

8 ♕e2

In a previous game I had played 8 ♘c3 ♗e7 9 ♕e2 cxd4 10 ♖d1, giving my opponent the extra possibility of 10...e5. After 11 exd4 exd4 12 ♘xd4 ♘xd4 13 ♕e5 ♕d6 14 ♕xd4 ♕xd4 15 ♖xd4 0-0 16 ♗f4 a draw was agreed in Collins-Izsak, Torokbalint 2005.

8...cxd4 9 ♖d1 ♗e7

Of course here 9...e5?? simply loses to 10 exd4 +−.

10 exd4 0-0 11 ♘c3 ♘d5 12 ♗e3

Not forced, but a solid developing move. White doesn't fear the capture on e3 since fxe3 would strengthen his centre (although Black trades pieces and gains the bishop-pair, so he can't be too unhappy either).

12 a3 b6 was played in Mozharov-Stukopin, Moscow 2009. I think Black should have exchanged on c3 first,

since after the weakening of the c-file 13 ♘xd5! exd5 14 ♘e5 ± gives White a pleasant edge with no risk.

12 ♗d2!? is not bad either, followed by ♖ac1.

12...♘xc3 13 bxc3 ♘a5 14 ♗c2 ♕c7

Black's play makes a slightly odd impression – he seems to be spending time aiming for control of c4, but has failed to address his lack of development. Around here I became quite optimistic.

15 ♗g5

This seemed like a natural response to Black removing defenders from the kingside. However, I probably should have played the more positional 15 ♘e5! ±. Black struggles to equalize here; for instance, 15...♘c6 16 ♗f4 ♗d6 17 c4 and White has an active game with good prospects of a kingside attack.

15...♗xg5 16 ♘xg5

16 ♗xh7+ was extremely tempting. Unlike in my game with Teeuwen (Game 30), however, here it is only good enough for a draw: 16...♔xh7 17 ♘xg5+ ♔g6! (the only move since after 17...♔g8? 18 ♕h5 ♖d8, the calm 19 ♖d3!!, followed by swinging the rook to f3 or h3, wins in all lines; 17...♔h6? 18 ♕g4 ♕d8 19 ♕h4+ ♔g6 20 ♕h7+!! is a resource that, as far as I recall, I didn't spot; taking the knight leads to a decisive attack after ♕xg7+, while after 20...♔f6 21 ♖d3! White's initiative is unstoppable) 18 ♕g4 f5 19 ♕h4 ♕d8 and White has to take a draw by perpetual check; for instance,

20 ♕h7+ ♔f6 (taking the knight leads to mate after ♕xg7+ and ♖d3) 21 ♕h5 g6 22 ♕h6 ♖h8 23 ♘h7+ ♔f7 (or 23...♖xh7 24 ♕xh7 ♗d7 25 ♖e1 ♕e7 26 ♕h4+ ♔f7 27 ♕h7+ is also perpetual) 24 ♘g5+.

16...h6 17 ♘e4 ♗d7 18 ♘f6+?!

This should have led to an immediate draw. White has a few ways to maintain an advantage; for instance, 18 ♕d3 ♖fe8 19 ♘c5 f5 20 ♖e1 with good chances.

18...gxf6 19 ♕g4+ ♔h8 20 ♕h4 ♔g7 21 ♕g4+ ♔h8 22 ♕h4 ♔g7 23 ♖d3 *(D)*

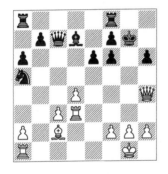

Having spent a lot of time to get to this position, I needlessly gambled. Although my chosen move doesn't lose, I should have simply taken the draw.

23...♖g8! 24 ♖ad1

This is still enough for equality, but things are getting needlessly complicated.

24...♔f8 25 ♕xf6

25 ♕xh6+ is better, with equal play.

25...♗c6?

25...♗b5 is correct.

26 ♕xh6+

Both during the game and in my initial notes I missed that Black's last move was actually a serious error! 26 d5! ♗xd5 27 ♕xh6+ ♔e7 28 ♖xd5 exd5 29 ♖e1+ ♔d8 and now 30 ♗h7! ♕c6 31 ♕xc6 ♖xg2+ 32 ♔xg2 bxc6 with an endgame in which White has good chances based on his passed h-pawn and superior minor piece.

26...♔e8 27 ♖g3??

I spent most of my remaining time calculating 27 d5 ♗xd5 28 ♖xd5 exd5, but couldn't find a continuation after 29 ♖e1+ ♔d8. As pointed out in the previous note, 30 ♗h7! is the answer.

27...♖xg3 ∓

The rest is agony.

28 hxg3?

28 fxg3 was the last chance, when at least White has a passed pawn and some prospect of play on the f-file. I was disappointed with my decision here.

28...♖d8 −+ 29 ♕g7 ♕e7 30 ♗d3 ♗d5 31 ♖b1 ♖c8 32 a4 ♖xc3 33 ♗xa6 bxa6 34 ♕h8+ ♔d7 35 ♖b8 ♖c7 36 ♔h2 ♘c6 37 ♖a8 ♘e5 38 dxe5 ♗xa8 39 ♕xa8 ♕c5 40 f4 a5 41 ♕g8 ♔c6 42 ♕a8+ ♔b6 43 ♕b8+ ♖b7 44 ♕d8+ ♔a7 0-1

A painful loss, and one which shows just how difficult these IQP positions can be to play with either colour.

2 1 e4 e5

1 e4 e5

One of the most important aspects of any 1 e4 repertoire is how it deals with 1...e5. For beginners, 1...e5 is a most natural move, competing for space in the centre and preparing the rapid development of the kingside. The Open Games (the general term for all positions arising after 1 e4 e5) are rightly considered to be an excellent training ground, featuring sharp tactical play and a strong introduction to such concepts as the centre, space and development.

However, 1...e5 does not diminish in importance as a player gains strength and experience. Many strong grandmasters have built their black repertoires around 1 e4 e5. Moreover, these lines are in the repertoires of all of the world's elite. The strength and soundness of 1 e4 e5 for Black (in particular, in lines like the Petroff, Berlin and Marshall) have caused headaches for top players and even for World Champions – Vishy Anand was notoriously unable to demonstrate anything against Magnus Carlsen's Berlin Defence in their first match, and switched to 1 d4 at the end of that match and throughout their second match, with considerably more success.

The choices I have made against 1 e4 e5 2 ♘f3 ♘c6 are as follows:

1 e4 e5 2 ♘f3 ♘c6 3 ♗c4 *(D)*

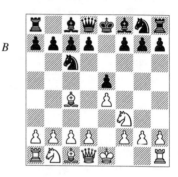

The Italian Game (as 3 ♗c4 is known) can give rise to sharp tactical play (after an early d4) or quiet positional play (after an early d3). It has a practical advantage over the Ruy Lopez in that play tends to be concentrated in a more limited range of structures, and there are considerably fewer variations to learn for both players. That said, it must be acknowledged that this line has traditionally been viewed as less critical than the Ruy Lopez. Other than relatively passive moves such as 3...♗e7 and 3...d6, Black has two main responses:

Giuoco Piano

3...♗c5

This, the Giuoco Piano, is the classical approach for Black and the normal choice of the world's elite. It has been recommended in a number of recent and prominent repertoire books and DVDs, notably including those by Marin, Gustafsson and Lysy. My recommendation is a relatively offbeat line which has long been championed by Swedish GM Jonny Hector and has recently become more fashionable, namely:

4 c3 ♘f6 5 d4 exd4 6 cxd4 ♗b4+ 7 ♘bd2!? *(D)*

It has long been known that Black can equalize fairly comfortably after both 7 ♗d2 and 7 ♘c3, but 7 ♘bd2 is much less known.

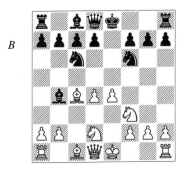

Indeed, despite playing these lines with Black for over a decade, this move was entirely unknown to me until I saw the game Y.Zhou-D.Howell, Leiden 2013. Black has two principal ways to respond: accepting the pawn sacrifice with the critical 7...♘xe4, or declining it with the sound 7...d5. In the latter case, as you might have guessed, we get an IQP position, and one in which White has reasonable prospects in my view.

Two Knights Defence

3...♘f6

This simple developing move introduces the Two Knights Defence. It is more aggressive than 3...♗c5, being based on a pawn sacrifice after 4 ♘g5 d5 (4...♗c5 is also possible, with enormous complications) 5 exd5 ♘a5 (5...♘xd5?! has long been known to be dubious after the precise 6 d4!) 6 ♗b5+ c6. Elite players seem to have shied away from this with Black, perhaps unwilling to have to demonstrate compensation for a pawn where there is a sound alternative like 3...♗c5. However, at 'normal' GM level the move is quite popular; for instance, it is the regular choice of English GM and 1 e4 e5 expert Mark Hebden.

Against the Two Knights Defence, White has a number of options. My suggestion is to play:

4 d4 exd4 5 e5 *(D)*

This typically gives rise (after the reply 5...d5) to positions in which White plays for a dark-squared blockade and Black has the bishop-pair but an inferior pawn-structure. Black has alternatives on move 5 (5...♘e4 and 5...♘g4) which also lead to interesting play. I like these positions since they contain some poison for Black (for instance, English GM Gawain Jones has been quite successful here with White) and are generally useful for 1 e4 players to know. In addition, they can also be reached by the Scotch Gambit move-order 1 e4 e5 2 ♘f3 ♘c6 3 d4 exd4 4 ♗c4, though here Black can try 4...♗c5 as well as 4...♘f6.

We shall now examine these variations in detail, starting with 3...♗c5 (Games 5-7) before moving on to 3...♘f6 (Games 8-11).

In addition to 2...♘c6, I have covered Black's other options, in particular the Petroff (2...♘f6) and the Philidor (2...d6) – see Games 12 and 13 respectively.

Giuoco Piano

Game 5
Hector – Rydström
Ballerup 2014

1 e4 e5 2 ♘f3 ♘c6 3 ♗c4 ♗c5 4 c3 (D)

White aims to play d4.
4...♘f6

This is well established as Black's best response. The passive 4...d6?! 5 d4 exd4 6 cxd4 ♗b6 has been played by some GMs but gives White a very pleasant position with a perfect centre; for instance, 7 ♗b5!? ♗d7 8 ♘c3

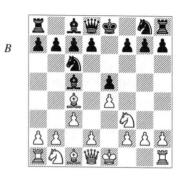

♘ge7 9 0-0 0-0 10 h3 ± was nice for White in Godena-Garcia Palermo, Italian Team Ch, Condino 2014.
5 d4 exd4 6 cxd4 ♗b4+
6...♗b6? 7 e5 ± is simply awful for Black.
7 ♘bd2
Smerdon: "An unusual sideline championed by the wild attacking Swedish GM Jonny Hector. Aussie GM Ian Rogers alerted me to the idea."
7...d5
Striking in the centre is logical, although at least White plays with equal material in this variation! For 7...♘xe4 (and 7...♗xd2+), see Game 7.
8 exd5 ♘xd5 9 0-0 0-0 10 a3 (D)

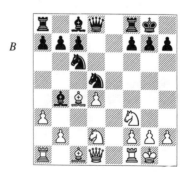

Putting the question to the dark-squared bishop.

10...♗e7

10...♗xd2 is the subject of Game 6.

11 ♖e1

Black now has three options for actively developing his light-squared bishop – to e6, to f5 or to g4.

11...♗g4

Or:

a) 11...♗e6 was Ivan Sokolov's preference in a game against Hector. 12 ♗a2 is a logical move, vacating the c4-square for the knight, improving the bishop (and avoiding ideas like 12 ♘e4 ♘e3!, which would equalize on the spot). Now:

a1) After 12...♕d7 I like 13 ♘e4!? (13 h3 ♖ad8 14 ♘c4 ♖fe8 15 ♗d2 ♗f6 was fine for Black in Fossan-Getz, Norwegian Ch, Trondheim 2014) 13...♖ad8 14 b4, when White intends to post a knight on c5, perhaps preceded by ♗g5. White has good play on the dark squares here. See line 'a2' for another example of a similar idea.

a2) 12...♘f4 and now I like Jeroen Bosch's idea of 13 ♘e4!? (13 ♘c4 ♘g6 14 ♗e3 ♗f6 15 ♕d3 ♗d5 was comfortable for Black in Hector-I.Sokolov, Malmö 2013) 13...♗xa2 14 ♖xa2 ♘d5 15 b4, when Bosch concludes "as odd as it looks, White still has a little something. He intends to double on the e-file and play ♕b3 and ♘c5."

b) 11...♗f5 *(D)* has been the most played move here.

The bishop is actively placed on f5. 12 ♗a2 is again a useful improving move. Then:

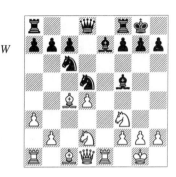

b1) 12...♘b6 is best answered by Bosch's suggestion of 13 ♘e4 (13 ♘f1 ♗f6 14 d5 ½-½ Chuprov-Azarov, Voronezh 2008) 13...♕d7 14 ♗f4 ♖ad8 15 ♖c1, when White has an edge, with extremely active pieces.

b2) 12...a6 13 ♘c4 ♗f6 14 h3 h6 15 ♘ce5 ♕d6 16 ♗d2 ♖ad8 and now 17 ♖c1 ♘ce7 18 ♘c4 ♕d7 19 ♘fe5 ♕c8 20 ♕f3 ♗e6 led to balanced play in Hector-Semcesen, Malmö 2012. Bosch notes that 17 ♕b3!, hitting the b7-pawn, would have been very strong. After 17...♗e6 I like the simple 18 ♘xc6 ♕xc6 19 ♖ac1 ♕b6 20 ♕c2 ♗xd4 21 ♘xd4 ♕xd4 22 ♗b1 ♖fe8 23 ♖cd1 ♘f6 24 ♗xh6 ♕h4 25 ♖xd8 ♖xd8 26 ♗c1, when White is better with the two bishops and a safer king in a wide-open position.

We now return to the position after 11...♗g4 *(D)*:

12 h3 ♗h5

This looks like a very solid idea, since White's typical plan of putting his queen on d3 and his bishop on c2 (or b1) will not achieve anything in view of ...♗g6. However, it turns out to be more significant that Black can no

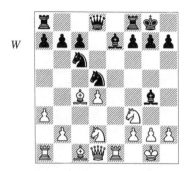

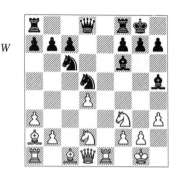

longer put his bishop on e6, meaning that White's c4-bishop becomes even more powerful.

While Black generally wants to exchange pieces in IQP positions, here 12...♗xf3? 13 ♘xf3 would be an unfavourable exchange. White's bishop-pair will be strong in the resulting open position and, in particular, his light-squared bishop will dominate the board, since it has no opponent. It is worth noting that if Black's c-pawn were on e6, at least some resistance could be put up on the a2-g8 diagonal, but here the bishop is extremely strong on this diagonal.

13 ♗a2

Again we see this useful waiting move. The bishop gets out of the way of ...♘b6 or ...♘a5 jumps and continues to exert strong pressure on the a2-g8 diagonal, especially since Black can't block with ...♗e6.

13...♗f6 (D)

14 ♕b3

We saw Hector miss this idea on move 17 of his game against Semcesen in Malmö 2012, but he has obviously learned from that game and finds

♕b3 easily here. This isn't forced and might not be the best move, but it is certainly logical. Other moves:

a) 14 ♘e4!? is an interesting pawn sacrifice. After 14...♗xf3 15 ♕xf3 ♘xd4 16 ♕g4 c6 (White threatened to take on d5 and f6) 17 ♗xd5 cxd5 18 ♘xf6+ ♕xf6 19 ♗g5 ♕g6 (19...♕f5 transposes) 20 ♕xd4 ♕xg5 21 ♖ad1 ♖fd8 22 ♖e5 ♕f6 23 ♖xd5 ♕xd4 24 ♖5xd4 ♖xd4 25 ♖xd4 Black needs to show some precision to draw this endgame, since White's rook will be very active on the seventh rank.

b) 14 g4 ♗g6 15 ♘c4 is also a strong idea, aiming to put the knight on a good outpost with ♘ce5. From there the knight will hit c6, f7 and g6, and if it is captured White can improve his pawn-structure with dxe5. White has a good advantage here.

14...♘b6 15 d5 ♘d4

15...♗xf3 16 ♘xf3 ♘e7 is the alternative, but after 17 ♖d1 I prefer White, who has more space and the bishop-pair; for instance, 17...♕d6 18 ♘g5 ♖fd8 19 ♕c2 ♗xg5 20 ♗xg5 ♖d7 21 ♖d4 ♘exd5 22 ♖e1 c6 23 ♖de4 with excellent compensation for the pawn in the form of a bishop-pair and more active pieces.

16 ♘xd4 ♗xd4 *(D)*

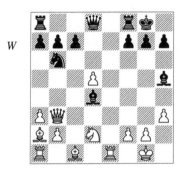

17 ♘e4

Instead:

a) 17 ♘f3 ♗xf3 18 ♕xf3 ♕d7 19 ♖d1 ♗e5 leads to a balanced position.

b) 17 ♕b4 is a strong computer suggestion. After 17...c5 (17...♗f6 18 ♘e4 ♗e7 19 ♕b5 ♗g6 20 ♗f4 followed by ♖ad1 leaves White extremely active) 18 dxc6 bxc6 Black's structure has been slightly compromised, so White should have an edge after, for instance, 19 ♕a5 ♘d5 20 ♕xd8 ♖fxd8 21 g4 ♗g6 22 ♘f3.

17...♖e8 18 ♗f4 ♗e5?

It seems logical to exchange dark-squared bishops, but in fact White gains a strong initiative after this. Black should have gone in for the complications after 18...♗g6 19 ♖ad1 ♖xe4 20 ♖xe4 ♗xf2+ (20...♗xe4 21 ♖xd4 leaves White with more space and the bishop-pair) 21 ♔xf2 ♗xe4 22 d6 ♕f6 23 ♕e3 ♗c2 24 ♖c1 cxd6 25 ♖xc2 g5 26 ♕g3 ♕xf4+ 27 ♕xf4 gxf4 28 ♖c7 d5 29 a4!, when White

retains a dangerous initiative in the endgame. Black needs to be precise to equalize here, despite his extra pawns; for instance, 29...♖d8 30 a5 ♘c4 is a good equalizing attempt.

19 ♗xe5 ♖xe5 20 ♕g3!

One of the advantages in having more space is that it is easier to switch your pieces from one side of the board to the other. Hector is extremely dangerous once he has the initiative, and here he attacks with energy and precision.

20...♘d7 21 f4! ♖e8 22 ♕f2 *(D)*

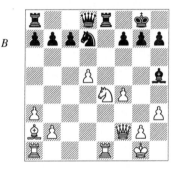

Suddenly the h5-bishop is in danger of being caught by g4 and f5.

22...f5

Stopping White's threat, but creating huge problems on the a2-g8 diagonal. Other defensive tries:

a) 22...h6 23 d6 gives White a strong attack; for instance, 23...♔h8 24 dxc7 ♕xc7 25 ♖ac1 ♕d8 26 ♘g3 ♗g6 27 f5 ♖xe1+ 28 ♖xe1 ♗h7 29 ♗xf7, winning a pawn with a much better position.

b) 22...f6 doesn't solve the problem either: 23 d6+ ♔h8 (23...♗f7 24 dxc7 ♕xc7 25 ♗xf7+ ♔xf7 26 ♖ac1 ♕b8 27 ♕d4 and Black can't defend his knight while avoiding ♘d6+) 24 g4 and the bishop is caught.

23 ♘g5 ♖xe1+ 24 ♖xe1 ♘f6 25 d6+

25 ♖e7! would have been a beautiful shot, but Hector's solution is more than good enough.

25...♔h8 26 ♗f7!

Introducing the threat of ♗xh5 and ♘f7+, winning the house.

26...h6 27 ♗xh5 hxg5 28 ♗g6 ♘e4

28...♕xd6 29 fxg5 ♘h7 avoids mate, but is still hopeless after 30 ♕xf5 ♕d4+ 31 ♔f2! ♕xf2+ 32 ♔xf2 ♘xg5 33 ♖e7, when the difference in piece activity and king safety is decisive, even in the endgame.

29 ♕f3 g4 30 hxg4 ♕h4 31 g3!

An elegant finish, breaking through to the h-file.

31...♘xg3

31...♕xg3+ 32 ♕xg3 ♘xg3 33 dxc7 and the pawn queens.

32 ♔g2 ♕f6 33 ♔xg3 1-0

White could have forced mate starting with 33 ♖h1+, but Black saw no reason to play on a piece down after Hector's simple move.

Game 6
Smerdon – Naumann
Bundesliga 2014/15

1 e4 e5 2 ♘f3 ♘c6 3 ♗c4 ♗c5 4 c3 ♘f6 5 d4 exd4 6 cxd4 ♗b4+ 7 ♘bd2 d5 8 exd5 ♘xd5 9 0-0 0-0 10 a3 ♗xd2

A critical continuation. Black enters into an unfavourable exchange (White's two bishops will be very effective in this position) but gains time to attack the d4-pawn.

11 ♗xd2

The slightly clumsy 11 ♕xd2 has also been tested, aiming to defend the d4-pawn, but based on this game and the accompanying analysis I think White should prefer the recapture with the bishop.

11...♗g4 12 h3! *(D)*

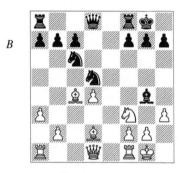

12...♗h5

12...♗xf3 is critical. After 13 ♕xf3 ♘b6 14 ♗d3 White seems to have strong compensation after either capture on d4:

a) 14...♘xd4 can be met by Bosch's 15 ♕xb7. Smerdon's more ambitious suggestion of 15 ♕h5 g6 16 ♕h6, where he believes that White has excellent compensation for the pawn, looks unconvincing.

b) 14...♕xd4 was tested in a game between two strong GMs, where White gave a model performance: 15 ♗c3 ♕h4 16 ♖fe1 ♖ae8 17 ♗e4 ♖e6 18 ♗xc6! ♖xc6 19 ♖e4 (White has given up one half of his bishop-pair, but his dark-squared bishop is dominant and his remaining pieces are very active) 19...♕d8 (19...♕h6 20 ♖d1 also leaves Black with problems) 20 ♗b4 ♖e8 21 ♖d1 ♕c8 22 ♖xe8+ ♕xe8 23 ♕e4! ♖e6 24 ♕xb7 c5? (24...c6 25 ♕xa7 ♘d5 was the last chance) 25 ♕c7 cxb4 26 ♖d8, winning the queen and the game in Smirnov-Bukavshin, Khanty-Mansiisk 2013.

13 ♗a2

13 g4 is also interesting, resulting in a pawn sacrifice for two bishops in an open position. 13...♗g6 14 ♖e1 ♘b6 15 ♗b3 (a possible improvement on Bosch's analysis, which ran 15 ♗a2 ♘xd4 16 ♘xd4 ♕xd4 17 ♗b4 ♕xd1 18 ♖axd1 ♖fe8, with equality) 15...♘xd4 16 ♘xd4 ♕xd4 17 ♗b4 ♕xd1 18 ♖axd1 ♖fe8 19 a4!? (this is an extra resource at White's disposal by virtue of having played 15 ♗b3 instead of 15 ♗a2; also interesting is 19 ♗e7!?, preventing exchanges and retaining enduring compensation for the pawn) 19...c6! 20 a5 ♘d5 21 ♗xd5 cxd5 22 ♖xd5 ♖xe1+ 23 ♗xe1 and the players soon agreed a draw in Brkić-Bosiočić, Croatian Team Ch, Bol na Bracu 2014.

13...♕d6 *(D)*

14 ♕b3

14 ♖c1 was played in a previous GM encounter: 14...♖ad8 15 ♖e1 ♘xd4 16 g4 ♘f4 17 ♗xf4 ♕xf4 18 ♘xd4 ♖xd4 19 ♕b3 ♗g6 20 ♕xb7 with an equal position, Gallagher-Michalik, Mitropa Cup, Ruzomberok 2014.

14...♖ad8 15 g4 ♗g6 16 ♖fe1 ♘f4

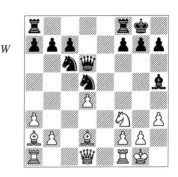

Smerdon suggests that 16...h5 is better, hitting the slightly exposed white kingside.

17 ♗xf4 ♕xf4 18 d5 ♘b8 19 ♕e3!

An excellent practical decision. Smerdon notes as follows: "I'm not sure White should go into the endgame, as the queen is really doing quite well harassing Black's queenside pawns. But I was getting a bit low on time, and saw that the endgame was comfortable for White."

19...♕xe3 20 ♖xe3 ♖fe8

Smerdon: "Now things get difficult for Black, whose pieces become quite passive."

During the game Smerdon mainly analysed 20...c6, concluding that after 21 ♖e7 cxd5 22 ♖xb7 d4 23 ♖xa7 d3 "White has won a pawn, but Black's passer looks dangerous." This certainly looks like a better attempt at counterplay.

21 ♘e5! c6?! 22 d6! ♔f8

This loses, but Black was in trouble in any case. 22...♖xd6 23 ♘xf7!, winning, is a pretty variation given by Smerdon.

23 ♖ae1

Smerdon: "Black is pretty much in zugzwang. White threatens d7, f4 and also the simple ♘xg6+ followed by ♖e7."

23...♗c2

Smerdon analyses 23...f6 24 ♘xg6+ hxg6 25 ♖e7!, threatening to win with ♖f7+.

24 ♘xf7 ♖xe3 25 ♖xe3 ♖d7 26 ♗e6 ♖xf7 27 ♗xf7 ♔xf7 28 ♖e7+ ♔f6 29 g5+ 1-0

Black resigned since, as Smerdon notes, "White will next play ♖xb7 and then queen the d-pawn."

Game 7
Hector – Hraček
Bundesliga 2012/13

1 e4 e5 2 ♘f3 ♘c6 3 ♗c4 ♗c5 4 c3 ♘f6 5 d4 exd4 6 cxd4 ♗b4+ 7 ♘bd2 ♘xe4

In his book on the Open Games, Viktor Bologan recommends the very unusual move-order 7...♗xd2+!? 8 ♗xd2 (8 ♘xd2 runs into 8...d5! 9 exd5 ♕e7+) 8...♘xe4 9 d5 ♘e7 *(D)* (9...♘xd2 10 ♕xd2 ♘e7 11 d6 leads to similar play as analysed below).

Here I think White should simply play for compensation based on his bishop-pair – Black will have to spend more time with the knight on e4 and, generally speaking, his position feels slightly cramped with three minor pieces. 10 ♗c1!? 0-0 11 0-0 and now:

a) 11...♖e8 12 ♖e1 ♘d6 13 ♗b3 b6 is possible, but seems to give White more chances of a kingside attack, since Black's pieces are bunched together on the queenside. After 14 ♗d2 ♗b7 15 ♗c3 this is not a position I would enjoy with Black.

b) 11...d6 12 ♖e1 ♘f6 gives White decent positional compensation with his space advantage and bishop-pair, although Black is very solid.

8 d5 *(D)*

8 0-0 is an interesting alternative, as in Shomoev-Khairullin, Vladivostok 2014, but I shall focus on the text-move, which cuts across Black's plan to play ...d5.

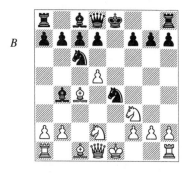

8...♘e7

In view of the move-order considerations set out at Black's 9th move, it is worth asking whether the immediate

8...♘xd2 9 ♗xd2 ♗xd2+ 10 ♕xd2 ♘e7 is possible. Now 11 0-0 d6! would be comfortable for Black, but in this move-order White has a better option: 11 d6! cxd6 12 ♕xd6 (12 0-0 transposes to the note to Black's 9th move below). This strikes me as less comfortable than the main lines for Black, for the somewhat bizarre reason that he finds it more difficult to give back his extra d-pawn! As we shall see, ...d6 and ...♗e6/g4 is a reliable equalizer in these lines, so being forced to fianchetto the bishop actually makes Black's task slightly harder.

a) 12...0-0 13 0-0 and Black's position is harder to handle; for instance, 13...♘f5 14 ♕f4 d6 15 ♖fe1 ♗e6 (not forced, but 15...d5 16 ♖ad1 ♘e7 leaves Black under some mild pressure) 16 ♗xe6 fxe6 17 ♖xe6 ± and completion of development had come at a structural cost (in addition to returning the pawn) in Westerberg-Ornstein, Swedish Team Ch 2014/15.

b) 12...b5!? (taking advantage of the impossibility of 13 ♗xb5? in view of the reply 13...♕a5+) 13 ♗d3 ♗b7 (after 13...♕a5+ 14 ♔f1 White retains some initiative; he can bring his queen's rook to e1 and, perhaps, his king's rook into play after h4 and h5) 14 ♘d4 0-0 15 0-0 a6 16 ♖fe1 ♖e8 17 h4 ♘c6 18 ♖xe8+ ♕xe8 19 ♘f5 g6 and now:

b1) After 20 ♕g3?! ♕e5! White's compensation is objectively dubious, although after 21 ♘d6 ♕xg3 22 fxg3 ♖b8 23 ♖e1 ♘b4 24 ♗e4 ♗xe4 25 ♖xe4 ∓ he ultimately managed to

escape in Smerdon-Breder, Bundesliga 2014/15.

b2) Probably White should force a draw by 20 ♕f6! gxf5 21 ♕g5+ ♔h8 (but not 21...♔f8? 22 ♕h6+ ♔g8 {or 22...♔e7 23 ♖e1+ +−} 23 ♗xf5 with a decisive attack) 22 ♕f6+ ♔g8 23 ♕g5+, with perpetual check.

9 0-0 *(D)*

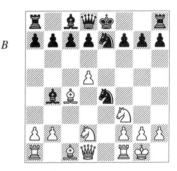

9...♗xd2

Forcing exchanges at the expense of giving up the bishop-pair, which will leave White with at least some compensation in this semi-open position. Black can retain the bishop-pair with 9...♘xd2 10 ♗xd2 ♗xd2, but this runs into the typical 11 d6!. By temporarily sacrificing a second pawn, White renders the development of Black's queenside more difficult since ...d6 is impossible. 11...cxd6 12 ♕xd2 d5 13 ♗xd5 0-0 and then:

a) 14 ♖ad1 was played in the first game I saw with this line, between the promising English IM Yang-Fan Zhou and one of the stars of the new generation of English players, GM David Howell. Recently it was given a whirl

by Nakamura too. 14...♘xd5 15 ♕xd5
d6 16 ♕xd6 (16 b3 h6 17 ♖fe1 ♖e8 18
♖xe8+ ♕xe8 19 ♖e1 ♕d8 20 h3 ♖b8
21 ♘d4 ♗d7 22 ♖d1 ♕c7 23 ♘f3
♗e6 24 ♕xd6 ♕xd6 25 ♖xd6 led to
equality in Y.Zhou-D.Howell, Leiden
2013) 16...♕xd6 17 ♖xd6 ♗e6 18 a3
♖fd8 19 ♖d4 ♖xd4 20 ♘xd4 ♖d8 21
♖d1 f6 22 f3 ♔f7 23 ♔f2 ♖d5 24 ♔e3
♖e5+ 25 ♔d3 ♖c5 26 ♖e1 ♗d7 27
♔d2 ♖d5 28 ♔c3 ♖c5+ 29 ♔d2 ♖d5
30 ♔c3 ♖c5+ 31 ♔d2 ½-½ Naka-
mura-Giri, Grand Prix, Khanty-Mansiisk 2015.

b) 14 ♗b3 retains White's strong
bishop, but Black should be able to
equalize without much trouble after
14...d5!. If this pawn falls, the position
will be symmetrical and equal, so
Black needs to display only modest
care here. 15 ♖fe1 a5!? (15...♗g4 16
♕b4 ♗xf3 17 ♕xe7 ♗e4 18 ♕xd8
♖fxd8 19 ♖ad1 ♔f8 20 f3 ♗g6 21
♖xd5 ♖ac8 was equal in Hector-
S.Haslinger, Bundesliga 2013/14) 16
♖ad1 ♖a6 (a creative way to develop
the rook) 17 ♗xd5 ♘xd5 18 ♕xd5
♕xd5 19 ♖xd5 (all other things being equal, one would expect that the
bishop would be more effective than
the knight in such an open position;
here, however, White has a useful
lead in development which is sufficient to level the chances, and the
players force a draw in an instructive
way) 19...♗e6 20 ♖b5 ♗xa2 21 b3!
(the bishop is now trapped, and free-
ing it will lead to the liquidation of the
queenside) 21...a4 22 bxa4 ♖xa4 23
♖xb7. Black now took the opportunity

to compromise White's structure with
23...♗d5 24 ♖be7 ♗xf3 25 gxf3 g6,
but after 26 ♖e8 the position with a
rook each and pawns on one side of
the board was dead equal and was
soon agreed drawn in Ponkratov-Alek-
sandrov, St Petersburg 2011.

**10 ♘xd2 ♘xd2 11 ♗xd2 d6 12
♖e1 0-0 13 ♕h5 ♘g6 14 ♗d3 ♗d7 15
♖e4 ♖e8 16 ♗g5** (D)

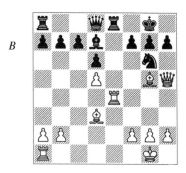

16...♕c8

16...f6! is the strongest move, but it
requires excellent preparation or nerves
of steel to find this. At first sight 17
♖h4 looks very dangerous, but it turns
out that Black can defend: 17...♘xh4
18 ♕xh7+ ♔f8 19 ♗xh4!? (more interesting than 19 ♕h8+, which forces
an immediate draw unless Black wants
to get mated by putting his king on e7)
19...♔e7! (absolutely the only move)
20 ♕h8+ (playing on with, for instance, 20 h3, seems to risk more for
White than for Black after 20...♕f7)
20...♔f7 21 ♕h5+ and a draw was
soon agreed in Gallagher-Zilka, Mitropa Cup, Ruzomberok 2014.

17 ♖h4

Now White has a strong initiative, and Black's position is tough to handle.

17...h6! 18 ♗xh6 ♖e5 19 ♗g5 ♖xg5!

Hraček defends excellently, finding the only moves.

20 ♕xg5 ♘xh4 21 ♕xh4 ♗f5 22 ♕c4 ♗xd3 23 ♕xd3 ♕d7 *(D)*

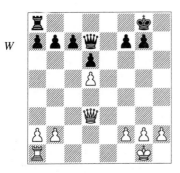

While this position is very close to equal, I prefer White based on the pawn-structure. Even though he has three pawn-islands, White has the safer king, and his 'isolated' d5-pawn is actually doing a good job holding back the c7-pawn, which is the only target for frontal attack in the position.

24 h3 ♖e8 25 ♖c1 c5! 26 dxc6 bxc6

Hraček activates his position at the cost of a technical structural weakening although, as noted at move 23, I didn't particularly like Black's structure even though he had only two pawn-islands.

27 b4 ♖e5

This operation seems time-consuming and puts the rook slightly offside.

27...d5 is more straightforward, followed by ...♖e4 or ...♖e6. Black is no worse here.

28 a4 a5 29 bxa5 ♖xa5 30 ♖c4!

Defending a4 and creating a well-concealed threat to go to the h-file.

30...c5 31 ♕c2 ♕d8 32 g3 *(D)*

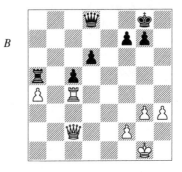

32...♖a8??

Amazingly, this move loses. Black could have taken prophylactic measures against White's h-file threats with 32...g6, though I have no doubt that Hector would have kept trying to open lines by 33 h4!, with some initiative.

Had Black realized that this was a critical position, he might have found the courage to go for 32...d5! 33 ♖xc5 ♖xc5 34 ♕xc5 d4 35 ♕b4 d3 36 ♕d2, when both 36...♕d4 and 36...♕d5 lead to equality – the passed d-pawn fully compensates for White's extra pawn.

33 ♖h4! +−

Now the black king is subject to an attack, and it's appropriate to notice that Black's major pieces, located on their starting squares, are not well placed for defence.

33...f6

33...Rb8 is more tenacious, but after 34 Wh7+ Kf8 35 a5! Black can't simultaneously defend his king and deal with the a-pawn.

34 Wh7+?

A very natural move, but a mistake. The beautiful computer move 34 We4!! is stronger, threatening We6+. Dealing with this threat will break Black's coordination; for instance, 34...Ra7 35 Wh7+ Kf7 36 Wh5+ Ke7 37 Re4+ Kd7 38 Wf7+ and the rook drops.

34...Kf7 35 Wh5+ Ke6 36 Re4+ Kd7 37 Wg4+ Kc6 38 Wxg7

White 'only' has an extra pawn and an initiative. Hraček makes a good practical decision, giving up more material to protect his king and get the c-pawn running. The rest isn't perfect but Hector's technique seems good enough to me.

38...Wg8!? 39 Wxf6 Wd5 40 We7 c4 41 Re1 Wd3 42 Rc1 Rb8 43 We1 Kd7 44 a5 Rb2 45 a6 Ra2 46 Wb4 Wd4 47 Rf1 d5 48 Wb1 Ra3 49 Wf5+ 1-0

Two Knights Defence

Game 8
M. Pap – Anagostopoulos
Rethymnon 2014

1 e4 e5 2 ᐃf3 ᐃc6 3 ᐃc4 ᐃf6 (D)

The Two Knights Defence is an aggressive line where Black (normally) wants to sacrifice a pawn for the initiative after 4 ᐃg5 d5 5 exd5 ᐃa5!.

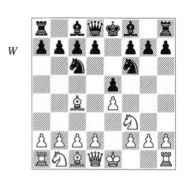

White has several options here, including the quiet 4 d3, but this is not practical given our repertoire since 4...ᐃc5 (4...ᐃe7 is also fine) transposes to quiet lines of the Giuoco Piano where White has foregone the opportunity to play c3 followed by d4 in one go.

My proposed answer, 4 d4, leads to positions that can also be reached via the Scotch Gambit: 1 e4 e5 2 ᐃf3 ᐃc6 3 d4 exd4 4 ᐃc4, and now 4...ᐃf6 transposes (4...ᐃc5 is the other main move, but then 5 c3 leads us back to the Giuoco Piano after 5...ᐃf6! 6 cxd4 since 5...dxc3? is far too risky).

4 d4 exd4 5 e5 d5

This is Black's traditional main line, striking in the centre and exploiting the position of the bishop on c4. White is never better after 6 exf6 dxc4 (here or in similar positions), since Black has excellent central control and the bishop-pair.

For 5...ᐃe4 see Game 10, while 5...ᐃg4 is examined in Game 11.

6 ᐃb5

Hence this move, planning to take on c6.

6...♘e4 7 ♘xd4 ♗d7 *(D)*

The most natural and perhaps the soundest move. We shall examine the more dynamic 7...♗c5 separately – see Game 9.

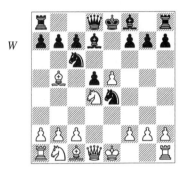

W

8 ♗xc6 bxc6

This is the most ambitious and popular move.

8...♗xc6 avoids being saddled with a bad light-squared bishop, but also gives up Black's main advantage in the position (namely his bishop-pair). The character of the position is also changed compared to the main game, since it is less likely that White will be able to dominate the dark squares once his knight is exchanged for the bishop. After something like 9 ♘xc6 bxc6 10 0-0 ♗c5 (10...♕e7 looks risky in view of 11 c4!, opening the centre and preparing ♕a4) 11 ♘d2 ♘xd2 12 ♗xd2 0-0 13 ♕g4 White has the easier game since his structure is healthier and more mobile.

9 0-0 ♗c5 10 f3 ♘g5 11 ♗e3

In this position Black has a wide choice.

11...♗b6

Other moves:

a) 11...♕e7 12 f4 ♘e4 13 ♘d2 f5 14 ♘xe4 fxe4 15 ♕d2 ♗b6 16 ♘b3 g5?! was T.Petrosian-Navara, Mainz rapid 2007 and now 17 ♕c3 ± would have given White excellent control of the dark squares.

b) 11...♘e6 12 f4 ♗xd4 13 ♗xd4 c5 14 ♗f2 ♗b5 15 f5! ♗xf1 16 fxe6 fxe6?! (16...♗a6 17 exf7+ ♔xf7 18 ♕f3+ ♔g8 19 ♘d2 gives White excellent compensation for the exchange since Black's pieces are horribly misplaced, while White has a simple plan of ♖e1 and pushing the e-pawn) 17 ♕xf1 and White's pieces were worth more than Black's rooks in Sengupta-Saptarshi, Indian Ch, Aurangabad 2011.

c) 11...0-0 12 f4 *(D)* and then:

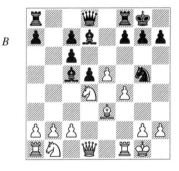

B

c1) 12...♘e4 13 ♘d2 ♕e7 (after 13...♘xd2 14 ♕xd2 ♖e8 15 ♘b3 ♗b6 16 a4 a5 17 ♗c5 White had a typical edge for this variation in T.Petrosian-S.Sethuraman, Dubai 2006) 14 ♘xe4 dxe4 15 ♕e2 f6 16 ♕c4+ ♔h8 17 ♘f5 ♗xe3+ 18 ♘xe3 was better for White in Carleton-Horner, Islington 1971.

c2) 12...♘e6 13 c3 ♕e8 14 ♘d2 ♗b6 15 ♘2b3 (Pap subsequently varied with 15 b4 in M.Pap-Kostopoulos, Anogia 2014) 15...f6 16 ♕d2 fxe5 17 fxe5 was M.Pap-B.Vučković, Serbian Team Ch, Kragujevac 2013 and now 17...♕g6 would have led to a balanced game.

12 f4 ♘e4 13 ♘d2 ♘xd2

13...c5 14 ♘4f3 will transpose.

14 ♕xd2 c5 15 ♘f3 d4 16 ♗f2 ♗c6 *(D)*

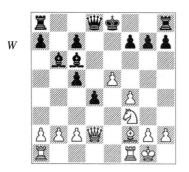

This is an unclear position with substantial risk for White, since the bishop on c6 is an extremely strong piece. On playing through the games which have been played from this position, I particularly don't like (for White) the lines where Black castles queenside and launches a kingside attack. Hence I suggest:

17 ♗h4

This has been played several times by GMs Zoran Jovanović and Misa Pap.

17 a4 is a move your computer may well advocate, but it's far from simple. 17...a5 18 f5!? (White tries to blast open the position, which is justified in view of his lead in development and the – perhaps temporarily – horrendous bishop on b6) 18...♕d5 19 ♕g5 h6 20 ♕xg7 0-0-0 and Black went on to win in G.Jones-L'Ami, Wolvega 2014. Over the board, I would prefer Black's position.

17...♕d7

17...♕d5 18 f5! leads to a strong attack: 18...♔d7 (18...0-0 19 f6 ± places the black king in serious danger) 19 b3 ♖ae8 20 c4 dxc3 (otherwise the b6-bishop is buried) 21 ♕xc3 ♔c8 22 ♗f2 ♖d8 23 ♖ac1?! (23 a4!) 23...♖he8 24 ♗xc5?! ♕xc5+ 25 ♕xc5 ♗xc5+? (25...♗xf3! 26 ♖xf3 ♖xe5 is OK for Black) 26 ♖xc5 ± M.Pap-Abramović, Serbian Team Ch, Kragujevac 2009. Now Black should have taken on f3 and sought drawing chances in a complex, pawn-down double-rook endgame.

18 ♖ad1 *(D)*

Pap's improvement over 18 h3, as played in M.Pap-Brenjo, Serbian Team Ch, Valjevo 2011.

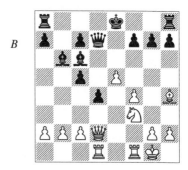

18...♕g4

Other moves:

a) 18...♗d5? 19 f5 gives White a strong initiative. Black can't castle queenside because of the h4-bishop, while kingside castling can be met by f6. Leaving the king in the centre runs into e6 or f6 breaks; e.g., 19...♗c4 20 e6 ♕d5 was Jovanović-Pokorna, Zadar 2011 and now 21 exf7+ ♔xf7 22 ♖f2 +− gives White a decisive attack.

b) 18...0-0 19 f5 ♕xf5 (19...f6 is solid, when 20 e6 ♕d5 21 b3 leads to a complex struggle where I slightly prefer White's chances) 20 ♘xd4 ♕h5?! 21 ♘xc6 ♕xh4 22 ♕d5 c4+ 23 ♔h1 ± and White was on top in Jovanović-Sarić, Croatia Cup, Šibenik 2012.

19 h3 ♕h5 20 ♕e2 0-0?

Missing White's threat. 20...♕f5 would have been OK for Black: 21 ♕c4 ♕e6 (after 21...0-0 22 ♗e7 White starts breaking down the c5-d4 pawn-chain) 22 ♕d3 0-0 (22...c4 23 ♕a3 and Black can't castle) 23 b3 with a balanced game.

21 ♘xd4! ±

Winning an important pawn for free.

21...♕xe2 22 ♘xe2 ♗b5

22...♖ae8 is a better attempt at creating counterplay, aiming for ...f6. For instance, after 23 ♖fe1 f6 24 exf6 gxf6 25 ♗f2 ♔f7 26 ♘g3 White still has work to do to convert his extra pawn. With a bishop-pair I think Black has reasonable drawing chances.

23 ♖fe1 ♗a5 24 c3 ♖fb8 25 ♘g3 ♗c4 26 ♖d2 ♖b6 27 ♘e4 +−

White has consolidated his extra pawn and went on to win smoothly.

27...♖ab8 28 b3 ♗e6 29 ♗f2 ♗f5 30 ♗xc5 ♗xe4 31 ♖xe4 ♖c6 32 ♗xa7

♖a8 33 b4 g5 34 ♗d4 ♗b6 35 fxg5 ♖xc3 36 ♗xb6 cxb6 37 e6 fxe6 38 ♖xe6 b5 39 ♖b6 ♖ca3 40 ♖xb5 ♔g7 41 ♖d7+ ♔g8 42 ♖bb7 ♖g3 43 ♖g7+ ♔f8 44 ♔h2 1-0

Game 9
G. Jones – Hebden
Kilkenny 2011

1 e4 e5 2 ♘f3 ♘c6 3 ♗c4 ♘f6 4 d4 exd4 5 e5 d5 6 ♗b5 ♘e4 7 ♘xd4 ♗c5 *(D)*

This is an interesting alternative to 7...♗d7 (which we examined in Game 8), which can be connected with a pawn sacrifice.

W

8 ♘xc6? leads to complications that don't favour White, who should prefer the sober...

8 ♗e3 ♗d7

8...0-0!? is an interesting pawn sacrifice which was played against me recently by English GM Peter Wells (and subsequently in the higher-profile US Championship final-round clash between Nakamura and Onischuk). White needs to be precise to get anything here. He should start by taking the pawn: 9 ♘xc6 bxc6 10 ♗xc5 ♘xc5 11 ♗xc6 ♖b8. Now Nakamura and I both obtained nothing after castling, but 12 ♕xd5 is the critical move. 12...♕e7 13 0-0 ♖xb2 14 ♘c3 and then:

a) 14...♖xc2 15 ♕d4 ♗e6 was Balint-Lyell, Budapest 2013, and now I like 16 ♖fd1 ±, taking control of the d-file.

b) 14...♖d8 15 ♕f3 ♖xc2 16 ♖fd1 gave White slightly the better chances in view of his more active pieces in M.Neubauer-Van Riemsdijk, São Paulo 2002.

c) 14...♗a6 15 ♖fc1! (the best move, although several subsequent games have continued 15 ♖fd1) 15...♖d8 16 ♕f3 ♕xe5 17 ♗d5 ♕f6 18 ♕e3 (White can also play for an endgame edge by taking on f6, but there Black's activity gives reasonable chances to hold the balance) 18...♘e6 19 ♗b3 (the rook is trapped on b2 and Black needs to be careful) 19...♘d4? (19...♗b7 20 ♖d1 ± still leaves White with an edge) 20 ♖e1 h6 21 ♘d5 ♕h4 22 ♖ad1 ± (White has completed development and Black lacks coordination) 22...c5? (Svidler blunders in a very difficult position; Ftačnik gives 22...♖xb3! as the most tenacious defence – then 23 ♘e7+ ♔f8 24 cxb3 ♘e2+ 25 ♕xe2 ♗xe2 26 ♖xd8+ ♔xe7 27 ♖d2 ± gives White good winning chances with two rooks against the queen) 23 ♘e7+ ♔h7 (after 23...♔f8 24 ♘c6 White wins as 24...♘xc6 fails to 25 ♕xc5+) 24 ♗xf7 ♖d6 25 ♘f5 ♘e2+ 26 ♔h1 ♖xd1 27 ♗g6+! and Black resigned in

Ye Jiangchuan-Svidler, China-Russia, Shanghai 2001.

9 ♗xc6 bxc6 10 ♘d2 (D)

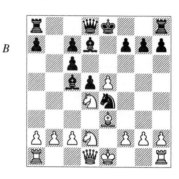

10...♕h4

The critical move, increasing the activity of Black's pieces. However, the black queen is likely to lose time after either ♘f3 or ♘xe4 ♕xe4 ♖e1.

10...♘xd2 11 ♕xd2 0-0 12 0-0 gives a position which is objectively balanced but offers White a clear plan of trying to dominate the dark squares. Black needs to be careful to avoid falling into passivity, especially in view of his d7-bishop. The most important aspect of the position is for White to keep the c7-, c6- and d5-pawns blockaded. Now:

a) 12...♕e7 13 ♘b3 ♗b6 14 ♕c3 ♖ae8?! (14...f6!?) 15 ♗c5 ♗xc5 16 ♘xc5 ♗f5 17 ♖fe1 gave White a very pleasant advantage in Westerberg-I.Agrest, Växjö 2015.

b) After 12...♗b6 White's attacking chances are quite real. 13 ♗g5 ♕e8 14 ♖fe1 and now:

b1) 14...c5 is the thematic move, but after 15 ♗f6! Black only has one move to avoid losing on the spot, namely 15...h6!. Now several games, including Bakalarz-Miron, Agneaux 2012 continued 16 ♖e3, but 16 ♘c6! is stronger. After 16...♔h7 (this is the only move; 16...♗xc6? 17 ♖e3 and the attack cuts right through) 17 ♘e7 (the knight controls some pretty important squares from e7) 17...c6 (17...gxf6? loses to 18 ♘xd5) 18 ♕d3+ g6 19 ♕g3 White has a continuing attack. The computer suggests that the position is equal but I think that over the board Black's position is almost unplayable.

b2) 14...♗e6 *(D)*.

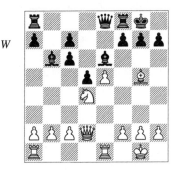

15 ♖e3! (bringing the rook into the attack; 15 a4 is a good positional solution) 15...♔h8 16 ♖g3 ♖g8 17 a4 a5 18 h4?! (18 ♖e1 ± keeps a solid edge) 18...c5 19 h5?! (19 ♘xe6 is objectively better, with a balanced game after 19...fxe6) and then:

b21) 19...c6?? 20 h6 ♗d8 21 ♘xc6 causes Black's position to collapse: 21...♕xc6 22 ♗xd8 ♖axd8 (White mates after 22...♖gxd8 23 ♕g5) 23 hxg7+ ♖xg7 24 ♖xg7 and 24...♔xg7 drops a rook with check after 25 ♕g5+,

or 21...f6 22 hxg7+ ♔xg7 23 exf6+ 1-0 Gaponenko-Wallace, Palma de Mallorca 2009.

b22) 19...cxd4! is a robust computer defence: 20 h6 f6! (20...♗f5? 21 hxg7+ ♖xg7 22 ♗f6 ♗g6 23 ♕h6 ♕f8 24 f4 with a strong initiative) 21 hxg7+ ♔xg7 22 ♗xf6++ ♔f7. White has interesting compensation for the piece but it seems that Black should be able to weather the storm.

11 0-0 *(D)*

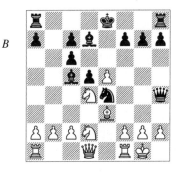

11...♗b6

This was English GM Mark Hebden's previous preference, with which he lost to Nakamura at Gibraltar 2008. It took a hammering in our main game, which I watched live.

Hebden subsequently switched to 11...0-0 12 ♘xe4 ♕xe4 13 ♖e1 ♕g6 (13...♖fe8 14 ♘b3 ♗xe3 15 ♖xe3 ♕b4 16 c3 ♕b6 17 ♕d4 gave White a pleasant bind on the dark squares in Salomon-Hebden, Oslo 2013). Here White hasn't demonstrated anything especially convincing over several games, and I would like to propose a novelty, viz. 14 e6!?, and then:

a) 14...♗xd4 15 ♗xd4 fxe6 (the alternative 15...♗xe6 16 ♖e3 is similar) 16 ♖e3 gives White excellent attacking chances on the dark squares, with more than enough compensation for the pawn.

b) 14...fxe6 15 ♘xe6 and here:

b1) 15...♗xe3 16 ♘xf8 ♗xf2+ 17 ♔xf2 ♖xf8+ 18 ♔g1 gives Black insufficient compensation for the exchange.

b2) 15...♗b4 16 ♘xf8 ♖xf8 17 ♖e2! (17 c3 ♗h3 18 g3 ♕e4 leads to a strong attack on the light squares) 17...♗g4 (now 17...♗h3 18 f3! simply doesn't work for Black) 18 ♕f1 ♗xe2 19 ♕xe2, with perhaps a tiny edge for White based on his superior pawn-structure.

b3) After 15...♗xe6 16 ♗xc5 ♖f4 17 ♖e3 I prefer White based on his superior structure, though Black should be able to hold the balance.

12 a4! *(D)*

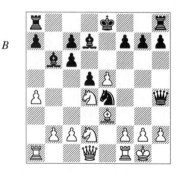

An extremely strong novelty from Gawain, the point of which is revealed on move 17.

12...a5

The most natural response, but as we shall see, it runs into a very strong rejoinder.

12...0-0 is a computer recommendation, but after 13 a5 ♗c5 (13...♗xd4 14 ♗xd4 gives White undisputed control over the dark squares) 14 ♘xe4 ♕xe4 15 ♖e1 we have the position in the note to Black's 11th move, but with a5 included for White. This has to be in his favour, since his rook gains active prospects on the a-file (♖a3 or ♖a4 followed by a rook-lift to the kingside isn't out of the question). Moreover, the weak a7-pawn is now fixed, and if it drops, White's a-pawn will be likely to become a queen.

13 e6!

Black's king is still in the centre so this move, blasting open the position, is certainly what White wants to play. However, working out the details (which I'm pretty sure Gawain had checked at home with his computer) is the difficult part.

13...♗xe6

13...fxe6 *(D)* is the most tenacious, although the bishop on d7 is extremely passive.

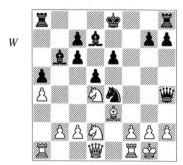

White retains a strong initiative. 14 ♘4f3! (trading the active minor pieces on b6 and e4, in order to leave a poor bishop on d7 against a strong white knight) 14...♕g4 15 ♗xb6 and then:

a) 15...♘xd2 16 ♕xd2 cxb6 17 ♘e5 ♕b4 18 ♕e3 obviously offers White excellent compensation as Black is unable to castle. The next move will probably be 19 ♖fe1.

b) 15...cxb6 16 ♘xe4 ♕xe4 (it doesn't take a GM to observe that 16...dxe4?? fails to 17 ♕xd7+ ♔xd7 18 ♘e5+, winning a piece) 17 ♖e1 ♕g4 (so that the queens will be exchanged if the white knight occupies e5) 18 ♕d3 ♕b4 19 ♘e5 ♕e7 gives White outstanding compensation for the pawn; he now has several promising options. Perhaps the simplest is 20 ♕b3 0-0 (20...♖b8 is risky in view of 21 ♕f3, when Black won't be able to castle) 21 ♕xb6 ± with a better structure and a position where White has risk-free winning chances.

14 ♘xe4 ♕xe4

After 14...dxe4 15 ♘xe6 fxe6 16 ♗xb6 ♖d8 (16...cxb6 17 ♕d6) 17 ♗d4 c5 18 ♕e2 cxd4 19 ♕b5+ White easily regains his pawn and Black will struggle to coordinate his pieces. For example, 19...♔f7 20 ♕xa5 ♖d7 21 ♕c5 and the passed a-pawn is extremely dangerous.

15 ♖e1 *(D)*

The white battery along the e-file is extremely dangerous and it is possible that the black position can't be saved.

15...♗xd4

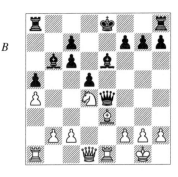

Black can try to solve his problems by tactical means: 15...♕g4 16 f3 (16 ♕xg4 ♗xg4 is still better for White but he doesn't have a devastating discovered check) 16...♕h4 17 ♘xe6 ♗xe3+ 18 ♖xe3 fxe6 19 ♖xe6+ ♔d7. Black isn't losing here but his position is much harder to play, with an inferior structure and a weaker king. A good line for White begins 20 ♖e4 ♕f6 21 c4! ±, trying to open the centre.

16 ♗xd4

If White takes on g7 he will have a large advantage with no risk. Accordingly Hebden tried to retain his extra pawn but the cure proves worse than the disease.

16...♕g6 17 ♖a3!

A devastating rook-lift. Comparing the activity of the rooks tells you everything you need to know about this position.

17...♔d7 18 ♖g3 ♕f5 19 ♕d2! +−

Gaining further time by threatening to collect the queen with 20 ♖e5.

19...♕h5 20 ♗xg7

From here on, the computer suggests various alternative ways to win, but Gawain's treatment is easily good enough.

20...Rhg8 *(D)*

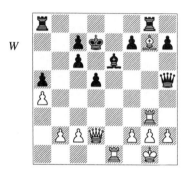

21 Qd4

Opening lines with 21 c4! is extremely strong.

21...Qf5 22 c4 Rab8 23 h4

23 Be5! cuts the black queen off from the defence.

23...Rb4 24 b3 Kc8

Black's king tries to get to safety on the queenside. However, his four split pawns on that side don't afford adequate protection.

25 Qa7 f6 26 Qxa5 Rb8 27 cxd5 cxd5

Other captures also lose – amongst other things, White is now material up.

28 Rc1!

Starting a devastating attack on the c7-pawn.

28...Qf4 29 Bh6!

A nice shot, deflecting the queen and protecting the c1-rook.

29...Qd6 30 Rgc3 Rb7 31 Qa8+ 1-0

A really powerful game by Gawain.

Game 10
G. Jones – S. Ernst
Wolvega 2014

1 e4 e5 2 Nf3 Nc6 3 d4 exd4 4 Bc4 Nf6 5 e5 Ne4

A good move with a solid reputation. However, Black needs to be precise over the next few moves since he loses some time with this knight.

6 Qe2! *(D)*

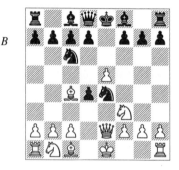

Immediately putting the question to the knight.

6...Nc5

6...Bb4+ is never a problem for White, since after 7 Kf1! Black loses coordination and will struggle to get his pieces safe. In particular, 7...Nc5? now drops a piece after 8 a3.

7 0-0

White can also play the enterprising sacrifice 7 c3. Interested readers can look up the excellent game Nakamura-Fressinet, Wijk aan Zee 2004. However, I'm recommending the main line instead since White's position appears quite promising to me.

7...Be7

7...♘e6 8 ♗xe6 dxe6 (the untested 8...fxe6!? looks like a decent alternative) 9 ♖d1 ♗e7 10 ♗e3 0-0 11 ♘xd4 ♕d5 12 f4 has been played in a couple of games. While one must always respect the latent power of the bishop-pair, here I think White's position is easier to play because of his space advantage. After something like 12...♗c5 13 ♘c3 ♘xd4 14 ♖xd4 ♕c6 15 ♖d3 White keeps an edge.

8 ♖d1 *(D)*

8 c3!? is again possible.

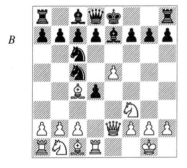

8...d5

This is always a principled move for Black in the Open Games, but here he needs to be careful about the position of his king in the centre. Other moves:

a) 8...0-0 9 ♘xd4 gives White a risk-free advantage based on his extra space. Perhaps Black should try to equalize gradually after 9...♘xd4 10 ♖xd4 c6, since 9...d5 10 ♘f3! ♗e6 11 ♘c3! d4 put Black's centre under strong pressure in Huschenbeth-Kahlert, Hamburg 2014, and now 12 ♘b5 ♗g4 13 c3 ♗xf3 14 gxf3 d3 15 ♗xd3

♘xd3 16 ♖xd3 would have won a pawn for insufficient compensation.

b) 8...♘e6 was the recent choice of GM Dejan Bojkov, who has extensively tested this 5...♘e4 line with Black. 9 c3 d5 10 exd6 cxd6 11 cxd4 d5 was Karpatchev-Bojkov, 2nd Bundesliga 2012/13 and now the simplest would have been 12 ♗b3 0-0 13 ♘c3 ♘c7 14 ♗f4 ± with the better-placed pieces in a symmetrical IQP structure.

9 exd6 ♕xd6 10 b4 ♘e6

Black can also try to keep the position closed with 10...d3 11 cxd3 *(D)*, and now:

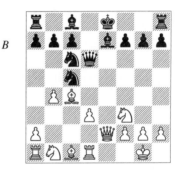

a) 11...♘a4?! 12 b5 ♘d4?! 13 ♘xd4 ♕xd4 14 ♗a3 ♗e6 15 ♗xe6 fxe6 16 ♕xe6 ♘c5 17 ♗xc5 ♕xc5 18 ♖e1 and White was winning in Stević-Beliavsky, Slovenian Team Ch, Celje 2004.

b) 11...♘xb4? 12 d4 and then:

b1) 12...♗e6 13 dxc5 ♗xc4 14 cxd6 ♗xe2 15 ♖e1 ♗xf3 16 ♖xe7+ ♔d8 was Tzermiadianos-Cela, Athens 1997. Now the game's 17 ♖xc7 was good enough but 17 gxf3! would have won easily; for instance, 17...cxd6 18 ♖xf7 ♘c2 19 ♘a3 ♘xa1 20 ♘c4 +−

and the black king can't save himself from the combined attack of White's three pieces.

b2) 12...♘d7 13 ♖e1 and then 13...0-0 14 ♕xe7 ♕xe7 15 ♖xe7 ♘c2 16 ♗b2 is much better for White, while after 13...♘b6, as in Nogueiras-Mikhalchishin, Mexico City (team event) 1977, the strongest would have been 14 ♗g5! ♘c6 15 d5 h6 16 ♗h4 ± with a powerful initiative.

c) I haven't found any games with 11...♘e6, but the forcing variation given by Oliver Renet, 12 d4!? (White can also play 12 ♘c3 with a promising position) 12...♘cxd4 13 ♘xd4 ♘xd4 14 ♕e4 ♗f5 15 ♕xd4 ♕xd4 16 ♖xd4 ♗f6 17 ♖f4 0-0-0 (17...g6 18 g4 is also better for White) 18 ♘d2 ♗xa1 19 ♖xf5, leads to an unbalanced endgame where the white minor pieces should probably be more effective than the rook and pawn.

11 b5 *(D)*

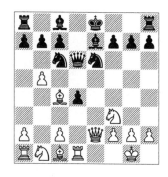

This position has arisen several times in grandmaster practice.

11...♘a5

Or:

a) 11...♘b4 was a recent GM choice in Kashtanov-Ehlvest, Jurmala blitz 2015. Here White has an excellent option in 12 ♘c3!; for instance, 12...c6 13 ♘e4 ♕c7 14 ♗xe6 ♗xe6 15 ♘xd4 0-0 16 a3 ♘d5 17 bxc6 bxc6 18 c4 ♘b6 19 ♘xe6 fxe6 20 ♗d2 and Black struggles to display dynamic compensation for his structural weaknesses.

b) 11...♘cd8? is, unsurprisingly, too passive to be attractive for Black. 12 ♗a3 and then:

b1) Black could try 12...c5 but after 13 bxc6 ♕c7 (not 13...♕xc6?? 14 ♗b5 +−) 14 ♘xd4 ♗xa3 15 ♘xe6 ♘xe6 16 cxb7 ♗xb7 17 ♘xa3 0-0 18 ♗xe6 fxe6 19 ♕xe6+ ♔h8 his compensation for the pawns is insufficient.

b2) 12...♕b6 13 ♗xe7 ♔xe7 14 ♘xd4 ♖e8 and here:

b21) 15 ♘b3?! (a slight misstep from the Aussie GM, who is normally surgical with the initiative) 15...♔f8 16 ♕h5? (16 ♖e1 ± would have kept Black under severe pressure) 16...h6 17 g3? (after 17 ♘c3 I still prefer White) 17...♘g5 18 ♗f1 and at this point a draw was agreed in Smerdon-Bojkov, Canberra 2011. Black would be better after 18...♕f6 but he was presumably delighted to see the back of this game.

b22) Completing development with 15 ♘c3 +− is decisive; for instance, after 15...♔f8 16 ♘d5 ♘xd4 (16...♕c5 17 ♘b3 ♕a3 18 ♕e4 with a decisive difference in piece activity) 17 ♕xe8+ ♔xe8 18 ♘xb6 White wins the exchange and should win the game.

12 ♗a3 ♕b6 13 ♗xe6 ♗xe6

13...♕xe6 is asking for trouble on the e-file after 14 ♕d3, but this might have been a better bet. After 14...♕f6 15 ♘bd2 ♗xa3 16 ♕xa3 b6 17 ♖e1+ ♗e6 ± Black is better coordinated than in the game, and is ready to offer a queen exchange with 18...♕e7.

14 ♗xe7 ♔xe7 *(D)*

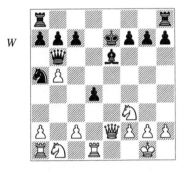

15 ♖xd4?!

Although this works out well in the game, I don't think it's objectively strongest.

After 15 ♘xd4 I think it's clear that White has a pleasant edge. Black's king is in the centre and cannot be conveniently brought to safety. The problem with the king position is not so much that it is subject to a direct attack (though Gawain has launched vicious attacks from less promising positions than this!), but rather that it gets in the way of the pieces – Black's rooks are harder to coordinate than White's, and the e6-bishop is awkwardly pinned. Moreover, Black's knight on a5 is clearly misplaced and will need some time to return to play, while it is not yet clear if the queen on b6 is a good piece.

The game could continue along the following lines: 15...♖hd8 16 ♕e5 ♔f8 (getting the king out of the centre at the cost of some time) 17 ♘c3 ♗g4 18 ♘f5 ♗xf5 (18...♗xd1? loses to 19 ♕xg7+ ♔e8 20 ♕e5+!, when both 20...♔f8 and 20...♔d7 lead to quick mates, while after 20...♕e6 White's strongest is to ignore the queen and simply leave it blocking the king's exit via e6: 21 ♕h8+ ♔d7 22 ♖xd1+, winning decisive material) 19 ♕xf5 ♔g8 (perhaps Black should try to suffer for a draw in an inferior endgame after 19...♕f6) 20 ♖d7 with a strong initiative.

15...♖ad8?

This extremely ambitious move should have been punished. Black wants to keep the other rook free for the e-file, but it was more important to connect the rooks so that ...♔f8 can be played quickly.

After 15...♖hd8 followed by ...♔f8 Black has reasonable chances of getting coordinated. 16 ♖a4 a6!, protecting the knight, reveals a hidden benefit of keeping the rook on a8.

16 ♖a4! *(D)*

Targeting the trapped black knight. 16 ♖e4 was also promising, but Gawain's move looks more incisive.

16...♕c5?

16...♘c6! is a cute defensive try, when the knight can't be taken in view of 17 bxc6? ♕b2 (and 18 ♕e5?? would lead to disaster on the back rank). After 17 ♘bd2 ♘d4 18 ♕e4 White retains strong pressure but nothing decisive is immediately apparent.

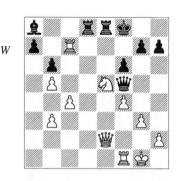

17 ♘bd2 b6 18 ♘b3!

Beautifully converting one advantage (misplaced knight on a5) into another (winning material).

18...♘xb3 19 axb3 ♖he8 20 ♖c4 ♕d6 21 ♖c6 ♕f4 22 g3 ♕f6 23 ♘e5 ♔f8

White has played powerfully and now taking either the a7- or the c7-pawn would lead to a large advantage. Instead Black gradually gets back into the game and even wins in the end. In view of my suggested improvement at move 15, the rest isn't especially relevant for our purposes, so I shall present the remaining moves with minimal notes.

24 f4?! ♕f5 25 ♖xc7 f6 26 ♖f1 ♗d5?

26...♕h3 offers Black sufficient counterplay.

27 c4 ♗a8 *(D)*

28 ♖xa7

28 g4! ♕e6 29 ♘d7+ ♔g8 30 ♕xe6+ ♖xe6 31 ♖xa7 +−.

28...h5! 29 c5 ♗d5 30 c6 ♔g8 31 g4?

31 c7.

31...♕e6! 32 g5 fxe5 33 f5 ♕d6

White has compensation for the piece in an unclear position but goes on to lose.

34 f6 ♕c5+ 35 ♕f2 ♕xf2+ 36 ♖xf2 gxf6 37 gxf6 ♖f8 38 ♖f5 ♖f7 39 ♖a6 ♗e6 40 ♖g5+ ♔h7 41 ♖g7+ ♖xg7+ 42 fxg7 ♖d2?!

42...♔xg7.

43 c7 ♖c2 44 ♖xb6 ♗c8 45 ♖c6??

Various moves draw, including 45 ♖g6!.

45...♖xc6 46 bxc6 ♔xg7 47 b4 ♔f6 48 b5 ♔e6 49 b6 ♔d6 50 b7 ♔xc7 51 bxc8♕ ♔xc8 52 ♔f2 ♔c7 53 ♔g3 ♔xc6 54 ♔h4 e4 55 ♔g3 ♔d5 56 ♔f2 ♔d4 57 ♔e2 e3 58 ♔d1 ♔e4 59 ♔e2 ♔f4 60 ♔e1 ♔f3 61 ♔f1 h4 62 h3 ♔g3 63 ♔e2 ♔xh3 64 ♔f3 e2 65 ♔f2 e1♕+ 0-1

Game 11
Jasny – Vul
Tatranske Zruby 2014

1 e4 e5 2 ♘f3 ♘c6 3 d4 exd4 4 ♗c4 ♘f6 5 e5 ♘g4 *(D)*

To me, this move (which has been played by many strong players, including Magnus Carlsen) seems a lot riskier than 5...♞e4 (and, of course, than 5...d5).

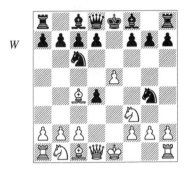

W

Black is relying on specific tactical features of the position to get away with this knight jump. Nevertheless, I have little doubt that if he plays correctly he should be fine.

6 0-0

6 ♛e2 has also been extensively tested. However, against such a provocative move, my preference is for simple development.

6...d6

Immediately striking at White's important e5-pawn. Black seems to have enough resources to get away with this. Other moves:

a) As you might have guessed, 6...♞gxe5?? just loses a piece to 7 ♞xe5 ♞xe5 8 ♜e1 d6 9 f4 +–.

b) 6...♝c5 7 ♝f4 0-0 8 h3 ♞h6 9 ♝xh6 gxh6 10 c3 d5 (10...dxc3 is critical, but after 11 ♞xc3 White has overwhelming compensation for the pawn) was Leygue-Flear, Saint Affrique 2001 and now 11 ♝b3 ♝f5 (11...dxc3 12 ♞xc3 ♞e7 13 ♛c1 ± followed by ♛xh6 is excellent for White)

12 cxd4 ♝b6 gives White a pleasant advantage.

c) After 6...♝e7 7 ♜e1 d6 8 exd6 ♛xd6 9 h3 ♞f6 it might seem as though Black has almost consolidated his extra pawn, but now a new avenue of pressure opens: 10 b3! 0-0 11 ♝a3 ♛d8 12 ♝xe7 ♞xe7 13 ♛xd4 ♛xd4 14 ♞xd4 ♞f5 was Tzermiadianos-Yuldachev, World Cities, Al Ain 2012 and now I would recommend 15 ♞f3. The position is either equal, or White has a minimal edge, but either way Black has to find a few precise moves to draw.

7 exd6 *(D)*

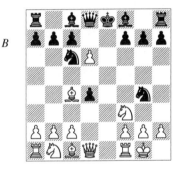

B

7...♝xd6

Developing another piece, but now the position of the black king will cost further time.

7...♛xd6 is probably sounder. 8 ♞a3 a6 9 h3 ♞h6 (9...♞f6 10 ♞g5 ♛d8 11 ♝b3 ♞e6 12 ♜e1, as in Roji-ček-Kociscak, Slovakian Team Ch 2013/14, gives White good compensation according to GM Niclas Huschenbeth) 10 ♜e1+ ♝e7 11 ♝g5 ♞f5 was Efimenko-Short, Mukachevo (6)

2009. Now Huschenbeth recommends 12 ♗d3 with an initiative; for instance, 12...0-0 13 ♗xf5 ♗xf5 14 ♗xe7 ♘xe7 15 ♕xd4 ♘c6 (after 15...♕xd4 16 ♘xd4 ♖ad8 17 c3 White wins material) 16 ♕xd6 cxd6 17 ♖ad1 ± and White has the more pleasant endgame.

8 ♖e1+ ♔f8 9 ♘bd2 ♘ge5

9...♗f5 10 ♘b3 ♕f6 was O.Schlesinger-Beha, Germany (team event) 2005/6 and now I like 11 ♗d5 ♘ce5 12 ♘bxd4 with an edge.

10 ♘xe5 ♘xe5 11 ♗b3 *(D)*

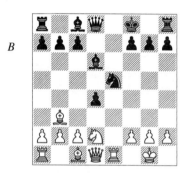

11...♗g4

This has been played in both of the games which reached this position.

11...♕h4 starts a forcing sequence where White comes out on top: 12 h3 ♗xh3! (otherwise Black will be pushed back) 13 ♖xe5! (13 gxh3?! ♕xh3 gives Black at least enough compensation) 13...♗xe5 14 ♕f3 ♗f6 (14...♗e6 15 ♗xe6 ♕h2+ 16 ♔f1 ♕h1+ 17 ♔e2 ♗f6 18 ♕h3! ♕xh3 19 ♗xh3 also looks better for White) 15 gxh3 ♖e8 with a complex position where I prefer the pieces to the rook and two pawns.

12 f3 ♗f5 13 ♘e4 *(D)*

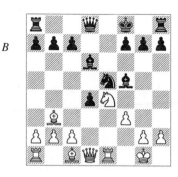

White is still a pawn down but Black really struggles to complete his development and, in particular, to activate his rooks and bring his king to safety.

13...h6

13...♕d7 14 ♗f4 ♖e8 15 ♕d2 ♗xe4 16 ♖xe4 ♘c6 17 ♖ae1 ♖xe4 18 ♖xe4 gave White more than enough compensation in Gochev-Kizov, Macedonian Team Ch, Struga 2012.

14 ♗f4 ♗xe4

This is a major concession but it's hard to offer Black good advice.

15 ♖xe4 ♘c6 16 ♕d3!

Bringing the queen into the attack and making room for the a1-rook.

16...g5 17 ♕c4 ♖h7 18 ♗xd6+ ♕xd6 19 ♖ae1

White has an extremely strong initiative.

19...♖d8

Trying to exchange with 19...♘a5? fails to 20 ♕b5 ♘xb3 21 ♕xb7 ♖d8 22 ♕xb3 ±.

20 ♕b5 a6 21 ♕f5 ♕g6 22 ♕xg6 fxg6

Black has defended excellently but White's initiative persists into the endgame.

23 ♖e6 ♖e7 24 ♖f6+ ♔e8 25 ♗f7+
♔d7 *(D)*

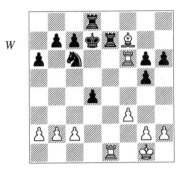

26 ♗e6+

26 ♖d1 ♔c8 27 ♗xg6 ± would have
left Black with an uphill defensive
task – the white bishop is by far the
stronger minor piece in a position with
an open centre and pawn-majorities
on opposite wings.

26...♔d6! 27 ♗c8+

27 ♗f7+ would have enabled White
to transpose into the previous line.

**27...♔c5 28 ♖xe7 ♘xe7 29 ♗xb7
♖b8 30 ♗e4 ♖b6?!**

30...♖xb2 is equal. The rest isn't
relevant for our purposes.

**31 ♖f7 ♔d6 32 b3 ♔e6 33 ♖f8 h5
34 ♖e8 ♔d7 35 ♖a8 ♘f5 36 ♗d3
♘e3 37 ♔f2 ♖c6 38 ♖xa6 ♖xa6 39
♗xa6 ♘xc2 40 ♗d3 ♘b4 41 ♗xg6?!
♘xa2 42 ♗xh5 ♘c1 43 ♗f7 ♘d3+ 44
♔f1 ♔d6 45 g3?! ♘e5 46 ♗h5 ♘d3?!
47 ♗g6 ♘c1?! 48 ♗f7 ♔e5 49 ♔e1
♘d3+ 50 ♔e2 ♘b4 51 h3 c5 52 ♔d2
♔f6 53 ♗c4 ♘c6 54 ♗d5 ♘e5 55
♗e4 ♔e6 56 f4 gxf4 57 gxf4 ♘d7 58
♔e2 ♘b6 59 h4 ♘c8?! 60 h5 ♘d6 61
h6 ♔f6 62 ♗d3 ♘b7 63 ♔f3 ♘a5 64**
f5 ♘c6 65 h7 ♔g7 66 f6+ ♔h8 67
♔f4 ♘d8 68 ♔e5 ♘f7+ 69 ♔d5 c4 70
♔xc4 1-0

1 e4 e5 2 ♘f3: Other Moves

Game 12
Korneev – T. Mamedjarova
Gjøvik 2009

1 e4 e5 2 ♘f3 ♘f6

The Petroff used to be the bane of a
1 e4 player's life, before it was largely
displaced by the Berlin and the Marshall. Since I am recommending the
Italian Game, you needn't concern
yourself with the Berlin and the Marshall at this point, but the Petroff remains a popular choice at all levels
and requires serious consideration.

My recommendation is 3 d4 ♘xe4
4 ♗d3 d5 5 dxe5, which leads to a
structure you might recognize from
the Two Knights. This is a sideline relative to 3 ♘xe5 or 5 ♘xe5, but one
which has been quite popular recently
amongst strong and experienced 1 e4
players like Guseinov, Safarli, Korneev and others.

3 d4 *(D)*
3...♘xe4

3...exd4 used to be regarded as a
secondary variation, but has since been
defended by the elite Chinese GMs
who regularly play the Petroff, like Bu
Xiangzhi and Wang Hao. I thought
that 4 ♗c4 was an interesting answer
(since Black's most common response

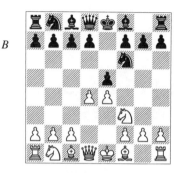

B

is 4...♘c6, transposing to the Two Knights), but failed to find anything clear after 4...♗c5. So I think White should choose the natural 4 e5 ♘e4 5 ♕xd4 d5 6 exd6 ♘xd6. Here I like 7 ♗f4 ♘c6 8 ♕d2; then Black's most common reply is 8...♗e7 9 ♘c3 0-0 10 0-0-0, when White has good attacking chances; for instance, 10...♗f5 11 ♗d3 ♕d7 12 ♘d5 and White was doing well in B.Smith-M.Mihalj, Veliko Gradište 2015.

4 ♗d3 d5

4...♘c6 was a stunning novelty when it was unleashed by GM Jacob Murey in 1993. It is still a respectable line, but much less popular than 4...d5. White can try a dangerous gambit as follows: 5 ♗xe4 d5 6 ♗g5 ♕d6 7 dxe5 ♕b4+ 8 ♘c3 dxe4 9 a3 ♕a5 (after 9...♕xb2 10 ♘d5 ♗c5 11 ♘xc7+ ♔f8, as in Oleksienko-Rakhmanov, Moscow 2007, White should play 12 0-0! exf3 13 ♕xf3 with a powerful initiative; e.g., 13...♕xe5 14 ♗f4 ♕f5 15 ♖ad1) 10 ♘d4 ♘xe5 (10...♕xe5?! 11 ♘xc6 ♕xg5 12 ♘xe4 was much better for White in I.Almasi-Seres, Budapest 2005) 11 0-0 ♗g4 12 ♕e1 f6 13 b4 (an

attempted improvement over 13 ♕xe4, as played in P.Carlsson-Minhazuddin, World Cities, Al Ain 2012) 13...♕a6 14 ♕xe4 0-0-0 15 ♗f4 h5 16 ♗xe5 fxe5 was played in Rausis-G.Pap, Chemnitz 2014. The game seems dynamically balanced after both 17 ♘f3 and 17 ♘b3.

5 dxe5 *(D)*

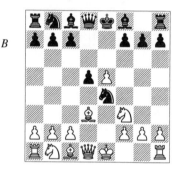

B

5...♗e7

Or 5...♘c5 6 ♗e2, and now:

a) 6...♗g4 7 ♘c3 c6 8 0-0 ♗e7 9 ♘d4 ♗xe2 10 ♕xe2 g6 (10...0-0 is better, but after 11 ♕g4 ♕d7 12 ♕g3 White has chances of developing an initiative on the kingside) 11 ♗h6 was much better for White in Safarli-Bezgodov, Khanty-Mansiisk blitz 2013.

b) 6...♗e7 7 0-0 0-0 8 ♗e3 and then:

b1) 8...♘e4 9 c4 c6 10 ♕c1 ♗g4 11 h3 ♗xf3 12 ♗xf3 ♘g5 13 ♗g4 was good for White in Guseinov-Khouri, Abu Dhabi 2010.

b2) 8...c6 9 c4 dxc4 10 ♗xc4 ♕xd1 (after 10...♘bd7, as in Neiksans-Nouro, Finnish Team Ch, Jyväskylä 2013/14, 11 b4 ♘e6 12 ♕b3 is nice for White)

11 ♖xd1 gives White some chances of an edge in this endgame; for instance, 11...♗g4 (11...♘bd7 12 ♘c3 {12 b4!?} 12...♘b6 13 ♗xc5 ♗xc5 14 ♗b3 ♗g4 15 ♘e4 ♗e7 with balanced play in Safarli-Kamarunsalehin, Sharjah 2014) 12 ♗xc5 ♗xc5 13 ♘c3 ♗e7 (Guseinov-Bu Xiangzhi, Istanbul Olympiad 2012) 14 h3 ♗xf3 15 gxf3 gives White an edge since Black struggles to develop his queenside.

b3) 8...♘c6 9 ♘c3 ♗e6 10 ♗b5 ♘d7 (10...♘e4 11 ♘xe4 dxe4 12 ♗xc6 bxc6 13 ♕xd8 ♖fxd8 14 ♘d4 ♗d5 15 c4 ♗xc4 16 ♖fc1 ♗d5 17 ♘xc6 ♖d7 18 ♘xa7 gave White an extra pawn and some winning chances in Safarli-Trusheliov, St Petersburg 2009) 11 ♗f4 a6 (after 11...♘b6, as played in the game Guseinov-Abasov, Sharjah 2014, White can obtain similar play to our main game with 12 a4 a6 13 ♗xc6 bxc6 14 a5 ♘c4 15 b3 ♘a3 16 ♘d4) 12 ♗xc6 bxc6 13 ♘d4 ♘b8 14 ♘xe6 fxe6 15 ♕g4 ♔h8 (after the more active 15...♖f5 16 ♘e2 ♕f8 17 ♗e3!? ♖xe5 18 ♘g3 Black is a pawn up, but his misplaced pieces promise White good compensation) 16 ♘e2 ♕d7 17 ♘d4 ♗c5 18 ♗e3 ♗xd4 19 ♕xd4 and White has achieved his aim (in both this opening and the Two Knights) of seizing control of the dark squares. Black's structure is compromised and his knight is obviously horrendous. White went on to win in Safarli-Aleskerov, Nakhchivan 2013.

6 0-0 *(D)*
6...0-0
Or:

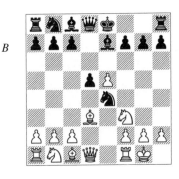

a) 6...♘c6 7 ♘c3 ♘xc3 (7...♘c5?! 8 ♗b5 ♗e6 9 ♘d4 ♗d7 10 ♗xc6 bxc6 11 f4 led to a rout in Shankland-J.Lampert, Biel 2014: 11...0-0 12 f5 ♘e4? 13 ♘xe4 dxe4 14 ♕g4 ♗c5 15 c3 g6? 16 ♗h6 ♖e8 17 e6! 1-0) 8 bxc3 ♗g4 9 ♖e1 0-0 10 h3 ♗h5 11 ♗f5 ♗g6 12 g4 ♖e8?! (12...♘a5!?) 13 ♕d3 was slightly better for White in Korneev-Debray, Lille 2011.

b) 6...♗g4 7 ♘c3 ♘xc3 8 bxc3 ♘d7 9 ♖e1 ♘c5 10 h3 ♗h5 11 ♗f5 g6 12 ♗d3 g5?! 13 ♗f5! was pleasant for White in Korneev-Espejo Montagut, Seville 2011.

7 ♘c3 ♘xc3 8 bxc3 c5 9 c4

Black faces a fundamental decision concerning which central structure to play.

9...d4

Other moves:

a) 9...♗e6? 10 cxd5 ♗xd5 11 ♕e2 ♕c7 (missing a tactic, but otherwise ♖d1 was coming) 12 ♗xh7+! ♔xh7 13 ♕d3+ ♔g8 14 ♕xd5 ± left White a pawn up for nothing in Neiksans-Klimakovs, Latvian Ch, Riga 2013.

b) 9...dxc4 10 ♗xc4 ♕xd1 11 ♖xd1 ♘c6 12 ♗d5 ♗e6 13 ♗e4 h6 was level

in Movsesian-Harikrishna, Greek Team
Ch, Kallithea 2008.

10 ♕e2 *(D)*

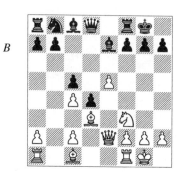

10...f5?!

10...♘c6 seems more circumspect.

**11 exf6 ♗xf6 12 ♕e4 g6 13 ♗h6
♖e8 14 ♕f4 ±**

White has generated a serious kingside initiative while Black's entire
queenside is undeveloped.

14...♘c6 15 ♖fe1 ♗e6 16 h4

16 ♗g5! +–, exchanging a key de-
fender of the dark-squares, is strong.

**16...♘b4 17 ♗g5 ♘xd3 18 cxd3
♔g7?**

Black had to try 18...♗xg5 ±.

19 h5!

Now White wins material by force.

19...gxh5

19...♗xg5 20 ♘xg5 ♗f5 21 g4! is
winning for White.

20 ♖e5!!

A beautiful exploitation of the pins.

20...♗f7 21 ♖xc5

21 ♗xf6+ ♕xf6 22 ♖f5 ♕e7 23
♖e1 +– is even clearer.

**21...♗e6 22 ♖d5 ♕e7 23 ♘xd4
♖e1+ 24 ♔h2 ♗xd5 25 ♖xe1 1-0**

Game 13
A. Sokolov – Naiditsch
French Team Ch 2015

I saw a lot of this game online as it
was played. Naiditsch was having an
horrendous event, but this takes nothing away from Sokolov, who was once
World Number 3 and remains a force
to be reckoned with.

1 e4 e5 2 ♘f3 *(D)*

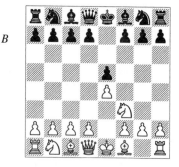

2...d6

The Philidor Defence has never
been at the forefront of theory or opening fashion, but it remains a respectable opening. Via this move-order, I
recall it being used extensively by a
whole generation of French super-
GMs (including Bacrot and Fressinet),
while my occasional Olympiad team-
mate IM Gavin Wall has played it for
his whole life.

The most popular Philidor variation
is the Hanham, which is more typically reached via the move-order 1 e4
d6 2 d4 ♘f6 3 ♘c3 e5 4 ♘f3 ♘bd7.
Since our repertoire against the Pirc is
3 ♗d3, we conveniently avoid the

Hanham by that move-order. Also, as will appear, Black can't reach the Hanham by the 'pure' Philidor move-order (as in this game), since White has attractive alternatives at various points.

A question arises as to which moves are sufficiently dubious or second-rate so that they may safely be ignored. For instance, 2...f6? and 2...♕e7?! are poor moves for reasons the reader can probably work out on his own. I've decided just to include light coverage of the Latvian Gambit (2...f5?!), since it crops up from time to time. 2...f5?! 3 ♘xe5 *(D)*.

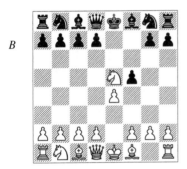

3...♘c6?! (3...♕f6 is the main line, when 4 d4 d6 5 ♘c4 fxe4 6 ♘c3 ♕g6 7 ♘e3 c6 8 d5 gives White a pleasant position, as in Warakomski-Dionisi, Warsaw rapid 2011) 4 d4! (this move was suggested by John Nunn a few years ago in *Secrets of Practical Chess*; Black's position looks horrible to me) 4...fxe4 5 ♘c3 ♘f6 was Korneev-V.Kalinins, Bunratty 2014 and now 6 ♗c4 ± gives White a serious advantage; for instance, 6...d5 7 ♘xd5 ♘xd5 8 ♕h5+ g6 9 ♘xg6 hxg6 10 ♕xg6+!

♔d7 11 ♗xd5 +− with three pawns and a serious initiative for the piece. The game might continue 11...♘xd4 12 ♗g5 ♗e7 13 ♗e6+!! ♘xe6 14 ♖d1+, winning the queen.

3 d4 *(D)*

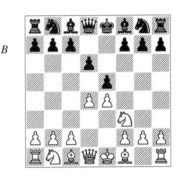

3...exd4

Other moves:

a) After 3...♘d7 4 ♗c4 Black has no good method to reach the Hanham:

a1) 4...♗e7? 5 dxe5 ♘xe5 (5...dxe5 6 ♕d5 +− ends the game immediately) 6 ♘xe5 dxe5 7 ♕h5 costs Black a pawn.

a2) Black's most common option is 4...c6 5 0-0 ♗e7, when the minitactic 6 dxe5 dxe5 7 ♘g5! ♗xg5 8 ♕h5 ♕e7 9 ♕xg5 ± gives White the bishop-pair for free.

b) 3...♘f6, which would transpose to the Hanham after 4 ♘c3 ♘bd7, allows 4 dxe5 ♘xe4 5 ♕d5 ♘c5 6 ♗g5 ♕d7 7 exd6 ♗xd6 8 ♘c3 0-0 9 0-0-0, when White seems to have the better chances in a sharp position. For instance, look up the game Quesada Perez-Sambuev, Havana 2014.

4 ♘xd4 ♘f6 5 ♘c3 ♗e7 6 ♗e2

White has more ambitious set-ups available, but simple development should be enough for an edge since he has extra space in the centre.

6...0-0 7 0-0 ♖e8 8 f4 ♗f8 9 ♗f3 *(D)*

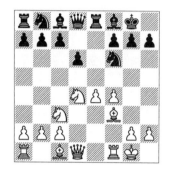

9...c5

By far the most popular move. Quiet approaches like 9...c6 are less challenging and give White chances to consolidate; for instance, 10 ♖e1 a5 11 ♗e3 a4 12 a3 ♘bd7 13 ♗f2 ♘c5 14 h3 and White's strong centre promised him the easier play in D.Vera-Granda, Montevideo 2015.

10 ♘de2 ♘c6 11 f5!?

This is a relatively rare move but seems quite strong to me. At the cost of giving Black one good square (e5), White gains kingside space and restricts the c8-bishop.

11...♘e5

Naiditsch plays logically, putting his knight on a strong outpost. Other moves:

a) 11...h6 12 ♘f4 ♘d4 13 ♘fd5 ♘xf3+ 14 gxf3 g6 15 ♘xf6+ ♕xf6 16 ♘d5 ♕d8 17 ♔h1 gave White a strong

attack in A.Kuzmin-Seel, Catalan Bay 2004.

b) 11...♘d7 12 ♘d5 ♘b6 13 ♘ef4 ♘e5 14 b3 ♘xd5 15 ♘xd5 b6 was Brenjo-Stojanović, Belgrade 2006. Now I like the simple 16 ♗b2, when White has a very pleasant position. Black must always watch out for the f6 break, and if he stops it by playing ...f6 himself, the e6-square will be chronically weak.

c) 11...d5 12 exd5 ♘d4 13 ♘xd4 cxd4 14 ♕xd4 ♗xf5 15 ♗f4! ♗xc2 16 ♖ac1 ♕a5 17 d6 led to a quick rout in V.Georgiev-Scalcione, Genoa 2001.

12 ♘f4 ♗d7 13 ♘fd5 ♘xd5 14 ♘xd5 ♗c6 15 ♗f4 *(D)*

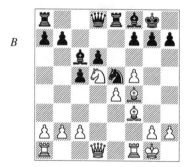

15...b5

Naiditsch seeks queenside counterplay. Black can consider 15...♘xf3+ 16 gxf3 g6. This is a better version than A.Kuzmin-Seel, analysed in the previous note, since his kingside hasn't been weakened by ...h6. The game might continue 17 ♕d2 ♗xd5 (otherwise ♗g5 would have been annoying) 18 ♕xd5 with balanced chances.

16 b3 a5 17 ♕d2 a4 18 ♖ad1

I find White's build-up very appealing – he simply posts his pieces in the centre. As it turns out, they are perfectly placed when the position opens.

18...♖a7 19 ♕f2 axb3 20 axb3 ♖a2 21 ♘c3 ♖a3 22 ♘d5 ♔h8

Repeating with 22...♖a2 appears more prudent, but I have no doubt that Naiditsch was playing to win at this stage.

23 ♗h5 ♕d7 24 h3 ♕a7 25 ♔h2 b4 26 ♕h4 ♖a2 *(D)*

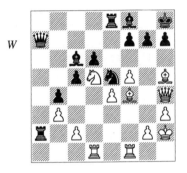

27 ♖d2

27 ♖f2 is also possible, when the position remains balanced.

27...♗xd5

Black doesn't have to do this and can continue manoeuvring, but exchanging on d5 certainly isn't a mistake.

28 ♖xd5! *(D)*

28 exd5?! is just bad for White, since he closes the attack on the d6-pawn and the bishop-pair does not function well in the resulting structure.

28...♘c6?!

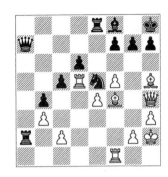

It is understandable that Naiditsch wasn't attracted by 28...♖xc2 29 ♗xe5 ♖xe5 (29...dxe5? 30 f6 gives White a very dangerous attack) 30 ♖xe5 dxe5, when White can force a draw with 31 ♕d8 ♕e7 32 ♕xe7 ♗xe7 33 ♗xf7. However, after his move he risks being worse.

29 ♗xd6 ♗xd6+ 30 ♖xd6 ♕c7 31 ♕g3 ♘d4?

31...♘e5 looks better, playing for positional compensation, though White's position must be preferable here.

32 e5!

Now the e-pawn starts running. Sokolov plays very dynamically.

32...♖xc2 33 e6 ♖c3 34 exf7!

Not a difficult tactic for a GM of Sokolov's calibre, but pleasing nonetheless.

34...♖f8 35 ♕e5

Impressive centralization.

35...♖xb3 36 f6 g6 37 ♕e7 ♕b8 38 ♖e1 ♖a3 39 ♕xf8+! ♕xf8 40 ♖d8!!

The final flourish. White had to avoid 40 ♖e8?? ♖a8!, when the position is very unclear.

1-0

3 c3 Sicilian

1 e4 c5 2 c3 *(D)*

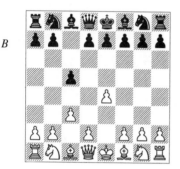

The Sicilian is the most popular defence to 1 e4. White's approaches vary from the most principled (the heavily theoretical lines with 2 ♘f3 and 3 d4, especially those where White castles queenside) to a range of 'Anti-Sicilians', such as those based on ♗b5(+), which have become more popular recently due to Magnus Carlsen's phenomenal results (admittedly, from rather equal positions).

The c3 Sicilian was the obvious choice for our repertoire. Firstly, as we shall see, it often leads directly to an IQP or a related structure. Secondly, White's sound and active set-up is easy to play and often leads to promising attacking chances in my view. There are more detailed introductions in each of the games, but you might

note that Black's two main defences begin with 2...♘f6 (Games 14-18) and 2...d5 (Games 19-23); other moves are covered in Games 24-26.

You might also note that several of the games begin with 1 e4 c5 2 ♘f3 e6 (or 2...♘c6) 3 c3, but I recommend that you play c3 on move two, since otherwise you will need a separate opening for Black's main response to 1 e4 c5 2 ♘f3, namely 2...d6.

2...♘f6

Game 14
Naroditsky – Oparin
Riga 2014

1 e4 c5 2 c3 ♘f6 3 e5 ♘d5 4 d4 cxd4 5 ♘f3 ♘c6

For lines where Black plays an early ...e6 together with ...d6, see Game 15. For the line with ...e6 and ...b6, refer to Game 18.

6 cxd4 d6

Black's rapid development has put immediate pressure on White's centre.

7 ♗c4

Developing and hitting the knight.

7...♘b6 *(D)*

This is by far Black's most popular continuation. 7...dxe5 is the subject of Game 17.

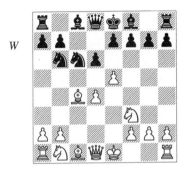

8 ♗b5

I have had good results with the enterprising gambit variation 8 ♗b3!? dxe5 9 d5! since it was suggested to me by GM John Shaw about 10 years ago. For this book, however, I have decided to recommend the main line, which is much less risky and leads to a pleasant IQP position for White.

8...dxe5

Or:

a) 8...d5 is actually quite an annoying continuation after 8 ♗b3, but here I think the bishop is better placed on b5, preparing to take on c6. A good recent example between two strong GMs proceeded as follows: 9 ♘c3 g6 10 0-0 ♗g7 11 ♗xc6+ bxc6 12 h3! (limiting the c8-bishop and protecting the important f3-knight, which guards the centre and helps restrain Black's dark-squared bishop) 12...a5 13 b3 0-0 14 ♖e1 a4 15 ♗a3 axb3 16 axb3 ♗h6 17 ♖e2! (an elegant regrouping) 17...♖e8 18 ♖ea2 ♖b8 19 ♗b4 ♗f5 20 ♖a7 ♘c4 21 bxc4 ♖xb4 22 cxd5 cxd5 23 ♕e2 ♗e6 24 ♘a4 ♕b8 25 ♘c5 and White was more comfortable in Stević-Kožul, Croatian Ch, Opatija 2015.

b) 8...♗d7 *(D)* is a tricky move-order, intending to take on e5 next move.

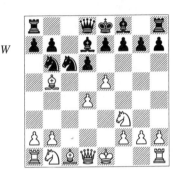

Here 9 ♘c3 is good but White can play for a decent IQP position, following the example of former World Junior Champion Peter Acs: 9 exd6!? e6! (a standard intermezzo; 9...exd6 is quite passive, leaving Black with less space for no compensation) 10 0-0 ♗xd6 11 ♘c3 ♘b4 12 ♗g5 (12 ♘e5) 12...f6 13 ♗d2 0-0 14 ♕b3 ♘4d5 15 ♘e4 ♗xb5 16 ♕xb5 ♖c8 17 ♖ac1 ♖xc1 18 ♖xc1 and Black gradually equalized in Acs-Sarić, Bundesliga 2013/14 but at the moment I slightly prefer White. Playing ...f6 has pros and cons – Black takes control of the important e5- and g5-squares, where he is traditionally weak in IQP positions, but the e6-pawn is slightly weakened. Thanks to his extra space, White's pieces seem slightly more active, and he can consider targeting the b6-knight and b7-pawn with a4-a5, gaining space on the queenside.

9 ♘xe5 ♗d7 *(D)*
10 ♘xd7

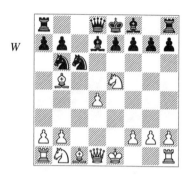

W

White has also tried 10 a4 and 10 ♘c3 but I am recommending the main line. It is worth noting that, while exchanging pieces is normally in Black's favour, here White gets the bishop-pair in an open position, which should certainly count for something.

10...♕xd7 11 ♘c3 e6 12 0-0 ♗e7

This is the main move, preparing to complete development. Other lines:

a) 12...♖c8 has been played by several strong GMs. White has a number of sensible moves like 13 ♗e3 but I would like to suggest a novelty: 13 d5!? (opening the position for the bishops at the cost of a pawn) 13...♘xd5 (not 13...exd5? 14 ♖e1+ ♗e7 15 ♗g5 f6 16 ♗e3 ± and White is much better, since he threatens ♗xb6 and ♘xd5) 14 ♘xd5 exd5 (the queenless middlegame after 14...♕xd5 15 ♕xd5 exd5 16 ♗f4 is surprisingly difficult for Black; for instance, 16...♗e7 17 ♖fe1 ♔f8 18 ♖ad1 ♖d8 19 ♖c1 with at least enough compensation in the form of the bishop-pair and superior activity) 15 ♗g5 f6 16 ♗e3 ♗e7 17 ♕h5+ g6 18 ♕f3 0-0 19 ♖fe1 with enduring compensation for the pawn.

b) 12...♖d8 13 ♕h5!? (I was very impressed with the Vajda-Shirov game {line 'b14'} when I first saw it, and I see no reason not to recommend this move, although White has lots of alternatives) 13...♗e7 (13...♕xd4 loses on the spot to 14 ♖d1 ♕c5 15 ♖xd8+ ♔xd8 16 ♕xf7 ♕e7 17 ♕f3, when the black position is collapsing) 14 ♖d1 (D) and then:

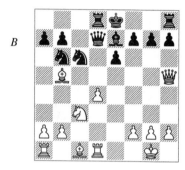

B

b1) 14...♘d5 15 ♕g4 and here:

b11) 15...0-0 16 ♗h6 ♗f6 17 ♘e4 transposes to line 'b12'.

b12) 15...♗f6 16 ♘e4 0-0 17 ♗h6 ♕e7 18 ♗xc6 bxc6 19 ♖ac1 ±. White has more active pieces and no structural disadvantage.

b13) Black might consider 15...♔f8 to avoid any weakening of the kingside, but after 16 ♕f3 g5!? 17 ♗a4 ♔g7 18 ♗b3 White's chances are to be preferred.

b14) 15...g6 16 ♗h6 (keeping the king in the centre) 16...f5 17 ♕e2 ♔f7 (Black has connected his rooks and gained space, but the e6-pawn and e5-square have been permanently weakened) 18 ♖ac1 ♗f6 19 ♘a4 ♕d6 20

♗xc6 bxc6 21 ♘c5 ♖b8 22 ♘b3 ♖he8 23 ♘a5! ♖bc8 24 a3 (White has manoeuvred excellently and stands much better thanks to Black's ragged structure and passive pieces; Shirov tries to change the character of the position, but this isn't sufficient to equalize) 24...e5 25 ♘c4 ♕b8 26 dxe5 ♗xe5 27 ♘xe5+ ♕xe5 28 ♕d2, Vajda-Shirov, Zurich 2012. In my notes to this game for Chess Publishing, I noted "Better structure, better minor piece, safer king." I stand by this assessment. White was clearly better and went on to win after further adventures.

b2) Black improved with 14...0-0 in a later game. White continued in direct fashion with 15 ♖d3!? (calmer moves like 15 ♗e3 and 15 ♗f4 were also possible). Then:

b21) 15...♘d5 is very solid. 16 ♗h6 (White can also play in more straightforward fashion with 16 ♖g3 g6 17 ♕h6 f5 {the threat was ♘xd5 and ♖h3} when he should probably secure the draw by capturing on g6) 16...♘f6 17 ♕g5 ♘e8 18 ♕g3 ♗d6 19 ♗f4 ♗xf4 20 ♕xf4 with balanced chances.

b22) 15...g6 16 ♕h6 f5 17 ♗g5 ♗xg5 18 ♕xg5 a6 (18...♕e7!?) 19 ♗xc6 ♕xc6 20 ♖e1 ♘c4 21 b3 ♘b2 22 ♖de3 ♖xd4 23 ♖xe6 ♕xc3 24 ♖xg6+ hxg6 25 ♕xg6+ ♔h8 and a well-played game ended in a draw in Torma-Kantor, Budapest 2013.

13 ♕g4 0-0 14 ♗xc6 bxc6 15 ♗h6 ♗f6 16 ♖fd1 *(D)*

About 100 games have been played from this position on my database. I think it's fair to say that White is

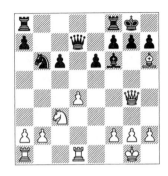

slightly better. His pieces are more active and the structure is not unfavourable for him.

16...♖fd8

Or:

a) Black can immediately shore up the kingside with 16...♔h8 17 ♘e4 ♖g8 (17...♕d8 18 ♗f4 ♗e7 19 ♕g3 ♘d5 20 ♗d6 ♗xd6 21 ♘xd6 ♕c7 22 ♖ac1 ♖fd8 23 ♘c4 ± and White was pressing in Nevednichy-Mamedov, World Cities, Al Ain 2012) 18 ♗g5 (White can also retain the bishops but his position remains preferable after their exchange, since Black has important weaknesses on the dark squares) 18...♗xg5 19 ♘xg5 h6 20 ♖ac1 ♘d5 21 ♘f3 ♘f6 was Piorun-Miton, Polish Ch, Chorzow 2013 and now 22 ♕g3! ± followed by ♘e5 would have left White pressing with no risk – all of his pieces are more active than their counterparts.

b) Black can also attempt to equalize immediately with 16...e5 which, interestingly, was Naroditsky's choice with Black in a game three years previously. 17 ♕xd7 ♘xd7 18 ♗e3 (18 dxe5 was played in Bojkov-Naroditsky,

Berkeley 2011) 18...exd4 19 ♗xd4 ♖fd8 20 ♔f1 ♗xd4 21 ♖xd4 ♘b6 22 ♖ad1 ♖xd4 23 ♖xd4 with a pleasant endgame edge thanks to White's superior structure in V.Belov-Hausrath, Biel 2009.

17 ♘e4 ♕e7 18 ♖ac1 ♖ac8 19 ♖d3 *(D)*

White's most common move here has been 19 h4, with which he has scored well, but I like Naroditsky's positional treatment.

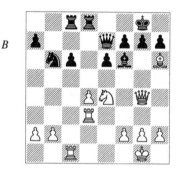

19...♖d5

19...♗xd4? 20 ♖xd4 f5 fails to 21 ♖xd8+ ♖xd8 22 ♕g3 with decisive material gain.

20 ♗e3

In Denny-Farley, Bridgetown 2010, White missed Black's threat and after 20 h4 ♗xd4 21 ♖xd4 f5 22 ♕xg7+ ♕xg7 23 ♗xg7 Black could have equalized with 23...fxe4 24 ♖xd5 exd5.

20...♖a5

Against neutral play White would continue as in the game with a3 and b4.

21 a3 ♖b5 22 b4 a5 23 ♗d2 a4?

Ignoring a basic tenet of defensive play (with which a strong GM like

Oparin is obviously familiar), namely that the weaker side should try to exchange pawns. Now the a4-pawn is a potential target.

Instead, 23...axb4 24 ♗xb4 ♕d8 would have limited White to a small advantage.

24 ♗e3 ± ♖d5 25 ♕f3 h5 26 h3 e5

As good or bad as anything else – Black doesn't want to be slowly tortured and makes an immediate break to free himself.

27 ♖c5! *(D)*

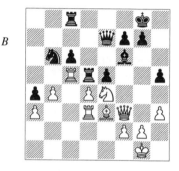

Increasing the tension.

27...♘d7

27...exd4 was the lesser evil, but after 28 ♘xf6+ ♕xf6 29 ♕xf6 gxf6 30 ♖xd4 Black's structure is riddled with weaknesses.

28 ♖xd5 cxd5 29 ♘xf6+ ♘xf6 30 ♕f5!

Even stronger than taking on e5.

30...♕e6 31 ♕xe6 fxe6 32 dxe5 ♘d7 33 f4

33 ♗d4!?.

33...g5! 34 g3

Black is doing a good job of complicating matters at the cost of a pawn.

However, Naroditsky's technique is impressive.

34...♖c2?!

Immediately activating the king by, for example, 34...♔f7 makes White's task harder.

35 ♗d4!

Cementing the position and preparing to occupy the c-file.

35...gxf4 36 gxf4 ♔f7 37 ♖c3 ♖d2 38 ♗e3 ♖b2 39 ♖c7 ♔e8 40 ♖c6 ♔f7 41 ♗d4 ♖d2 42 ♗c3 ♖d1+ 43 ♔f2 d4

The best defence against White's threat of f5 exf5 e6+, winning the knight.

44 ♖d6 ♘b6 45 ♔e2 ♖b1 46 ♗xd4 +−

White picks up a second pawn and only basic care is required to bring home the full point.

46...♘c4 47 ♖c6 ♘xa3 (D)

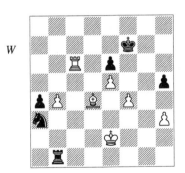

48 f5!

Using all the resources in the position.

48...♘b5

48...exf5 49 e6+ ♔g6 50 ♗c5 and the e6-pawn can't be stopped.

49 fxe6+ ♔g7 50 ♗c5 ♖xb4

A cute tactic, but far too little too late.

51 e7

51 ♗xb4 ♘d4+ was Black's idea, though White is still winning comfortably here.

51...♖e4+ 52 ♔d3 ♖xe5 53 ♖c8 1-0

A positional masterclass by the young American GM.

Game 15
Mamedov – Wojtaszek
Gashimov Memorial, Shamkir 2014

1 e4 c5 2 c3 ♘f6 3 e5 ♘d5 4 ♘f3 e6 5 ♗c4

I recommend the immediate 5 d4 but against the ...e6 systems these moves normally transpose.

5...d6 6 d4 cxd4 7 cxd4 (D)

7...♗e7

7...♘b6 is another serious move. White has several options including 8 ♗d3 dxe5 9 dxe5, but I like the IQP approach: 8 ♗b3 dxe5 9 ♘xe5 ♘c6 10 ♘xc6 (White can also play 10 ♘f3, with typical IQP play) 10...bxc6. As we can see from other examples in this book, this structural change leads to subtle positional play. White can't push d5 and instead will rely on his space advantage and Black's potential weaknesses on the c-file (especially the c6-pawn and the c5-square). A recent example went 11 0-0 ♗e7 12 ♘c3 0-0 13 ♘e4 ♗a6 14 ♖e1 ♘d5 15 ♕f3 ♕b6 16 ♖d1 with level chances in Mamedov-Khurtsidze, Nakhchivan 2015.

8 0-0 0-0 9 ♖e1 ♘c6

This leads to an important position which can be reached from several move-orders. Importantly, this defensive set-up is suitable for those who play the black side of both 1 e4 c5 2 ♘f3 e6 and 1 e4 c5 2 ♘f3 ♘c6, and seems quite popular at the moment (at least judging from my recent games).

Alternatively:

a) 9...a6 10 exd6 ♕xd6 11 ♘c3 ♘c6 transposes to note 'd' to Black's 11th move.

b) 9...b6 is a logical try, but Black must be precise to equalize in the symmetrical IQP position resulting from 10 ♗xd5 exd5 11 ♘c3 ♗e6 12 ♗f4 (I got nothing special after 12 exd6 ♕xd6 13 ♗g5 ♘c6 14 ♗xe7 ♘xe7 15 ♘e5 ♖fc8 in Collins-Adair, Ascot 2013); for example, 12...dxe5?! (12...♘c6 13 ♘b5 dxe5 14 ♘xe5 ♘xe5 15 ♗xe5 was roughly equal in Pavasović-A.Horvath, Slovenian Team Ch, Ljubljana 2012) 13 ♘xe5 a6 (Stević-Kožul, Croatian Ch, Poreč 2014) 14 ♖c1 ± gives White a solid plus.

10 exd6 (D)

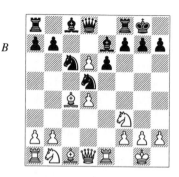

10...♕xd6

10...♗xd6 is much less popular, but has been essayed by several GMs with good results. 11 ♘c3 and now:

a) 11...b6 was played in Zumsande-P.H.Nielsen, Bundesliga 2014/15. Here White can continue in normal IQP style with 12 ♗d3 or change the structure with 12 ♘xd5 exd5 13 ♗b5 followed by ♗g5, when Black needs to be precise to equalize.

b) 11...♘ce7 can be met by 12 ♕d3. Now 12...h6 transposes to line 'c' (and was the actual move-order of Stević-Janković). Instead 12...♘g6 led to a quick draw in Poluliakhov-Skorchenko, Sochi 2005, but here I like 13 ♗g5 ♕a5 14 ♗d2 (14 ♘xd5 exd5 15 ♗b3 ± is also possible, with the more active pieces in a symmetrical pawn-structure) 14...♘xc3 15 ♗xc3 ♕h5 16 ♕e4 and White is fully prepared for d5, when his bishops will be extremely active (and his other pieces aren't poorly placed either). This looks like a tough defensive chore for Black.

c) 11...h6 (D) has scored well and been played repeatedly by strong GMs like Kožul.

W

Protecting the g5-square from a white knight or bishop makes sense now that Black's dark-squared bishop has left e7. I think White should try to exploit the weakening of the b1-h7 diagonal in direct fashion: 12 ♕d3 ♘ce7 13 ♗b3 b6 (13...♗d7 14 ♗c2 ♘f6 15 ♘e5 ♖c8 16 ♗d2 ♘f5 17 h3 with strong pressure) 14 ♗c2 ♘f6 15 ♘e5 (15 ♘e4 was Stević's later 'improvement', played in Stević-Janković, Croatia Cup, Šibenik 2010, but I think this gives White less after 15...♘f5 =) and here:

c1) 15...♗xe5 16 dxe5 ♕xd3 17 ♗xd3 ♘fd5 and White can press in the endgame with his bishop-pair, though Black has strong defensive chances based on his d5 outpost.

c2) 15...♗b7 was played in a clash between two strong GM specialists in this line, Stević-Kožul, Stari Mikanovci rapid 2010. Here I would like to suggest the improvement 16 ♕g3; for instance, 16...♔h8 17 ♕h3 looks extremely dangerous for Black in my view, since he has exchanged no pieces and ♗xh6 is a constant menace. Indeed, 17...♔g8? 18 ♗xh6! gxh6 19

♕xh6 followed by a rook-lift is winning for White.

11 ♘c3 (D)

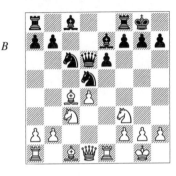

B

In this game we look at Black's early attempts to develop his light-squared bishop.

11...b6

Preparing a typical and ambitious development of the bishop to b7. There are a number of other lines to consider:

a) For 11...♖d8 see Game 16.

b) 11...♗d7 develops the bishop and prepares to put a rook on the c-file. Once Black has developed his f8-rook (for instance, to d8), ...♗e8 might look passive but is actually very solid. Here I like 12 a3, which has been played in two games so far. In both Black chose 12...♘xc3 13 bxc3 *(D)* and now the paths diverge:

b1) In Stripunsky-Smirin, Arlington 2014 Black chose 13...♖ac8 but after 14 ♕d3 ♕c7 15 ♗a2 ♕a5 16 ♖b1 White had an excellent position based on the superior activity of his pieces. After 16...b6 17 ♖b5 ♕a6 18 ♗c4 g6, instead of the game's 19 ♖b1 (which also retained some advantage),

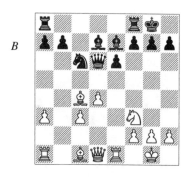

B

Black's position would have been critical after 19 d5! ♘d8 20 ♖b4 b5 (after 20...♖xc4 21 d6! White wins material) 21 ♗xb5 ♗xb5 22 ♖xb5 ♗f6 23 c4 with an extra pawn and a dominating position.

b2) 13...♘a5 14 ♗d3 ♖ac8 15 ♘e5 (Black's position is already difficult) 15...♘c6?! 16 ♗f4 ♘xe5 17 ♗xe5 ♕c6 *(D)* and then:

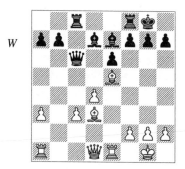

W

b21) In Collins-Snape, Hastings 2008 I couldn't resist the temptation to try a double bishop sacrifice: 18 ♗xh7+? ♔xh7 19 ♕h5+ ♔g8 20 ♗xg7 ♔xg7 21 ♖e3. Now Snape's 21...e5 allowed me to muddy the waters somewhat, but after the cold-blooded

21...♖h8 22 ♖g3+ ♗g5 23 ♕xg5+ (23 ♖xg5+? ♔f6 and Black wins – though this might be hard to see over the board!) 23...♔f8 White's initiative doesn't fully compensate for the piece.

b22) 18 ♗e4! ♕a6 19 ♕f3 and White wins material, as after 19...♗c6 20 ♕g4 g6 21 ♗xg6!! hxg6 (21...fxg6 22 ♕xe6+ exploits the undefended rook on c8) 22 ♖e3! Black has to give up his queen to avoid mate with ♖h3 and ♖h8.

c) To the unprepared, 11...♘xc3 12 bxc3 b6 looks extremely natural, preparing a queenside fianchetto and play against the isolated pawn couple on c3 and d4. However, this is effectively a trap (which I have both fallen into and sprung!), since after 13 ♘g5! *(D)* Black must make a concession to avoid a very strong attack:

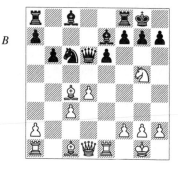

B

c1) 13...♗b7?? loses immediately to 14 ♘xe6!, with decisive threats.

c2) When I fell into this position with Black, I went for 13...g6 but after 14 h4! I came under a very strong attack. After 14...♘a5?! 15 ♗d3 ♗b7 (after 15...♕c7, White can play 16

♘xh7!, while the simple 16 h5 gives Black a lot of trouble too; I simply think that White has an overwhelming advantage in numbers on the kingside and Black can't equalize anywhere) 16 ♘xh7! ♕c6 (16...♔xh7 17 ♕h5+ ♔g7 18 ♕h6+ ♔g8 19 ♗xg6 fxg6 20 ♕xg6+ ♔h8 21 ♖xe6 is crushing) 17 ♗e4 ♕xc3 18 ♗d2 ♕xd4 19 ♗xb7 ♘xb7 20 ♘xf8 White was much better and went on to win in Landenbergue-Collins, European Clubs Cup, Saint Vincent 2005.

c3) The tempting 13...h6 led to a rout in a game between two young talents: 14 ♘e4 ♕c7 15 ♕g4 ♔h7? (Black needs to try 15...f5 but after 16 ♕g3 f4 {taking on g3 gives Black a clearly worse endgame in view of his weaknesses on the e-file} 17 ♕d3 White was better in Zelbel-Tvarijonas, European Clubs Cup, Bilbao 2014) 16 ♗xh6!! ♔xh6 17 ♕h3+ ♔g6 18 g4 and Black resigned in view of mate in four in D.Howell-Bitalzadeh, Wijk aan Zee 2009.

c4) After my 2005 ECC debacle, I was delighted to be able to play the white side of this line in another important team competition, the Turin Olympiad in 2006. My opponent defended better than I did: 13...♗xg5!. I think this is a necessary concession, but with the bishop-pair and more active pieces White has a very pleasant advantage. 14 ♗xg5 ♗b7 and I went on to win after 15 ♕h5 in Collins-Nokes, Turin Olympiad 2006 but 15 ♕g4! is even stronger, with serious kingside threats including ♗f6.

d) 11...a6 12 ♗b3 b5 *(D)* (12...♖d8 and 12...♘f6 13 ♗e3 ♖d8 should be compared with Game 16) and now White has a pleasant choice:

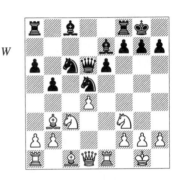

d1) In a couple of games White has gone for 13 ♘xd5 exd5 14 ♘e5 ♗e6 15 ♗f4 ♘xe5 16 ♗xe5 ♕d7. If anyone is better, it's White, but Black should be able to hold the balance with a few accurate moves.

d2) As far as I can tell, 13 ♘e4!? is a novelty, but seems like a very logical one. Black has weakened his dark squares (especially c5) and trading bishops makes a lot of sense. 13...♕c7 (13...♕d8 14 ♗g5 is similar) 14 ♗g5 ♗xg5 15 ♘exg5 and then:

d21) 15...♗b7?! 16 ♖c1 and it's too late for 16...h6?! (16...♕d7 17 ♕d3) in view of 17 ♘xe6!! fxe6 18 ♖xe6 ♕d7 (18...♖ad8 19 ♘e5 +−) 19 ♖exc6! ♗xc6 20 ♘e5 ♕f5 and now 21 ♘xc6 is good for White but even better is the stunning move 21 f3!! +−, when Black's position collapses, since trying to hold his minor pieces with 21...♗b7 22 ♖c7 ♖ab8 fails to 23 ♖xb7!.

d22) 15...h6 pushes White's knight where it wants to go, but leaving the knight on g5 would be perilous for the black king, as we have just seen. After 16 ♘e4 White's play is easier. He will follow up with ♖c1 and ♘c5 while the bishop on c8 is passive. Black also has to look out for ♗xd5 at all times. The weakness of the d4-pawn isn't felt at all.

We now return to 11...b6 (D):

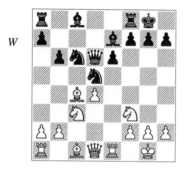

12 ♗b3

A typical continuation, improving the bishop and awaiting developments.

In a recent game, I tried to exploit the use of ...b6 before ...♘xc3 with 12 ♘xd5 exd5 13 ♗b5 ♗b7 (13...♗f6 14 ♕a4 ♗d7 15 ♗g5 ♗xg5 16 ♘xg5 f6 17 ♘f3 a6 18 ♗xc6 ♗xc6 was also equal in Rozentalis-B.Lindberg, Stockholm 2012) 14 ♗xc6 ♗xc6 15 ♗f4 ♕xf4 16 ♖xe7 ♕d6 17 ♖e1 ♗d7. I thought that my 'superior' minor piece should count for something, but in fact the black bishop performs OK in this structure (and ♘e5 can always be met by ...f6), so I actually had nothing in Collins-Sipila, Lisbon 2014.

12...♘xc3

Wojtaszek clarifies the pawn-structure before committing his bishop to b7. Other moves:

a) 12...♗a6 looks more active, but after 13 ♘xd5 exd5 14 ♘e5 Black has some problems to solve since his minor pieces are insufficiently defended. The computer's top line is 14...♗b7, but White is obviously better. Instead 14...♗f6 15 ♗f4 ♖fe8? was played in Sedina-Atlas, Swiss Team Ch 2013 and here both players missed the shot 16 ♘xf7! ♕xf4 (16...♖xe1+ 17 ♕xe1 ♕xf4 18 ♗xd5 ± is similar) 17 ♗xd5 ±, when White is on top; for instance, 17...♘e7 18 ♖xe7 ♖xe7 19 ♘e5+ ♔h8 20 g3 ♕f5 21 ♗xa8 ♗xe5 22 dxe5 ♕xe5 with a healthy extra pawn.

b) 12...♗b7 13 ♘xd5 exd5 is perhaps what Wojtaszek wanted to avoid by taking on c3: the b7-bishop is restricted by the d5-pawn. White seems to have a small edge here; for instance, 14 g3!? followed by ♗f4 (and perhaps ♗a4), with pleasant play, although Black should certainly be able to hold if he plays carefully.

13 bxc3 ♗b7 14 ♗c2 (D)

Mamedov plays in aggressive style, preparing the standard set-up with ♕d3. However, he has lost quite a lot of time with his light-squared bishop, and Black should be fine here.

14...♕d5

14...♖ac8 looks sensible. White can win the bishop-pair with 15 ♘g5 ♗xg5 (15...g6? 16 ♘xh7! is a standard shot) 16 ♗xg5, but Black remains extremely solid.

15 ♗e4 ♕h5 16 ♗f4

Wojtaszek has avoided any kingside threats by bringing his queen into the defence, but this has cost time and slightly weakened his control of important central squares.

16...♖fd8

16...♖ac8 17 ♖c1 ♘a5 is a standard plan, aiming to exchange pieces. However, White has comfortable play after 18 ♗xb7 ♘xb7 19 ♕a4 ♘a5 (19...♕a5 is strongly met by 20 ♕d7) 20 c4 with a space advantage and more active pieces. Note how the hanging pawns on c4 and d4 control more squares (in particular, the d5-square) than the IQP would on its own.

17 ♕d2 ♘a5 18 ♗xb7 ♘xb7 19 ♘e5

Going for an original and aggressive plan, aimed at exploiting the position of the black queen.

19...♖ac8 *(D)*

20 g4!?

I like the more flexible 20 ♖e3, when White can play in the centre or on the kingside depending on Black's reaction.

20...♕h4 21 ♗g3 ♕h3?

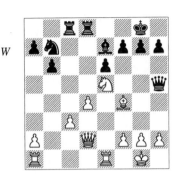

The black queen proves to be badly out of play on this square. 21...♕f6 is necessary, although White retains some initiative after 22 ♖e3.

22 ♕e2

22 ♘xf7 ♔xf7 23 ♕e2 is already possible, threatening ♕xe6+ and ♕f3+ (hitting the knight on b7), but I prefer Mamedov's approach.

22...♘d6 23 d5!

The thematic break, achieved under very favourable conditions.

23...♖e8 24 dxe6 fxe6 25 ♖ad1 ♗f8 26 ♖d3 ♘f7 27 ♘xf7 ♔xf7 28 ♖d7+ ♔g8 29 ♕f3 ♔h8 30 ♖xa7 +−

White has an extra pawn and a strong initiative. The rest of the game isn't flawless but Mamedov eventually converts his advantage into victory.

30...♕h6 31 ♗e5 ♖cd8 32 ♔g2 ♕g6 33 ♖e4 ♔g8 34 ♖f4 ♖e7 35 ♗c7 ♖c8 36 ♗d6 ♖ee8 37 ♗e5 ♖e7 38 ♗d6 e5 39 ♗xe7 exf4 40 ♗xf8 ♖xf8 41 ♖a8 ♕d6 42 c4 g5 43 ♖xf8+ ♔xf8 44 ♕d5 ♕e7 45 a4 h6 46 ♕c6 ♔g7 47 h3 ♕b4 48 ♕d7+ ♔g6 49 ♕c6+ ♔g7 50 ♕d7+ ♔g6 51 ♕c7 ♕b1 52 ♕c6+ ♔g7 53 ♕d7+ ♔g8 54 ♕f5 1-0

Game 16
Faizulaev – Khenkin
Agzamov Memorial, Tashkent 2013

1 e4 c5

To avoid confusion, I have tinkered with the move-order of this game. The game actually proceeded 1...c6 2 c4 d5 3 cxd5 cxd5 4 exd5 ♘f6 5 ♘c3 ♘xd5 6 ♘f3 ♘c6 7 ♗b5 e6 8 0-0 ♗e7 9 d4 0-0 10 ♖e1 ♕d6 11 ♗c4, transposing to the position after White's 11th move.

2 c3 ♘f6 3 e5 ♘d5 4 d4 cxd4 5 ♘f3 e6 6 cxd4 d6 7 ♗c4 ♘c6 8 0-0 ♗e7 9 exd6 ♕xd6 10 ♖e1 0-0 11 ♘c3 ♖d8

This is the most popular and perhaps the best move for Black, and was recommended by Rogozenko in this book *Anti-Sicilians: A Guide for Black*.

12 ♗b3 (D)

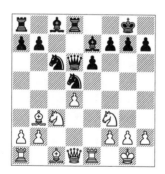

B

12...♘f6

Black directly attacks the d4-pawn. 12...a6 has also been played by several GMs. Most games have proceeded 13 ♘xd5 exd5 14 ♘e5 ♘xe5 15 ♗f4, which is basically a drawing variation,

but White can also continue in standard IQP fashion by 13 a3.

13 ♗e3

I like this continuation, which leads to typical IQP play. 13 ♘b5 ♕d7 14 ♗f4 is another attempt, seeking to make use of the concrete features of the position, but after the annoying 14...♗b4! Black has been doing well of late. However, this could be an interesting direction for research if you don't like 13 ♗e3 for some reason.

13...b6 14 ♕e2

White has scored very well with this move, and I would include our main game in that assessment, since Faizulaev manages to draw with a very strong GM who outrates him by 300 points.

14...♗b7 15 ♖ad1 ♘a5 16 ♗c2 ♖ac8 17 ♘e5 ♘c6 (D)

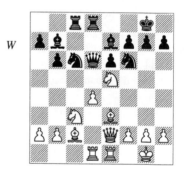

W

18 ♘e4

This allows Black some welcome exchanges. So what else? Certainly 18 ♗g5?! cannot be recommended, even though 18...♘xe5? 19 dxe5 ♕c6, as in Landenbergue-Pavlović, Biel 2007, should lead to a large advantage for

White after 20 ♕f1!. The problem is that this is rendered irrelevant by the fact that Black would be doing excellently after the critical 18...♘xd4!.

18 f4!? supports the knight and (on a good day) provides options of f5. I think this is a position which someone who likes an IQP should be happy to play. Black struggles to exchange pieces and White has decent chances in a double-edged fight. A sample line: 18...♘b4 19 ♗b3 ♘bd5 20 ♘b5 ♕b8 21 f5!? exf5 22 ♗g5 puts Black under heavy pressure.

18...♘xe4

18...♕d5 19 ♘xf6+ ♗xf6 20 ♗xh7+ ♔xh7 21 ♕h5+ ♔g8 22 ♕xf7+ ♔h7 23 ♕h5+ ½-½ Emms-Moiseenko, Bled Olympiad 2002.

19 ♗xe4 f5! *(D)*

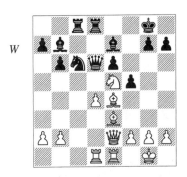

This is a typical idea in IQP positions, though one which is easy to underestimate. Black seizes space and reduces the risk of any kingside attack. The downside is the weakening of the e5-square and the e6-pawn, but this is not easy to exploit.

20 ♗f3 ♗f6 21 ♗f4?!

White goes for complications but these should work out in Black's favour.

After something like 21 g3!? the position remains dynamically balanced. Neither side has a great pawn-structure since e6 is weak in the long run. For example, 21...♕e7 (after 21...♗xe5 22 dxe5 ♕xe5 23 b4 White's bishop-pair on an open board, coupled with pressure on the e-file, gives White full positional compensation for the pawn) 22 ♗xc6 ♗xc6 23 ♘xc6 ♖xc6 24 ♖c1 ♖dc8 25 ♖xc6 ♖xc6 26 ♖d1 with dynamic equality.

21...♘xd4! 22 ♖xd4 ♕xd4 23 ♗xb7 ♕xf4 *(D)*

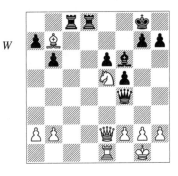

24 ♘f7?!

24 ♗xc8 is the lesser evil, but after 24...♖xc8 25 ♘d7 ♕c4 26 ♘xf6+ gxf6 Black has an extra pawn, although the conversion will be anything but easy given that only major pieces remain.

24...♖d2?!

While this is an inspired idea, it seems that it gives up most of Black's advantage. 24...♔xf7! was the best move, also based on a cute tactical point. 25 ♗xc8 ♖d2 26 ♗xe6+ (26 ♕xe6+ ♔g6 also, paradoxically, leaves Black with the safer king) 26...♔f8 27 ♕e3 and now the trick is 27...♖xf2! 28 ♕xf4 (of course after 28 ♕xf2? ♗d4 Black wins on the spot) 28...♖xf4 and White faces a long struggle for a draw in a dreadful position. Often people overestimate the drawing chances granted by opposite-coloured bishops – with the presence of rooks, Black has both an extra pawn and an attack.

25 ♕xe6 ♕xf2+ 26 ♔h1 ♕xe1+ 27 ♕xe1 ♖e2!! *(D)*

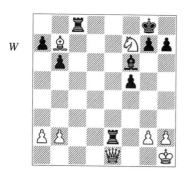

This was Khenkin's point. All other moves lose on the spot.

28 ♕f1 ♖cc2

After 28...♖ce8 29 ♗d5! ♔f8! (not, of course, 29...♖e1?? 30 ♘e5+, when White collects the rook on e1) White has some problems to solve.

29 ♗d5 ♔f8?

After 29...♖f2! White should take a draw, either by giving perpetual himself (with 30 ♘d8+ ♔h8 31 ♘f7+) or allowing a perpetual attack on his queen (e.g., 30 ♕e1 ♖fe2 31 ♕f1).

The ambitious 30 ♕g1 is well met by 30...♔f8! intending ...♗xb2 and ...♖c1 as well as a direct attack on the white king.

30 ♘g5?

30 h4 leaves White with a large advantage.

30...♗xg5 31 ♕xf5+ ♗f6

Now Black is much better again. We've gone a bit beyond the opening and I shall leave the rest of the game (possibly played in time-trouble) for you to enjoy without comments.

32 h4 ♖cd2 33 ♗b3? ♖d4? 34 h5 ♔e7 35 ♔g1 ♖dd2 36 ♔f1 ♖xb2?! 37 ♕d5 ♖f2+ 38 ♔g1 ♖xg2+ 39 ♔h1 ♖g5 40 ♕e6+ ♔d8 41 ♕d6+ ♔c8 42 ♗e6+ ♔b7 43 ♕d7+ ♔a6 44 ♕a4+ ♔b7 45 ♕d7+ ♔a6 46 ♕a4+ ♔b7 47 ♕d7+ ♔a6 48 ♕a4+ ½-½

Game 17
R. Antonio – Senador
Philippine Ch,
Boracay Island 2012

1 e4 c5 2 c3 ♘f6 3 e5 ♘d5 4 ♘f3 ♘c6 5 d4 cxd4 6 cxd4 d6 7 ♗c4 dxe5 *(D)*

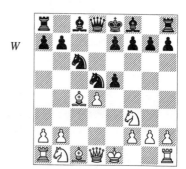

This is a move which, I must admit, I underestimated for a long time. Black starts direct play in the centre and White should be well-prepared here.

8 ♘xe5!?

Leading, in many lines, to our standard IQP positions. Alternatively:

a) I previously thought that 8 ♗xd5 ♕xd5 9 ♘c3 was some sort of refutation of 7...dxe5, but in fact things are quite double-edged after, for example, 9...♕d6 10 d5 ♘d4 11 ♘xd4 exd4 12 ♕xd4 e5 13 ♕e3 f5.

b) 8 dxe5 is the main line, when White normally enjoys an edge in the endgame after 8...♘db4 9 ♕xd8+ ♘xd8. While I have played this way myself (Collins-S.Novikov, Barcelona 2014), the positions become slightly non-standard and I wanted to recommend something else.

8...e6

This is the universal choice amongst strong players. 8...♘xe5 is much less ambitious and after 9 dxe5 e6 10 0-0 ± White has a space advantage, a lead in development and a pleasant advantage.

9 0-0 ♗d6

9...♗e7 leads to a tricky position. The point is that White's most natural move, 10 ♘c3, will lead to an endgame after knight exchanges on c3 and e5 (for instance, look up the game Friedrich-Nyzhnyk, Bad Wörishofen 2010). White has tried some other methods of using the active position of the knight on e5, such as 10 ♕g4 (10 ♕f3 is also interesting), but my recommendation is to head for standard

IQP play by playing 10 ♘f3 0-0 11 ♘c3 *(D)*.

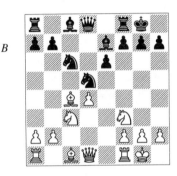

White is then actually a tempo down on some standard theoretical lines (for instance, Aronian-Giri, Stavanger 2014 went 1 ♘f3 c5 2 c4 ♘f6 3 ♘c3 d5 4 cxd5 ♘xd5 5 e3 e6 6 d4 ♘c6 7 ♗c4 cxd4 8 exd4 ♗e7 9 0-0 0-0, leading to the same position with White to move). However, I think he still has a reasonable position. A couple of examples:

a) 11...♘xc3 12 bxc3 b6 13 ♖e1 ♗b7 14 ♗d3 ♖c8 15 h4 ♘a5 16 ♘g5 ♗xg5 17 ♗xg5 ♕d5 18 ♗e4 ♕d7 was Cherniaev-Gharamian, Biel 2011 and now 19 ♗xb7 ♕xb7 20 ♕g4 ♔h8 21 ♖ad1!? would have been an interesting pawn sacrifice; for instance, 21...♖xc3 22 d5 exd5 23 ♖e7 ♖c7 24 ♗f6 gxf6 25 ♕d4 ♖xe7 26 ♕xf6+ ♔g8 27 ♕g5+ ♔h8 28 ♕f6+ with perpetual check.

b) 11...b6 12 ♘xd5 exd5 13 ♗b5 (in my game with Sipila in Lisbon 2014, the same position arose but with the white rook on e1 and the black queen on d6; that game quickly petered out to equality, but in the current position White seems to have more chances for an initiative since he can play ♗f4) 13...♗d7 14 ♗f4 a6 15 ♗d3 ♗g4 and now grabbing a pawn with 16 ♗xh7+ ♔xh7 17 ♕c2+ ♔g8 18 ♕xc6 ♖c8 19 ♕b7 ♗xf3 20 gxf3 gave Black excellent play in Zhigalko-Solodovnichenko, Dubai 2015. I like 16 ♖c1!?; for instance, 16...♘xd4 (or 16...♗xf3 17 ♕xf3 ♘xd4 18 ♕h3 g6 19 ♗c7 ♕c8 20 ♕e3 ♘e6 21 ♗xb6 ±) 17 ♗xh7+ ♔xh7 18 ♕d3+ ♗f5 19 ♕xd4 ♗c5 20 ♕d2 with some attacking chances against the slightly exposed black king.

We now return to the position after 9...♗d6 (D):

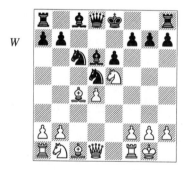

W

10 ♘f3

If you want to play a complex game, then this is again my suggestion.

White has tried a number of alternatives which I don't really like, such as 10 ♕h5. A few other moves are worth a brief mention too:

a) I should point out that 10 ♗b5? simply doesn't work after 10...0-0!; for instance, 11 ♗xc6 (11 ♘xc6 bxc6 12 ♗xc6? ♗xh2+ 13 ♔xh2 ♕c7+ 14

♔g1 ♕xc6 ∓ and Black regains the material with a superior structure and a very strong attack in prospect on the a8-h1 diagonal) 11...bxc6 12 ♘xc6 ♕c7 13 ♘e5 ♗xe5 (13...♗a6 14 ♖e1 ♖fc8 was also good) 14 dxe5 ♕xe5 ∓ Grekh-Baklan, Ukrainian Team Ch, Alushta 2009.

b) 10 ♗xd5 is certainly the safest approach – indeed, the game Chernaiev-Wells, London 2009 was agreed drawn in this position. After 10...exd5 11 ♗f4 ♗xe5 12 ♗xe5 (Rogozenko gives 12 dxe5 0-0 13 ♖e1 d4 14 ♘d2 ♕d5 as good for Black) 12...0-0 13 ♖e1 ♗f5 14 ♘c3 ♕d7 15 ♕d2, Rogozenko laconically observes, "Not much can happen in such a position." Indeed, the top-level game Nisipeanu-Radjabov, Bucharest 2013 ended in an uneventful draw.

c) 10 ♘xc6 bxc6 11 ♘c3, as in Halak-Simek, Liberec 2015, leads to a structure where Black is extremely solid. The e6- and c6-pawns restrain the d4-pawn and, if he's feeling ambitious, Black can ultimately aim for a ...c5 break.

10...0-0 11 ♘c3 (D)

B

We have an unbalanced IQP struggle. This position has been tried by a number of GMs with White, including the Philippine GM Rogelio Antonio Jr, who has used it to win some impressive attacking games.

11...a6

This is a logical move, and I wanted to annotate the present game because it beautifully illustrates many of White's ideas in this structure. Other lines:

a) Antonio previously enjoyed success from this position against a top GM: 11...♗b4?! (this looks like a waste of time, especially if Black then doesn't take on c3) 12 ♕d3 ♘ce7 13 ♗d2 ♘b6 14 ♗b3 ♘g6 was played in R.Antonio-Movsesian, Bled Olympiad 2002. Now I like simple development with 15 ♖fe1 ♗e7 (trying to develop with 15...♗d7 falls under a strong initiative after 16 ♘g5 and h4) 16 ♖ad1 with an ideal IQP position; for instance, 16...a5 17 a3 ♗d7 18 ♘e5 ♖c8 19 ♘xd7 ♕xd7 20 d5, opening the position for the bishop-pair.

b) 11...b6 12 ♘xd5 exd5 was agreed drawn after 13 ♗d3 in Bortnyk-Antipov, Moscow (Under-16) 2013 but White might try 13 ♗b5 with mild pressure.

c) 11...♘xc3 12 bxc3 (D) and now:

c1) 12...♘e7 13 ♗d3 ♘g6 14 ♕e2 b6 was played in Fressinet-Avrukh, Internet blitz 2004 and now I like 15 ♘g5!; e.g., 15...♗e7 (not 15...♗b7? 16 ♕h5 h6 17 ♘xf7) 16 h4 ♗b7 17 ♕g4 ± with strong pressure on the kingside.

c2) 12...b6 has been popular, and now I like the old move 13 ♕d3; for

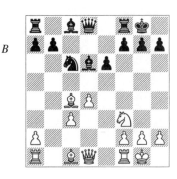

instance, 13...♘a5 (13...♗e7 14 ♕e4 ♗b7 15 ♗d3 g6 16 ♗h6 ♖e8 17 ♖fe1 with chances for both sides in Rossetto-O'Kelly, Buenos Aires 1948) 14 ♘g5 g6 was I.Novak-Hanko, Slovakian Team Ch 1996/7 and now I like 15 ♕h3 h5 16 ♗e2, when the black kingside structure is potentially vulnerable. After a logical sequence like 16...e5 17 ♕h4 ♕f6 18 ♗e3 the position is dynamically balanced.

c3) 12...e5 gives good chances of equality; for instance, 13 h3 (13 ♗d3 goes into a standard position a tempo down, but seems a decent alternative; for instance, 13...exd4 14 cxd4 h6 15 ♖e1 with unclear play) 13...♗f5 14 ♖e1 exd4 15 cxd4 ♖c8 with level chances in J.Cuartas-Lammers, Sitges 2010.

d) 11...♘ce7 (D).

12 ♕d3 (I like this move, solidifying c3 and preparing the standard ♗b3-c2 manoeuvre) 12...♘xc3 13 bxc3 ♘g6 14 ♗b3 (14 ♘g5!? is more aggressive, when Black should content himself with 14...♗d7 since continuing as in the game with 14...b6 runs into 15 h4! with some advantage after 15...h6 16

W

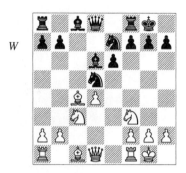

B

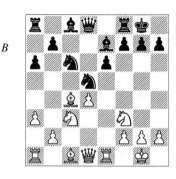

h5 hxg5 17 hxg6, since the g6-pawn is a bone in Black's throat) 14...b6 15 Rel Bb7 16 Ng5 (a standard manoeuvre, attacking the kingside – while looking at e6 and f7 – and allowing the white queen to transfer to g3 or h3) 16...Be7 and then:

d1) 17 Wg3 Bd5 18 h4 Nxh4 (this isn't forced but seems to be a good decision) 19 Bxd5 (19 Wxh4 h6 20 Nxe6 Bxh4 21 Nxd8 Rfxd8 is also level) 19...Wxd5 20 Re5 Wc4 21 Wxh4 h6 22 Wh3 hxg5 23 Bxg5 Bxg5 24 Rxg5 with a balanced position which White went on to win in Sanikidze-R.Ibrahimov, Turkish Team Ch, Konya 2011. An instructive GM struggle.

d2) The immediate 17 h4! is more ambitious. Perhaps White rejected this in view of 17...Bxg2, but it turns out that White is at least OK after 18 Rxe6! (not 18 Kxg2?? Nxh4+ −+ and 19...Bxg5) 18...fxe6?! (18...Bd5 is more solid) 19 Nxe6 Wc8 20 Nxf8+ Kxf8 21 Kxg2 Wg4+ 22 Kf1 with a messy position where the b3-bishop (and the white bishop-pair generally) is a major trump.

12 Rel Be7 13 a3 *(D)*

13...Nxc3

Black transforms the structure. Otherwise:

a) 13...Re8 14 Ba2 g6?! (Black could avoid weakening his kingside and prefer 14...Nxc3 15 bxc3 b5) 15 h3 Nxc3 16 bxc3 Bf6 17 Bh6 Ne7 18 Ne5 Nf5 19 Bf4 Wa5 20 Wf3 Bg7 21 Bh2 Wd8 22 Rad1 left White in a dominant position in I.Salgado-Matuszewski, Wroclaw rapid 2014.

b) 13...b5 14 Ba2 is likely to transpose after Black takes on c3, since 14...Bb7?! leaves the bishop passively placed after 15 Nxd5! exd5 16 Wd3 ±.

14 bxc3 Bf6 15 Wd3 b5 16 Ba2 Bb7 17 Bd2

17 h4!? is a typical sacrifice that might also be interesting; for instance, 17...Bxh4 18 a4 b4 19 Nxh4 Wxh4 20 Rb1 Rfe8 21 Re3 with complicated play.

17...Re8 18 Rad1 Rc8 19 Bb1

19 a4 is also possible, with balanced chances.

19...g6 20 Ba2 *(D)*

While the objective merit of White's last few moves can certainly be questioned, this is an absolutely standard

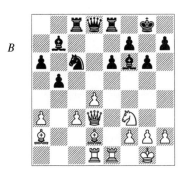

B

manoeuvre and one which should be remembered. The bishop went to the b1-h7 diagonal in order (in combination with the queen) to force a kingside weakening. If Black responds with ...h6, he normally falls under an extremely strong attack (as he would have here). If he responds with ...g6 (or the more aggressive ...f5), the bishop has nothing more to do on the b1-h7 diagonal and so switches back to the more active a2-g8 diagonal.

20...♕d6 21 ♗c1 ♖cd8?

The rook was already well placed. Black handles the position slightly too passively, and soon comes under a strong attack.

Black needed to get his own play going with 21...♘a5, unleashing the b7-bishop and intending ...♘c4 to clamp down on the white queenside. White needs to regroup here in a very unclear position where computers tend to like Black; for instance, 22 ♘d2!? (giving the white queen access to the kingside) 22...♗g5 23 ♕h3 ♕d8 24 ♖e2 ♗f4 25 ♖de1 with a tense manoeuvring battle with chances for both sides. He could also choose 21...♘e7, intending moves

like ...♗d5 or ...♘f5 with a robust position.

22 ♘g5! *(D)*

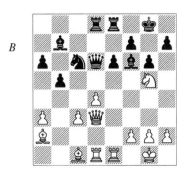

B

Starting strong play on the kingside. Black can hardly give up the f6-bishop for this knight since then the dark squares (including those around the black king) would be chronically weak. We can also notice that, while the ...a6 and ...b5 construction gains space and controls important light squares, it also weakens the black structure (the a4 break is sometimes possible, and the c5-square is weak) more than its more conservative ...b6 equivalent.

22...♕e7?! 23 ♕g3

23 ♘e4 is also nice for White, aiming at the dark-squared bishop or for the c5 outpost.

23...♘a5 24 ♕h4

White employs a thematic idea, but misses a good chance for 24 d5!.

24...h5 25 ♕g3

Like on moves 19 and 20, it is important to remember this idea and what it tries to achieve. ...h5 is enormously damaging for Black, since it weakens the kingside – specifically, it makes g6 much more brittle, and now sacrifices on e6 or f7 are in the air.

25...♗d5!

A good move, shoring up the kingside in view of the weaknesses described in the previous note.

26 ♗b1

The computer thinks Black is fine, but this is an extremely dangerous position to play in practice, since Black must be constantly on the lookout for tactical shots (such as the one which lands in a couple of moves). For such a position I would need to be at least a pawn up to be happy with Black, while all he has here is a slightly better structure as comfort for his practical problems.

26...♗g7? (D)

26...♘c4 would have kept the balance although, as I mentioned before, over the board I like White.

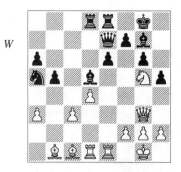

27 ♗f4?

27 ♘xf7! should be played now. After 27...♕xf7 28 ♗xg6 ♕b7 (or 28...♕f8 29 ♕g5! with a decisive attack) 29 ♕h3 (even better than taking on e8) White is attacking with material

equality (once he takes on h5) and is much better.

27...♖c8

Black should have admitted his mistake with 27...♗f6, when 28 ♘xf7 is fine for Black after 28...♕xf7 29 ♗xg6 ♕g7.

28 h4

Again 28 ♘xf7 should have been played.

28...♘c4

Finally!

29 ♘xf7

Having missed two opportunities, this is now only good enough for an unclear game.

29...♕xf7 30 ♗xg6 ♕f6 31 ♖e5?

31 ♗xh5 is better, with unclear play.

31...♘xe5 32 dxe5? (D)

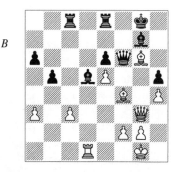

White has completely lost the thread and Black gets a winning position, before disaster strikes.

32...♕f8 33 ♕g5 ♖c4 34 ♖d4 ♖xd4 35 cxd4 ♖c8 −+ 36 ♗e3 ♕xa3 37 ♕xh5 ♖c1+

37...a5 −+.

38 ♔h2 ♕a1??

38...a5 −+.

39 ♔g3??

39 ♗h7+ ♔f8 40 ♕g5 is enough for perpetual.

39...♖c3 40 ♗h7+ ♔f8 41 ♕g5 ♖xe3+??

41...♕a5 −+.

42 fxe3 ♕e1+ 43 ♔h2 ♕f2??

Black walks into a mate in three. 43...♔e8 44 ♕g6+ ♔f8 45 ♕g5 would have drawn.

44 ♕d8+ ♔f7 45 ♗g8+ ♔g6 46 ♕g5# (1-0)

Despite the (time-trouble?) errors at the end, an instructive game in my view.

Game 18
D. Howell – Wallace
London rapid 2013

1 e4 c5 2 ♘f3 e6 3 c3 ♘f6 4 e5 ♘d5 5 d4 cxd4 6 cxd4 b6 *(D)*

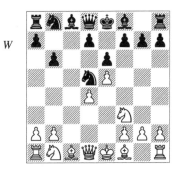

This system was recommended by Joe Gallagher in his book on the Anti-Sicilians many years ago. Black's set-up is logical but fails to place much pressure on the enemy centre, giving White a choice of promising ways to continue.

The variation I have suggested appears quite counter-intuitive (giving up the light-squared bishop in order to gain time) but I think it's rather promising.

7 ♗c4 ♗b7 8 0-0 ♗e7 9 ♗xd5!?

The point.

9...♗xd5

9...exd5 is principled, stabilizing the centre and keeping the bishop-pair. After 10 ♘c3 ♘a6 White has a couple of ways to play this position:

a) 11 ♘b5 0-0 12 ♗f4 ♗c6 13 ♕b3 ♘c7 14 ♘xc7 ♕xc7 15 ♗g5 ♗xg5 16 ♘xg5 with a better structure and a superior minor piece in Ghaem Maghami-Halay, Manila 2010.

b) 11 ♖e1 ♘c7 12 ♗f4 0-0 13 ♕b3 d6 14 ♖ad1 ♕d7 15 ♗g3 ♖ad8 16 ♖e3 and White was pressing in Degraeve-Kunin, Sables d'Olonne 2014.

10 ♘c3 *(D)*

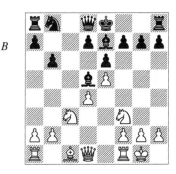

10...♗c4

A creative try, though the position as a whole is very difficult for Black. Otherwise:

a) 10...♞a6?! 11 ♘xd5 exd5 was much better for White in Can-Zubarev, Rethymnon 2011.

b) 10...♝b7 11 d5 exd5 12 ♘xd5 (12 ♘d4!?) 12...0-0 13 ♝f4 and White was comfortable in Sedina-Danielian, Istanbul Women's Olympiad 2012.

11 ♖e1 0-0 12 d5 exd5

12...d6?! 13 b3 ♝xd5 14 ♘xd5 exd5 15 ♕xd5 ± left White far more active in Kharchenko-Voloshin, Alushta 2011.

13 ♘xd5 ♘c6 14 ♖e4 ♝a6?!

14...♝xd5 15 ♕xd5 ♘b4 16 ♕b3 ♘a6 17 ♝e3 d5 18 exd6 ♝xd6 19 ♖d4 was Smagin-Kupreichik, Eupen rapid 1994. White has a serious advantage in piece placement with an open centre.

15 ♖g4 *(D)*

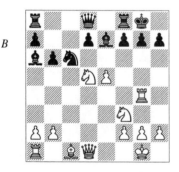

15...♚h8

The legendary Tony Miles once even managed to win with 15...f5 in Schweber-Miles, Buenos Aires 1979, but this move is busted by 16 exf6 ♝xf6 17 ♝h6 ♖f7 18 ♕b3 ♘a5 19 ♘xf6+ ♕xf6 20 ♝xg7 ♕g6 21 ♕xf7+! ♕xf7 22 ♝e5+ ♚f8 23 ♝d6+ ♚e8 24 ♖e1+ ♚d8 25 ♖f4, winning back the queen with a material and positional advantage.

16 ♝f4 ♖c8 17 ♕d2 ±

Even with a rapid time-limit, David Howell has an excellent feel for the initiative, and plays convincingly here.

17...f6 18 exf6 ♝xf6 19 ♖e1 ♖f7 20 ♝d6 ♕g8 21 ♖ge4!

The rooks have a bright future on the e-file.

21...♝b7 22 ♘g5 ♝xg5 23 ♕xg5

Opposite-coloured bishops favour the attacker, and here it is hard for Black to avoid disaster on g7.

23...♘a5 24 ♘e7 ♖xe7 25 ♖xe7 ♘c4 26 ♝g3 h6 27 ♕g6 1-0

2...d5

The basic position of this line emerges after 1 e4 c5 2 c3 d5 3 exd5 ♕xd5 4 d4 *(D)*.

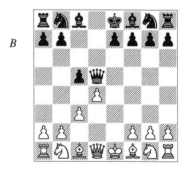

I have organized the material as follows:

a) 4...g6: Game 23

b) 4...♘c6 5 ♘f3 and then:

b1) 5...e5: Game 22

b2) 5...cxd4 6 cxd4 e5: Game 22

b3) 5...♘f6: Game 20
b4) 5...♗g4: Game 20
b5) 5...♗f5: Game 21
c) 4...♘f6 5 ♘f3 and here:
c1) 5...♘c6: Game 20
c2) 5...e6: Game 19
c3) 5...♗g4: Game 20

Game 19
Baklan – E. Romanov
Sitges 2014

1 e4 c5 2 c3 d5 3 exd5 ♕xd5 4 d4 ♘f6

See above to locate material on other moves.

5 ♘f3 e6 *(D)*

For 5...♘c6 and 5...♗g4 see Game 20.

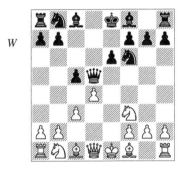

The text-move (5...e6) is a solid and sober approach by Black which is an excellent choice for ambitious players, as it avoids simplifications. This line frequently gives rise to IQP positions (after ...cxd4 cxd4) and so is an attractive one for White to face. However, Black has solidified his defences here over recent years.

The position White wants arises after 6 ♗e3 (apparently threatening to take on c5) 6...cxd4 7 cxd4 ♘c6 8 ♘c3 ♕d6 9 ♗d3 ♗e7 10 0-0 0-0 11 a3 b6 12 ♖e1 ♗b7 13 ♗c2. This is an extremely dangerous IQP to defend against since White is extremely well mobilized.

Players then realized that Black could change the character of the play by meeting 6 ♗e3 with 6...cxd4 7 cxd4 ♗b4+! 8 ♘c3 0-0, intending to meet 9 ♗d3 with 9...b6 (9...♗d7, intending ...♗b5, is similar) 10 0-0 ♗xc3 11 bxc3 ♗a6!. This position is quite playable for White (I won a decent game in an Olympiad from this position), and so this attempt wouldn't particularly scare me off.

However, it was then discovered that White isn't really threatening to take on c5 after ♗e3, since his lack of development means that Black will either regain the pawn or get excellent compensation for it. For instance, see the game D.Howell-Carlsen, London 2009, where Black played 6...♗e7 and got a fine position after White took on c5. White can play more conservatively with 7 ♗e2, but then his pieces are less actively placed than he would like and Black can comfortably take on d4.

Similar considerations apply to the sophisticated move-order 6 a3 (aimed against the ...♗b4+ line) – White is not yet threatening to take on c5 and Black can wait for a concession before taking on d4. Unfortunately I speak from experience here, having lost with

White in the game Collins-Bern, Norwegian Team Ch 2014/15.

So what's White to do? He needs to play moves that make sense with or without Black capturing on d4. The system used in our main game seems to me to meet these requirements quite nicely – it was overlooked when White was trying to force Black into an IQP, but has become more popular now that White is tired of playing passive IQP positions.

6 ♗d3 ♗e7

Obviously we'd be delighted if Black were to take at any point over the next couple of moves, when White could castle and gain time with ♘c3.

7 0-0 0-0 8 ♕e2 *(D)*

8...cxd4

Black aims to force the white rook to d1 (it would prefer to go to e1). This is a reasonable option, and is the second most popular in the position, but I think White gets a decent IQP here. Other moves:

a) 8...♖d8 is recommended by GM Smerdon on Chesspublishing.com. 9 ♖d1 and then:

a1) 9...cxd4 leads to similar play to our main game. 10 cxd4 ♘c6 11 ♘c3 ♕h5 12 ♘e4 ♘xe4 (12...♗d7 looks more solid) 13 ♗xe4 ♘b4 14 ♗f4 ♘d5 15 ♗e5 f6! 16 ♗g3 ♗d7 with a balanced game in Rozentalis-G.Papp, Oslo 2014.

a2) After 9...♘c6 10 dxc5 ♕xc5 11 ♘bd2 White seems to have a pleasant edge in this position (which is typical for some lines of the French Tarrasch), since his pieces are more active and Black will struggle to mobilize his queenside. He went on to win in Mamedov-Sadzikowski, European Ch, Jerusalem 2015.

b) 8...♘c6 is the most popular continuation here. I think now is a good time for White to change the structure with 9 dxc5!? *(D)*.

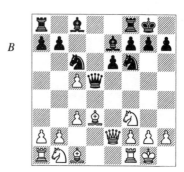

The knight on c6 isn't badly placed in itself, but it will block the light-squared bishop if (as is likely) it comes into play via b7. Now:

b1) 9...♖d8 10 ♖d1 transposes to Mamedov-Sadzikowski in line 'a2' – in fact that game followed this move-order.

b2) 9...♕xc5 10 ♘bd2 ♖d8 11 ♘e4 ♘xe4 12 ♗xe4 leads to a typical French Rubinstein position. White has more active pieces and an edge, though Black should be able to equalize with careful play. A couple of recent examples:

b21) 12...♗f6 13 ♗e3 ♕e7 14 ♖ad1 ♗d7 15 ♘d4 ♘xd4 16 ♗xd4 ♗xd4 17 ♖xd4 ♗c6 18 ♖fd1 was agreed drawn in Sebag-A.Mista, French Team Ch 2015. The position is certainly closer to a draw than anything else, but White retains marginally more active pieces and a queenside majority so she could have played on.

b22) 12...♗d7 13 ♗f4 ♗e8 14 ♖ad1 ♕h5 15 h3 ♖xd1 16 ♖xd1 ♖d8 17 ♖xd8. Here the players agreed a draw in Rozentalis-Krasenkow, Køge 2014, but I think White has an edge; for instance, 17...♘xd8 (17...♗xd8 18 b4! ± is similar, but on c6 the knight is likely to be hit by b5) 18 ♕d2 f6 19 b4 starts active play on the queenside. White's pieces are more active and his majority is easier to push, since he can do so without exposing his king.

9 cxd4 ♘c6 10 ♖d1 ♘b4

Starting a standard regrouping – the knight gains time on the bishop on d3 and intends a solid blockade of the d4-pawn by occupying the d5 outpost.

10...♖d8 transposes to line 'a1' of the previous note.

11 ♘c3 *(D)*

11...♕h5

11...♕d8 12 ♗b1 b6 13 ♘e5 ♗a6 14 ♕f3 ♖c8 was played in Vajda-C.Horvath, Budapest 2013 and now,

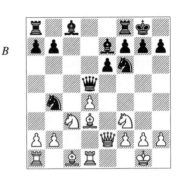

instead of Vajda's 15 ♗g5 (which is a perfectly reasonable move), I prefer 15 ♕g3. This position gives rise to some beautiful variations which are highly thematic for IQP structures:

a) 15...♘h5 16 ♕h3 ♘f6 is a typical device, but here allows 17 d5!, based on the tactical point 17...♘bxd5 18 ♘xd5 exd5 19 ♘d7 and the threat of mate collects the exchange (of course, Black won't fall for 19...♕xd7?? 20 ♗xh7+, when the queen is lost). With a pawn and active pieces, Black has some compensation for the exchange but White's game seems preferable.

b) 15...♖e8 16 ♗h6 ♗f8 (16...g6? loses to 17 ♗xg6! hxg6 18 ♘xg6 with a winning attack) 17 ♗g5 ♗e7. Now White could repeat with 18 ♗h6, but he has an active position and the better chances after 18 ♕h3:

b1) Of course 18...h6? loses after 19 ♗xh6!, although the follow-up is slightly unusual: 19...gxh6 20 ♕g3+ ♔f8 21 ♗g6!!. Taking the bishop leads to immediate mate, so Black has nothing better than 21...♗d6 22 ♗xf7 ♘c6 (22...♖e7 23 ♕g6 is winning for White) 23 ♗xe8 ♕xe8 24 ♘g6+ ♔g8

25 ♕xd6 ♕xg6 26 ♕xe6+ +− with a material advantage and an attack.

b2) 18...g6 19 a3 ♘bd5 20 ♘xd5 (D) and now Black has only one way to stay in the game:

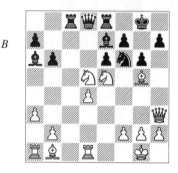

b21) 20...♘xd5?? loses on the spot to 21 ♘xf7!.

b22) After the alternative capture 20...♕xd5? 21 ♗a2 White develops overwhelming activity; for instance, 21...♕d6 (21...♕d8 22 ♗xe6 fxe6 23 ♕xe6+ ♔g7 24 ♘f7 is also winning for White) 22 ♕f3 ♔g7 23 ♗f4 and Black can't avoid ♘xf7, as 23...♕d8 24 d5! exd5 25 ♗h6+ ♔g8 26 ♖xd5 leads to a winning attack.

b23) 20...exd5! is essential, though after 21 ♕f3 White's pieces are better placed in this symmetrical structure; for instance, 21...♕d6 22 ♖e1 ♗d8 23 ♗a2 ♗b7 24 ♖ac1 with a comfortable advantage.

c) The solid 15...♘bd5! seems the most prudent, with balanced IQP play. An interesting computer suggestion is 16 a4!?, aiming to play on the queenside with a5 while enabling the bishop to come out via a2.

We now return to 11...♕h5 (D):

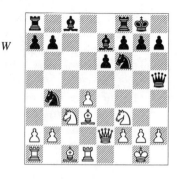

12 ♗c4

This position has been defended, as Black, by World Champions Mikhail Tal and Vasily Smyslov.

12 ♗b1 b6 13 a3 ♘bd5 14 ♘e4 ♘xe4 15 ♗xe4 ♗b7 is an alternative which has been played a couple of times by c3 Sicilian specialist Enrico Sevillano. I think Black should have no cause for complaint here.

Black now has a wide choice.

12...♖e8

A standard move, but White has a good response. Alternatives:

a) 12...♖d8 is logical, putting the rook on a half-open file and attacking the d4-pawn. However, as will appear, Black needs to be alert to d5 breaks as his bishop is undefended on e7. 13 ♗g5 and then:

a1) 13...h6 14 ♗h4 ♗d7? (after 14...♘fd5, as in Kranzl-Znamenáček, Prague 1992, 15 ♗xe7 ♘xe7 16 a3 ♘bd5 17 ♕e5! ± leads to similar play to our main game) has been played a couple of times, but no one has found 15 d5!, which works perfectly; for instance, 15...♘bxd5 16 ♘xd5 ♘xd5 17 ♖xd5! exd5 18 ♗xe7 ♖e8 19 ♗d3 with a material advantage since Black can't exploit the pin on the e-file.

a2) The interesting pawn sacrifice 13...b5!? 14 ♘xb5 ♗b7 was tried in the game Sveshnikov-Smyslov, Sochi 1974. Black has some compensation, but after 15 a3 ♘bd5 16 ♗d2 (preparing ♘c3) I would rather be White.

b) 12...♗d6 was the Magician from Riga's choice in Hamann-Tal, European Clubs Cup, Tallinn 1986. After 13 h3 b6 White played too passively with 14 ♘e4 and was soon worse. Instead 14 ♗g5 (14 ♘b5 ♗b8 15 ♗d2) 14...♗b7 15 ♗xf6 ♗xf3 16 ♕xf3 ♕xf3 17 gxf3 gxf6 18 d5 exd5 19 ♘xd5 ♘xd5 20 ♖xd5 would have led to a drawn endgame.

c) 12...♘bd5 is solid and consistent, after which White can continue in similar style to the game with 13 ♕e5!? or play for normal IQP pressure after 13 ♗g5.

13 ♕e5! *(D)*

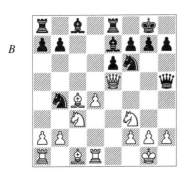

The queen is excellently placed on e5. An exchange on e5 can be met by dxe5, improving White's structure, while an exchange on h5 will misplace the black knight from f6.

13...♗d7 14 a3!

Forcing the black knight away from d5.

14...♘c6

Of course 14...♘bd5 simply loses a pawn after 15 ♕xh5 ♘xh5 16 ♘xd5 exd5 17 ♗xd5 ±.

15 ♕xh5 ♘xh5 *(D)*

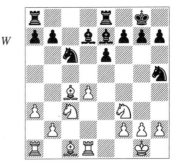

16 ♘e5!

A nice echo of move 13. Again the knight is dominant on e5, but a trade would improve the white structure.

16 d5! is also thematic and good. Presumably Baklan was worried that Black could gradually equalize after 16...exd5 17 ♘xd5 ♗g4, but he will certainly need to show some precision; for instance, 18 ♘xe7+ ♖xe7 19 ♗e3. The white bishop-pair is strong, and I would be reluctant as Black to commit to 19...♗xf3 20 gxf3, when the white pawns are weakened but White's control of the board is impressive.

16...♘f6

16...♖ad8 17 ♘xd7 ♖xd7 18 d5 is similar.

17 ♘xd7 ♘xd7 18 d5! ♘b6 19 ♗a2 exd5 20 ♘xd5 ♘xd5 21 ♗xd5 (D)

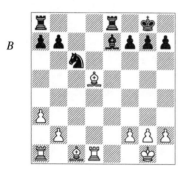

This is an unpleasant position for Black, since White has the bishop-pair for free in an open position. With limited material and no weaknesses, Black should be able to defend this position, but it's certainly no fun. Baklan gives an outstanding demonstration of how to play such positions with White.

21...♗f6 22 ♖b1!

The computer likes 22 ♗e3, but after 22...♗xb2 23 ♖ab1 ♗xa3 24 ♖xb7 ♘e7 the elimination of White's queenside has not helped his winning prospects (even after he takes the a7-pawn). Bishops are at their best when there is play on both sides of the board.

22...♗d4 23 ♗g5!?

Offering Romanov a chance to alter the nature of the position.

23...♖e5!?

Black could also have sat tight with 23...♗b6, but after 24 ♔f1 White retains a pleasant endgame advantage.

24 ♗xc6 bxc6 25 ♖xd4 ♖xg5

White has traded down into a superior rook endgame. The white rooks are more active and Black's queenside is vulnerable.

26 ♖c4! (D)

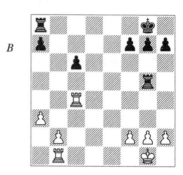

26...♖b5

A strong GM like Romanov knows that activity is key in rook endgames. (Full disclosure – Romanov has played two rook endgames against me, winning the superior one and drawing the inferior one!)

The alternative is 26...♖c8 27 ♖bc1, and then:

a) 27...♖d5 prevents the capture on c6, but only for a move: 28 g3. Now similar play develops unless Black goes passive with 28...♖d6 29 b4. This certainly doesn't look like an improvement compared to the game.

b) 27...♖b5 28 ♖xc6 ♖xc6 29 ♖xc6 leads to similar play to the game, since a pair of rooks are exchanged on move 31.

27 ♖xc6 a5 28 ♖bc1 ♖bb8

An interesting decision – Romanov doesn't want to allow the exchange of a pair of rooks. 28...♔f8 29 ♖c8+ ♖xc8 30 ♖xc8+ ♔e7 leads to similar play to the game.

29 ♔f1 g6 30 ♖1c2 ♖b3

30...♔g7 would have avoided the rook exchange, but after 31 ♖c7 White has ideas of ♖e2-e7.

31 ♖c8+ ♖xc8 32 ♖xc8+ ♔g7 33 ♖c2

White has an extra queenside pawn and good winning chances. A detailed analysis of this position would take us too far off course, but I was quite impressed by Baklan's technique.

33...h5 34 ♔e2 h4 35 h3 g5 36 ♔d1 f5 37 ♖c7+ ♔g6 38 ♔c2 ♖b5 39 ♖c4 ♖e5 40 b4 axb4 41 axb4 ♖e2+ 42 ♔c3 ♖xf2 43 b5 ♖e2 44 b6 ♖e8 45 ♔b4 ♔h5 46 ♖c5 ♖f8 47 b7 ♖b8 48 ♖b5 ♔g6 49 ♔c5 g4 50 hxg4 fxg4 51 ♔b6 h3 52 gxh3 gxh3 53 ♔a7 h2 54 ♖b1 1-0

Game 20
Tiviakov – Idani
Mashhad 2010

1 e4 c5 2 c3 d5 3 exd5 ♕xd5 4 d4

In this game we shall deal with Black's various knight developments, in conjunction with ...♗g4 plans.

4...♘f6

Black can also bring out his queen's knight before developing the bishop to g4: 4...♘c6 5 ♘f3 ♗g4 (for 5...♘f6 see the note to Black's 5th move). In this position 6 ♘bd2 cxd4 7 ♗c4 ♗xf3 doesn't work as well for White as in our main game, but 6 ♗e2! *(D)* is quite strong:

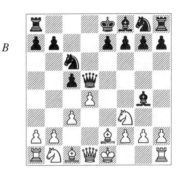

a) 6...e6 7 h3! ♗xf3 (if Black proceeds by analogy with the 4...♘f6 line and plays 7...♗h5, his c6-knight gets hit with 8 c4 and 9 d5; White has scored excellently from this position) 8 ♗xf3 ♕d7 9 dxc5 ♕xd1+ 10 ♔xd1 (recapturing with the bishop followed by castling also appears favourable for White) 10...♗xc5 11 ♖f1 ♘f6 12 ♘d2 0-0-0 13 ♔c2 gave White the bishop-pair and a queenside majority and, it seems to me, a very pleasant position in D.Howell-Guseinov, Dubai 2015.

b) Black can resolve the central tension with 6...cxd4 7 cxd4 e6, but this allows White an active development with 8 ♘c3 *(D)*.

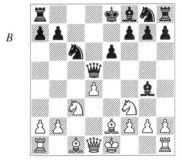

Then Black typically chooses between:

b1) 8...♕a5 9 h3 ♗h5 (this allows White a promising pawn sacrifice; after 9...♗xf3 10 ♗xf3 ♗b4 11 0-0 ♘ge7 White has a few promising continuations, but I like Szabo's treatment: 12 ♘a4 ♖d8 13 a3 ♗d6 14 ♗e3 0-0 15 b4 ♕f5 16 ♘c3 ♗c7 {16...♗b8 17 ♗e4 ♕f6 18 ♕g4 h6 19 ♖ad1 was similar in G.Szabo-Shishkin, Bucharest 2008} 17 ♗e4 ♕f6 18 ♕g4 h6, G.Szabo-Nikolova, Plovdiv 2011, and after 19 ♖fd1 White has the two bishops and an active set-up) 10 d5!?. White seeks to take advantage of Black's lag in development and, in particular, the presence of his king in the centre. While White's king is also in the centre, it can castle quickly, but the black king can only castle queenside (which is risky!). Now:

b11) 10...0-0-0? would be terrific if it worked, but it falls short for tactical reasons. 11 ♗d2! is a precise move, threatening the knight on c6 by blocking the d-file. Now Black has to capture on d5: 11...exd5 12 0-0 ♘f6 (this is the only move to have been played; Black has alternatives but his position is both bad and extremely difficult to play, while White's game plays itself) 13 ♖c1 ♗xf3 14 ♗xf3 ♕b6 15 ♗e3! ♕xb2 (this fails predictably, but Black had nothing playable at this point; after 15...d4 16 ♘a4 White wins back material with a crushing position) 16 ♗xa7 ♗b4 17 ♗g4+ with a winning attack in Penz-Schwarhofer, Austrian Team Ch 2013/14.

b12) 10...♖d8 has barely been tried but isn't that bad (and is certainly better than 10...0-0-0?). White should continue 11 ♗d2 exd5 12 0-0, with a strong initiative for the pawn; for instance, 12...♘f6 13 ♖e1 ♗e7 14 g4 ♗g6 15 g5 ♘g8 (15...♘h5 16 ♘h2 leaves the knight in trouble) and the black king remains stuck in the centre, promising White strong compensation.

b13) 10...exd5 is the best move, and the most popular. 11 ♘d4 (D) and here:

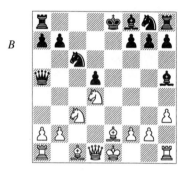

b131) 11...♗g6 was played in Collins-Cafolla, Kilkenny 2011. Now 12 0-0 is simplest, with a strong initiative for the pawn.

b132) 11...♘xd4 12 ♗xh5 ♘c6 13 0-0 ♘f6, as in Nayer-Lautier, World Cup, Khanty-Mansiisk 2005 can be well met by 14 ♕b3 0-0-0 (White threatened to take on b7) 15 ♗xf7 ±, regaining the pawn with some advantage.

b133) 11...♗xe2 12 ♕xe2+ ♗e7 13 ♘xc6 bxc6 14 0-0 ♖d8 (I once had the position after 14...♔f8 15 ♖e1 with White against a promising Irish junior, who played 15...♕d8 16 ♗e3 g6 17 ♖ad1 ♔g7 18 ♖d3 ♕f8 19 b4 ♗xb4 20 ♕b2 f6 21 a3 ♗xa3 22 ♕b7+ ♘e7; this was Collins-R.Griffiths, Kilkenny 2009 and now I should have played 23 ♗f4! ± with a very strong initiative) 15 ♗d2 d4 16 ♘e4 ♕b5 (after 16...♕d5 17 ♖fe1 ♔f8 18 ♕a6 h5 19 ♖ac1 h4 20 ♖xc6 White regained his pawn with a continuing initiative in Bedouin-Cossin, French Team Ch 2015) 17 ♕f3 ♔f8 18 ♖ac1 h5 19 ♖fe1 h4?! (19...♕d5) 20 b4?! (20 ♘c5!? ♗xc5 21 ♖e5 ♕xb2 22 ♖cxc5 ♕xd2 23 ♕a3 is a promising computer suggestion) 20...♕d5 21 ♕a3 ♖h5 22 ♕xa7 ♖e5 23 ♘c5 and a draw was agreed in Picard-Reinderman, Haarlem 2014, despite Black's 200 rating point advantage.

b2) 8...♗b4 9 0-0 ♕a5 *(D)* and now White has several promising continuations:

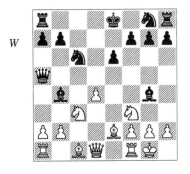

b21) 10 ♗e3 and then:

b211) 10...♘f6 11 ♕b3 0-0 gives White a similar set-up to a main line which I'm trying to avoid (i.e. 1 e4 c5 2 c3 d5 3 exd5 ♕xd5 4 d4 ♘f6 5 ♘f3 ♗g4 6 ♗e2 e6 7 h3 ♗h5 8 0-0 ♘c6 9 ♗e3 cxd4 10 cxd4 ♗e7 11 ♘c3 ♕d6 12 ♕b3 0-0). However, in that position Black's queen is on d6 and his bishop is on e7, which seems more solid to me than having these pieces on a5 and b4 respectively. For example, 12 a3 ♗xc3 13 bxc3 ♘d5 14 ♖fc1 ♕c7 15 c4 ♘f4 (15...♘xe3 16 fxe3 also looks slightly more comfortable for White) 16 ♗d1 ♖fd8 17 ♕c3 ♖ac8 was Al Qudaimi-Al Modiahki, Arab Ch, Abu Dhabi 2013 and now I like White's position after 18 ♖ab1 with space and the bishop-pair to compensate for his hanging pawns.

b212) 10...♘ge7 11 ♕b3 (White can also start with 11 h3) 11...0-0 12 ♖fd1 ♖fd8 13 h3 ♗h5 14 ♖ac1 ♖ac8 15 a3 ♗xc3 16 bxc3 ♕c7 (the following game is a model demonstration of White's chances) 17 g4 ♗g6 18 c4 ♗e4?! (18...f6! would have led to balanced play) 19 ♘g5 ♘a5 20 ♕b4 ♘ac6 21 ♕b3 ♘a5 22 ♕b4 ♘ac6 23 ♕c5 (23 ♕b5 ± is also strong) 23...b6 24 ♕b5 ♗g6 25 d5! (White has executed his standard break under ideal conditions) 25...h6 26 ♘f3 ♘e5 27 c5! ± (blasting open the position to the benefit of White's pieces, especially his bishop-pair) 27...♘xd5? (the alternative 27...♘xf3+ is more tenacious) 28 cxb6 ♘xf3+ 29 ♗xf3 ♕b8 30 ♖xc8 ♖xc8 31 b7 ♖c7 32 ♖xd5! exd5 33 ♗xd5 ♖e7 34 ♗xa7 1-0 Ghaem Maghami-Leon Hoyos, Khanty-Mansiisk Olympiad 2010. I'm really impressed by the energy with which White conducted this game.

b22) 10 h3 *(D)* actually sets a sophisticated trap.

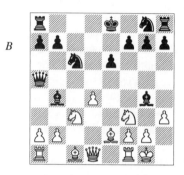

Only White can be better after 10...♗xf3, and 10...♗f5 11 ♕b3 also looks promising for him. However, 10...♗h5 is answered by 11 a3! ♗xc3 (11...♘f6 isn't playable in view of 12 axb4 ♕xa1 13 g4 +–, when Black will have to shed further material to free the queen from the corner) 12 bxc3 ♘ge7 13 ♖b1 ♕c7 (White has good chances here) 14 ♖b5 ♗g6 15 c4 0-0 16 ♕b3 b6 17 d5 exd5 18 cxd5 (the passed d-pawn is strong and White's activity is hard to control) 18...♘a5 19 ♕b4 ♕d8 (19...♖fd8 is stronger) 20 d6 ♘ec6 21 ♕f4 ♖e8 22 ♗e3 ♖e4 23 ♕g3 ♘c4 24 ♗xc4 ♖xc4 25 ♖d1 (the d6-pawn gives White the advantage, and Black now collapses in a few moves; 25 ♘e5! ♘xe5 26 ♖xe5 is even stronger) 25...♕d7? (25...f6 is only slightly better for White) 26 ♘e5 ♘xe5 27 ♖xe5 ± ♖e4 28 ♖xe4 ♗xe4 29 ♗d4 ♗g6 30 ♕e5 1-0 Sevillano-V.Georgiev, Los Angeles 2011. An instructive game.

5 ♘f3 ♗g4

This is the main line. The other main possibility is 5...♘c6, when I recommend 6 ♗e2 *(D)*.

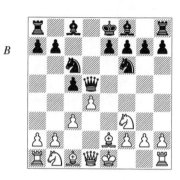

Then:

a) 6...♗f5 transposes to the note to Black's 6th move in Game 21.

b) 6...♕d6?! wastes a lot of time, and after 7 0-0 g6?! 8 ♘a3 cxd4 9 ♘b5 ♕d8 10 ♗f4 ♘d5 11 ♗g3 ♗h6 (otherwise c4 was a threat) 12 ♘fxd4 a6 13 ♘xc6 bxc6 14 ♘d4 ± Black was much worse in Bergez-Kurajica, Las Palmas 2013.

c) 6...cxd4 7 cxd4 ♗f5 8 ♘c3 ♕a5 9 0-0 e6 was Vysochin-Volokitin, Ukrainian Ch, Kiev 2011 and now I like 10 ♘h4!?, when the bishop-pair in a semi-open position should favour White; for instance, 10...♖d8 11 ♘xf5 ♕xf5 12 ♗e3 ♗e7 13 ♗d3 ♕h5 14 ♕xh5 ♘xh5 15 ♗e2 ♘f6 16 ♖fd1 followed by 17 ♗f3 with fairly good prospects in the endgame.

d) 6...e6 7 0-0 cxd4 (7...♗e7 8 ♘a3 0-0 9 ♘b5 ♕d8 10 dxc5 ♗xc5 and now, instead of the weakening 11 b4?!, as in Pandurević-Ferčec, Velika Gorica 2014, White could play 'with the draw in hand' after 11 ♗f4 a6 12 ♘bd4 ♘xd4 13 ♘xd4 ±) 8 cxd4 ♗e7 9 ♘c3 ♕d6 and here we see another motif in some IQP positions: 10 ♘b5!? ♕d8 11 ♗f4 ♘d5 12 ♗g3 *(D)*.

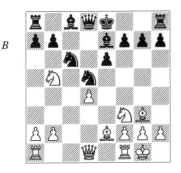

White has transferred his bishop to the g3-square and controls a lot of important squares on the queenside. This is an important position which has been tested in several GM encounters.

d1) 12...0-0 13 ♗c4 a6 14 ♘c3 (White has also tried 14 ♗xd5 axb5 15 ♗e4 without obtaining anything special) 14...♗f6 15 ♘e4 (15 ♖c1 ± is also logical, to avoid the repetition) 15...♗e7 16 ♘c3 ♘f6!? was Kosteniuk-Hou Yifan, Geneva (women) 2013 and now I like 17 ♖e1; for instance, 17...♘h5?! 18 d5 ♘xg3 19 hxg3 ♘a5 20 ♗d3 with some pressure – of course Black can't take twice on d5 in view of ♗xh7+.

d2) 12...a6 13 ♘c3 0-0 was M.Zaitsev-Danin, 2nd Bundesliga 2014/15, and now I like simple development with 14 ♕c2 and ♖fd1.

We now return to 5...♗g4 *(D)*:

6 ♘bd2

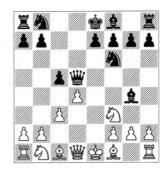

I'm quite fond of this move, which contains some early traps and leads to an endgame with a slight initiative for White.

6 ♗e2 is the traditional main line, leading to IQP positions after 6...e6 7 h3 ♗h5 8 0-0 ♘c6 9 ♗e3 cxd4 10 cxd4 ♗e7 11 ♘c3 ♕d6 12 ♕b3, but Black is well developed and very solid after 12...0-0!.

6...♘c6

Everything else looks somewhere between dubious and unplayable:

a) 6...cxd4 7 ♗c4 ♕d7 has been played in 35 games, but only in two in my database has White found the correct path: 8 ♘e5! ♗xd1 9 ♗xf7+ ♔d8 10 ♘xd7 ♘bxd7 11 ♔xd1 dxc3 12 bxc3 and the bishop-pair gave White the superior endgame in B.Gupta-Sarosi, Kecskemet 2012.

b) 6...e6 7 ♗c4 gains time on the black queen. Now 7...♕c6 is the move preferred by some engines. 8 h3 ♗h5 (after 8...♗xf3 9 ♘xf3 cxd4 10 ♕xd4 the bishop-pair gives White the better chances) 9 0-0 cxd4 10 ♘xd4 ♗xd1 11 ♘xc6 ♗a4 12 ♘d4 and White's lead in development, coupled with the misplaced bishop on a4, gives White slightly better chances. A few sample lines: 12...a6 (this seems the most accurate; 12...♗e7 13 ♘b5 is unpleasant, while after 12...♘c6 13 ♘xe6! fxe6 14 b3 ♘e5 15 bxa4 ♘xc4 16 ♘xc4 ♖c8 17 ♘e5 Black will struggle to complete his development) and then:

b1) 13 ♖e1 ♘c6 14 ♘2f3 (14 ♘xe6 fxe6 15 ♗xe6 ♗e7 16 b3 ♗b5 17 c4 ♘d4 18 cxb5 ♘c2 leads to unclear play which Houdini assesses as approximately level) 14...♘xd4 15 ♘xd4 ♗c5 16 ♗e3 ♖c8 and Black seems to have equalized.

b2) The slightly odd 13 ♘2b3!?, aiming for a5, is quite effective. After 13...♘c6 14 ♗e3 ♖c8 15 ♘xc6 ♗xc6 16 ♘a5 ♗d5 17 ♗b3 b5 18 ♗d4 White retains some pressure, and will play 19 a4 next.

7 ♗c4 ♗xf3 (D)

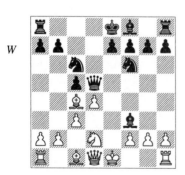

8 ♕b3

8 ♕xf3 is a sound but unambitious alternative; for instance, 8...♕xf3 9 ♘xf3 cxd4 10 ♘xd4 ♘xd4 11 cxd4 e6 12 ♗b5+ ♔d8 13 ♗g5 ½-½ Vlassov-Shipov, Internet rapid 2002.

8 ♕a4? is very plausible error that has been played by several strong players. Black is much better after the unexpected 8...♗d1!.

8...♘a5

Basically the only move. The queen sacrifice 8...♗xg2 falls short, though not by much: 9 ♗xd5 ♗xd5 10 ♕xb7 ♘xd4 (10...♖d8 hasn't been played, but 11 f3 ♘xd4 12 ♕a6 ♘c2+ 13 ♔f2 ♘xa1 14 ♕a4+ ♘d7 15 ♖d1 ± is excellent for White) 11 ♕a6 ♘c2+ 12 ♔e2 ♘xa1 was Dos Santos-D.Flores, São Paulo 2009 and now 13 ♕a4+ ♘d7 14 ♖d1 ± would have given White a powerful initiative with a favourable material balance. Obviously the c2-knight isn't long for this world, and the black kingside is unable to come to the defence of its king.

9 ♕b5+ ♕d7 10 ♘xf3 ♘xc4 11 ♕xc4 cxd4 12 ♘xd4 (D)

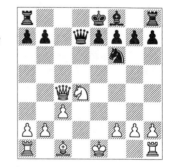

A long forced sequence has resulted in this position, where White has a slight lead in development (in that he can castle immediately) and his game is to be preferred. In particular, I would like to note that these positions are often underestimated by Sicilian players – it is true that Black isn't far away from equality, but White's initiative can quickly assume serious proportions if Black doesn't play accurately.

12...e6

12...e5 is far less popular, perhaps because it seems slightly loosening. A sound response is 13 ♘c2 ♕d5 14 ♘e3 ♕xc4 15 ♘xc4 ♘d7 16 f4 e4 17 ♗e3 ♖c8, as in Tiviakov-Aveskulov, Ottawa 2007, which proceeded 18 ♘e5 ♗c5 19 ♔e2 ♘b6 20 ♗xc5 ♖xc5 21 ♖hd1 g5 22 ♖d4 with a small endgame edge.

13 ♗g5 *(D)*

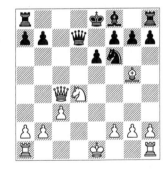

13...♖c8

Or:

a) 13...♕d5 14 ♕b5+ ♕d7 (Black could try 14...♕xb5 15 ♘xb5 ♘d5) 15 ♗xf6 gxf6 16 0-0-0 ♕xb5 17 ♘xb5 ± and White had a pleasant endgame in Sveshnikov-Nunn, World Over-50 Ch, Katerini 2014.

b) 13...♘d5 has also been played. Since the knight is now eyeing the queenside I would prefer not to castle

long, and I like 14 ♖d1 h6 15 ♗h4 followed by 0-0 and ♖fe1, with a slight pull for White.

14 ♕b3

This is Tiviakov's latest preference, but he has also won with 14 ♕e2, as has English GM and c3 Sicilian expert David Howell.

14...♘e4

Or:

a) 14...♗c5 15 ♗xf6 gxf6 16 ♖d1 0-0 17 0-0 ♕c7 18 ♖d3 gave White a pleasant advantage thanks to the superior structure and safer king in Osmak-Buksa, Lvov 2015.

b) Idani has also tried 14...♘d5. Then I like 15 0-0 followed by centralizing the rooks, with a slightly easier game for White. Instead 15 0-0-0 ♗e7 16 ♗xe7 ♕xe7 17 ♕b5+ ♕d7 18 ♖he1 a6 19 ♕xd7+ ♔xd7 was a pretty level endgame in Durarbayli-Idani, World Under-18 Ch, Porto Carras 2010.

15 0-0-0 ♘c5 16 ♕c2 *(D)*

This is more ambitious than immediately playing for the endgame with 16 ♕b5, as in Michalczak-Cacciola, Stein am Rhein 2014.

16...♗e7

16...♕d5?? 17 ♘xe6 1-0 was the abrupt finish of Grafl-Reschke, 2nd Bundesliga 2003/4.

17 h4 ♕a4 18 ♕xa4+

Keeping the queens on with 18 b3 is also possible, but Tiviakov always prefers a slightly superior endgame.

18...♘xa4 19 ♘b5 ♗xg5+

19...a6 is an alternative, but after 20 ♘d6+ ♗xd6 21 ♖xd6 White enjoys a long-term advantage since his bishop is the superior minor piece in an open position with asymmetrical pawn-majorities.

20 hxg5

Now the h7-pawn is a weakness, and Black also finds it less comfortable to play ...f6.

20...♔e7

Black could (and perhaps should) have forced matters with 20...♖c5. After 21 ♖h4 ♖xb5 22 ♖xa4 ♖xg5 23 ♖xa7 0-0 24 g3 b5 a complicated double-rook endgame has arisen. I prefer White since his rooks are more active and his queenside majority seems more mobile, but both sides have chances in such a position.

21 ♖h4! *(D)*

Showing another downside to the exchange on g5.

21...♘b6

21...♖c5 is clearly inferior to this option on the previous move. 22 ♖xa4 ♖xb5 23 ♖xa7 ♖b8 24 f4 ± leaves White with a healthy extra pawn.

22 ♘xa7 ♖c7

22...♖a8 23 ♖b4 ♖xa7 24 ♖xb6 ± leads to a double-rook endgame with

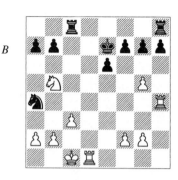

White being a pawn up and having excellent winning chances.

23 ♖b4 ♘d5 24 ♖b3 ♖a8

24...h6 is a better attempt at counterplay, although after 25 ♘b5 ♖cc8 26 gxh6 ♖xh6 27 g3 ± White's extra pawn gives him good chances.

25 ♘b5 ♖d7 26 c4 ♖c8 27 ♘a3 ♖cc7 28 g3 ±

White is a pawn up for no compensation and went on to win convincingly.

28...f6 29 ♖h1 fxg5 30 ♖xh7 ♔f7 31 ♖h1 ♘f6 32 ♖e1 g4 33 ♖c3 ♖c5 34 ♘b5 ♖f5 35 ♖e2 ♘h7 36 c5 ♔e7 37 ♘d6 ♖d5 38 ♔c2 ♖c7 39 b4 ♘g5 40 ♘b5 ♖c6 41 a4 ♘f3 42 ♖d3 ♖h5 43 a5 ♘e5 44 ♖d6 ♖xd6 45 ♘xd6 ♘c6 46 ♖e3 1-0

Game 21
Kryvoruchko – Negi
World Cup, Tromsø 2013

1 e4 c5 2 ♘f3 ♘c6 3 c3 d5 4 exd5 ♕xd5 5 d4

The 'pure' c3 Sicilian move-order would of course be 1 e4 c5 2 c3 d5 3 exd5 ♕xd5 4 d4 ♘c6 5 ♘f3. Now for the forcing lines 5...e5 and 5...cxd4 6 cxd4 e5 see Game 22. In this game we examine a more subtle way for Black to force the pace:

5...♗f5 *(D)*

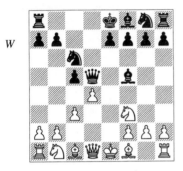

This is a move which has risen from near-obscurity to become one of Black's most popular responses to the c3 Sicilian. Part of the reason for this surge in popularity was undoubtedly how, in 2012-13, many players (including 2700-rated GMs) automatically replied 6 ♘a3?! cxd4 7 ♘b5? and couldn't understand why their positions immediately collapsed after 7...0-0-0!. Wang Yue has won several games as Black like this, as has Gawain Jones.

Looking at the position from first principles, it is clear that the bishop exerts less pressure on the centre than it would on g4 (where it pins the knight that is controlling the d4- and e5-squares). Black gets the additional option of ...♗xb1 but, in principle, White shouldn't be scared of this move, which gives up the bishop-pair in a semi-open position while spending

two moves to exchange a knight that hasn't moved. While this sequence could sometimes result in the fall of the a2-pawn (which is attacked by the black queen), this pawn cannot be captured without significant risk.

Anyway, our first job is (unlike Wang Yue's super-GM victims) to make a good choice at move 6.

6 ♗e2

As discussed above, 6 ♘a3?! cxd4 7 ♘b5? 0-0-0 8 cxd4 e5! is really unpleasant for White.

6 dxc5 is a possibility here (as in many lines after 2...d5), giving Black a choice between struggling to equalize after 6...♕xc5?! or dynamically playing for compensation in the endgame after 6...♕xd1+!.

Probably the main line is 6 ♗e3, which tends to give White slightly the better chances. However, I like the straightforward text-move, which aims to complete development as quickly as possible. It also often leads to promising IQP positions for White, and so is a natural repertoire choice for us.

6...cxd4

6...e6 (6...♘f6 7 0-0 e6 comes to the same thing) 7 0-0 ♘f6 is a solid option, delaying the capture on d4 so as to frustrate the development of the white knight to c3. 8 ♗e3 and here:

a) After 8...cxd4 9 cxd4 White has easy IQP play starting with the natural 10 ♘c3.

b) 8...♖d8 9 ♘a3 cxd4 (9...a6 10 dxc5) 10 ♘b5 ♗d6 11 ♘xd6+ ♕xd6 12 ♘xd4 and the bishop-pair should give White some advantage.

c) 8...♘g4 9 ♘bd2 ♗e7 10 ♘c4 and now:

c1) 10...♗g6 was played in Godena-Rombaldoni, Italian Ch, Boscotrecase 2014. Now is a good time to grab on c5: 11 dxc5!? ♘xe3 12 fxe3 ♗xc5 13 ♕e1 0-0 14 ♖d1 ♕e4 15 ♘d4 leaves the white pieces very well placed in the centre, and capturing on d4 will improve his pawn-structure.

c2) 10...0-0 is logical. 11 h3 ♘xe3 12 ♘xe3 ♕e4 13 ♘xf5 ♕xf5 14 ♗d3 ♕f4 15 dxc5 ♗xc5 16 ♕e2 is probably equal. White has a choice between playing a middlegame (♗e4) or an endgame (♕e4).

7 cxd4 *(D)*

The daring 7 ♘xd4 was essayed in Acs-A.Mista, Bundesliga 2012/13 but it's not necessary to go for these early complications.

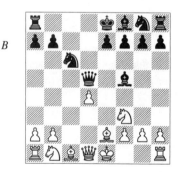

7...♗xb1

7...e6 8 ♘c3 ♕d7 was played in the game M.Zaitsev-Krejči, 2nd Bundesliga 2014/15. Now I like the natural 9 0-0 ♘f6 10 ♗e3, when White can play in standard IQP fashion with ♕b3, ♖fd1 and ♖ac1, or change the character

of the play with ♘e5, which is even possible after 10...♗d6 11 ♘e5!?:

a) 11...♘xe5?? 12 dxe5 ♗xe5? 13 ♗b5 is unfortunate for Black.

b) 11...♗xe5 12 dxe5 ♘xe5 13 ♕xd7+ ♘exd7 14 ♖fd1 a6 15 ♖ac1 and White's bishop-pair and superior development provides him with full compensation for the pawn.

c) 11...♕e7 is possible, but after 12 f4 White has cemented his knight on a powerful square. He can go on to seize additional space by g4!?, with promising chances.

8 ♖xb1 e6

8...♕xa2 has scored well in games between lower-rated players, and there is certainly an argument that having said A (7...♗xb1) Black should say B and grab the pawn. However, in addition to getting strong positional compensation after, for instance, 9 ♗d2 e6 10 0-0 ♕d5 11 ♕a4 followed by b4 and ♖fc1, White in fact has the strong novelty 9 0-0!. If Black plays a slow move like 9...♘f6 or 9...e6 White can develop his bishop more actively than to d2 (for instance, to e3), with excellent compensation. Accordingly 9...♕xb1 is the critical test, but after 10 d5 Black is in serious trouble, based on the beautiful point 10...♖d8 (after 10...0-0-0 11 ♕b3 Black's best is 11...♖xd5 12 ♕xd5, when his king is unlikely to survive; 10...♕e4 11 dxc6 bxc6 12 ♘g5 gives White a huge initiative; for instance, 12...♕b4 13 ♕c2! ♕b7 14 ♕c4 e6 15 ♗h5 g6 16 ♕c3 f6 17 ♗f3) 11 dxc6!! ♖xd1 12 cxb7 ♖xf1+ (12...♖d8 13 ♗b5+ ♖d7 14 b8♕#) 13 ♗xf1

♕xc1 14 b8♕+ ♔d7. White is technically material down here, but he can grab the bishop on f8 (in fact, he has time to take on a7 first), when Black is unlikely to complete his development without massive material loss.

9 0-0 ♗d6 10 ♕a4 ♘f6 *(D)*

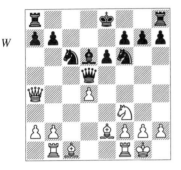

Negi is a strong theoretician and has gone for this position twice (according to my database). Accordingly, it is clear that Black can't be much worse here, but I still believe that White has chances to play for an edge.

11 ♗e3

Playing for normal development. I believe there is one very major alternative:

a) 11 ♕c4 0-0 12 ♗g5 ♘b4 13 ♗xf6 gxf6 14 a3 ♖ac8 15 ♕xd5 ♘xd5 was equal in Swathi-Negi, Indian Team Ch, Pune 2014.

b) 11 ♗c4! is my suggestion:

b1) 11...♕e4 12 ♗g5 0-0 13 ♖fe1 ♕f5 14 ♖bd1 gives White an ideal set-up while the black queen will be attacked again with ♗d3.

b2) 11...♕f5 12 ♗a6! (this is the point, trying to take advantage of the black king in the centre) 12...♕a5 (12...♕xb1 13 ♗xb7 0-0 14 ♗xa8 is better for White) 13 ♕xa5 ♘xa5 14 ♗b5+ ♘c6 with an interesting endgame. Of course, reaching an endgame is normally the dream scenario for someone playing against the IQP. Here, however, White has the bishop-pair and more active pieces after, for instance, 15 ♗d2 0-0 16 ♖bc1. Personally I think White can continue playing with no risk (thanks to his bishop-pair), although Black is extremely solid.

11...0-0 12 h3 a6 13 ♕c4 ♖ac8 14 ♖bc1

Black is certainly no worse in this position; hence my recommendation of 11 ♗c4!. I shall give the rest of the game with only light notes.

14...♕f5

14...b5 15 ♕xd5 ♘xd5 looks more solid.

15 ♕d3 ♕a5

I'm not completely sure why Black continues to avoid the exchange of queens which, as noted above, is generally in his favour. Taking on d3 would have led to a solid position.

16 a3 ♘d5 17 ♕e4 ♖ce8 18 ♗c4

Finally bringing the bishop into active play.

18...f5?

I really don't like this move, which makes the c4-bishop into a monster.

19 ♕d3 ♗b8 20 ♖fe1 ♕d8

20...♕c7 is more solid.

21 ♗xa6

Perhaps Negi simply missed this easy tactic.

21...♘xe3 22 ♕xe3 ♗a7

22...♘xd4 23 ♕xd4 ♕xd4 24 ♘xd4 bxa6 leads to the loss of Black's d-pawn.

23 ♗b5 ♕d5 24 ♗xc6 bxc6

White is a pawn up with a dominant position and converts his advantage into victory with ease.

25 ♕c3 e5 26 dxe5 ♔h8 27 ♕xc6 ♕b3 28 ♕c2 ♕b6 29 ♖ed1 ♖e6 30 ♖d7 h6 31 ♕d2 ♗b8 32 b4 f4 33 ♖d1 ♖g6 34 ♖d8 1-0

Game 22
Gochelashvili – Nechaev
Vladivostok 2014

1 e4 c5 2 ♘f3 ♘c6 3 c3 d5 4 exd5 ♕xd5 5 d4 cxd4

The immediate 5...e5 is also interesting. 6 ♘xe5 ♘xe5 7 dxe5 ♕xe5+ (7...♕xd1+ 8 ♔xd1 doesn't seem to give Black sufficient compensation) 8 ♗e2 ♗d7 was Dzhumaev-Kholmirzaev, Uzbek Ch, Tashkent 2015, and now I like the simple 9 0-0 0-0-0 10 ♘d2 ♗c6 11 ♗g4+ f5 12 ♖e1 ♕f6 13 ♗f3 with some initiative.

6 cxd4 *(D)*

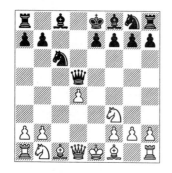

Black needs to play vigorously now, as otherwise the early exchange on d4 just allows White to develop rapidly and set up an ideal IQP position.

6...e5

6...♗g4 has its logic, but doesn't work very well tactically: 7 ♘c3 ♗xf3 (otherwise Black will be forced into full retreat) 8 ♘xd5 ♗xd1 9 ♘c7+ ♔d7 10 ♘xa8 ♗h5 11 d5 ♘d4 12 ♗f4 and since the a8-knight will not be trapped, White will gain a significant advantage.

7 ♘c3 ♗b4 *(D)*

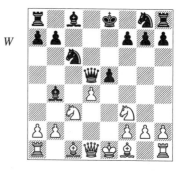

8 ♗e2!?

I was completely unaware of this move before I started preparing this book! However, it makes a great deal of sense to me. Black is blasting open the position while behind in development and with his queen about to come under attack. Accordingly, rapid development and castling has to be one of the critical continuations. It seems that many strong GMs have come to the same view.

8...exd4

Or:

a) 8...♘xd4 9 0-0 ♗xc3 10 bxc3 ♘xf3+ 11 ♗xf3 ♕xd1 12 ♖xd1 ♘f6 was Khamrakulov-Minzer, Albacete 2007. Here I like 13 ♖b1 e4 14 ♗e2 0-0 15 ♖d4, when White's bishop-pair is insurance against the extra pawn, which can be regained at any point, and I substantially prefer his position here.

b) 8...e4 looks logical but runs into the strong piece sacrifice 9 0-0! *(D)*.

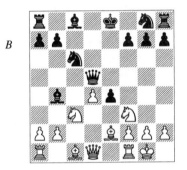

9...♗xc3 10 bxc3 ♘f6 (after accepting the offer by 10...exf3 11 ♗xf3 White's initiative is worth more than a piece; for instance, 11...♕d8 12 ♖e1+ ♘ce7 13 ♗a3 ♔f8 14 d5 and White was already winning in Kulitsov-V.Arkhipov, Suvorov 2012) 11 ♘d2 0-0 12 a4 ♗f5 13 h3 ♖fd8 14 ♘c4 ♗e6 15 ♖b1 with a pleasant 'isolated pawn couple' position in Starostits-Bernotas, Panevezys 2012.

9 0-0 ♗xc3

9...♕d8 10 ♘b5 ♘f6 has also been tested. Basically all of White's logical moves lead to an advantage here, including recapturing on d4. A recent example continued 11 a3 ♗e7 (11...♗c5

12 b4 ♗b6 13 ♗b2 doesn't change much) 12 ♘fxd4 ♘xd4 13 ♘xd4 0-0 14 ♗f3, when White had the more active pieces and an edge in Nisipeanu-O.Saez, Benasque 2013.

10 bxc3 ♘ge7 11 ♘xd4 0-0 *(D)*

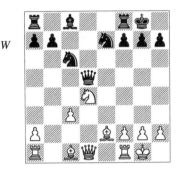

12 ♘xc6 ♕xc6

12...bxc6 seems more solid. After 13 ♗a3 ♖e8 14 ♗f3 ♕xd1 15 ♖fxd1 ± White's bishop-pair guaranteed him a very pleasant endgame in Vajda-Navrotescu, Romanian Ch, Baile Tusnad 2001.

13 ♗a3 ♖e8 14 ♖b1

14 ♗f3 might be even stronger. The position after 14...♕f6 15 ♖e1 ♗e6 16 ♗xb7 ♖ab8 17 ♕f3 was tested in two Ponomariov-Savić encounters: European Junior Ch, Siofok 1996 and World Junior Ch, Zagan 1997. I'm not sure how the (then) future FIDE World Champion scored only 25% in these games, since White is clearly better.

14...♕xc3??

This loses on the spot; after a move like 14...♕f6 White has an obvious plus.

15 ♗xe7 ♕e5

Not, of course, 15...♖xe7, which is met by 16 ♕d8+.

16 ♗b5

Maybe this is what Black missed. He gets a pawn for the exchange but no chances of survival given the open files and his development deficit.

16...♕xe7 17 ♗xe8 ♕xe8 18 ♖e1 ♗e6 19 ♖xb7 ♕c6 20 ♖xa7 ♖b8 21 ♕a4 ♕c8 22 h3 h6 23 ♕f4 ♖b2 24 a4 ♕c5 25 ♖xe6 ♕xa7 26 ♖e8+ ♔h7 27 ♕f5+ 1-0

Game 23
Ali Marandi – Van Foreest
World Under-14 Ch, Maribor 2012

1 e4 c5 2 c3 d5 3 exd5 ♕xd5 4 d4 g6 *(D)*

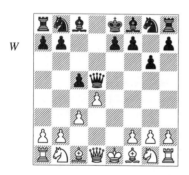

A logical and ambitious line, where Black takes on some risk in an attempt to unbalance the game. I have good memories here since I have (as far as I can recall) 2/2 here. In the first game, my win contributed to gaining my IM title (in the Calvia Olympiad in 2004), in the second, a win against the strong

GM Ivan Ivanišević in Tromsø 2010 helped me gain my second GM norm.

5 ♘f3 ♗g7 6 ♘a3 cxd4

6...♗d7? is the worst plausible move in the position, weakening b7 while getting nothing in return. 7 ♗c4 ± ♕d6 (7...♕e4+ 8 ♗e3 and ♗xf7+ is a threat) 8 ♕b3 e6 9 ♕xb7 ♕c6 10 ♕xc6 ♗xc6 11 dxc5 ♘d7 12 ♗e3 ♖b8 13 0-0-0 ♘e7 14 ♖he1 ♘d5 15 ♗xd5 ♗xd5 16 ♖xd5 exd5 17 ♗f4+ ♔d8 18 ♗xb8 ♘xb8 19 ♘b5 ♘c6 20 ♖d1 and Black resigned in Collins-Figueroa, Calvia Olympiad 2004.

7 ♗c4 ♕e4+ 8 ♗e3

A cute trick.

8...♘h6

8...dxe3 is not to be recommended: 9 ♗xf7+ ♔xf7 (9...♔f8 10 ♕d8+ doesn't change much) 10 ♘g5+ and the queen is lost.

9 ♘b5 0-0 10 cxd4 *(D)*

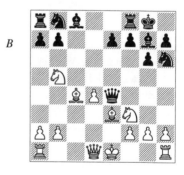

10...♘c6

Other moves:

a) After 10...♘f5, 11 ♘c7 is unclear so I suggest the more straightforward 11 ♕e2 a6 12 ♘c3 ♕c6 13 0-0 with active play in return for the IQP.

b) 10...♘a6 11 0-0 ♗g4 was played in D.Howell-Simonian, Warsaw rapid 2011 and now I like 12 ♘c3 ♗xf3 13 ♘xe4 ♗xd1 14 ♖axd1 ± with a pleasant endgame.

11 ♘c3 ♕f5 12 h3 ♕h5 13 d5 ♘e5 14 ♘xe5 ♕xe5 15 0-0 ♘f5 16 ♖e1

This position has been played several times with White by Turkish IM Cemil Can Ali Marandi, with impressive results, including against grandmasters.

The structure strongly resembles a Grünfeld Defence, and is defined by the white pawn on d5. This pawn cramps Black and enables White to exert pressure on the e7-pawn. Black aims to release the pressure through exchanges (as he has less space), or to set up a strong blockade (the knight would be perfectly placed on d6) followed by gaining counterplay on the flanks. Generally speaking, the play is very difficult and complex, which makes this line an excellent choice for players seeking winning chances with Black. Exchanging off the potentially strong e3-bishop is logical:

16...♘xe3

Black can keep the tension with 16...♕c7 17 ♗b3 (Ali Marandi recently changed his treatment of this line: after 17 ♕b3 ♗d7 18 ♖ad1 b5 19 ♗f1?! {19 ♘xb5 is more critical} 19...♖ab8 20 ♘e4 ♘xe3 21 ♖xe3 a5 Black had good queenside counterplay in Ali Marandi-Fier, Skopje 2014; I prefer the bishop retreat) and now:

a) 17...♗d7 18 ♗g5 ♖ae8 19 ♕d2 ♕b6 20 ♖ad1 h6 21 ♗f4 e5 22 dxe6 ♗xe6 23 ♘d5 ♕d4 24 ♕a5 b6 25 ♕xa7 ♗xd5 26 ♖xe8 ♕xd1+ 27 ♗xd1 ♖xe8 28 ♗b3 and White was winning in Pavasović-Bromberger, Austrian Team Ch 2010/11.

b) 17...♘xe3 18 ♖xe3 ♗f6 19 ♕f3 ♗g5 20 ♖e2 ♗f5 21 ♖ae1 ♖ad8 22 g4! (White plays in thematic fashion, gaining control of the e4-square, which is especially promising in light of the bishop on g5; Black is too passive to exploit the weakening of the white kingside) 22...♗c8 23 ♘e4 ♗h4 24 ♕e3 ♔g7 25 d6! ♕a5 (after 25...exd6 26 ♕d4+ f6 27 g5 White breaks through) 26 g5 e5 27 ♘c5 b6 28 ♕xe5+ f6 29 ♕e7+ and White won a good game in Ali Marandi-Dastan, Iasi (Under-15) 2012.

17 ♖xe3 ♕d6

Now White can simply build up on the e-file.

18 ♕e2 a6 *(D)*

Otherwise Black must constantly look out for ♘b5 tricks.

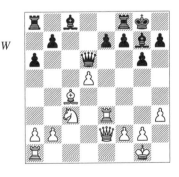

19 ♖e1

Taking the pawn by 19 ♖xe7 b5 20 ♗b3 b4 21 ♘d1 a5 gave Black more

than sufficient compensation in In't
Veld-Kevlishvili, Amsterdam 2013.

19...b5 20 ♗b3 b4?!

20...♗d7! 21 ♖xe7 (this isn't forced,
but there is nothing better for White)
21...b4 22 ♘d1 ♖ac8 gives Black full
positional compensation.

21 ♘e4 ♕c7?

21...♕d8 ± is more solid.

22 d6!!

An excellent move!

22...exd6

22...♕a7 23 ♖c1! exd6 24 ♘g5 ♗h6
25 ♖e7 forces Black to give up his
queen for insufficient compensation.

23 ♘g5 ♗e5

23...♗f6 24 ♘xf7! isn't much more
pleasant for Black: 24...♖xf7 loses to
25 ♕f3!.

**24 ♖f3 ♗f5 25 ♖xf5 gxf5 26 ♕h5
♔g7 27 ♗xf7 ♕a7 28 ♕xh7+ ♔f6 29
♕g6+ ♔e7 30 ♖xe5+ dxe5 31 ♕e6+
♔d8 32 ♕d6+ ♔c8 33 ♗e6+ ♔b7 34
♗d5+ 1-0**

It should be noted that the black
player in this game is now an extremely strong Dutch IM rated over
2500, so to win in such a fashion is impressive.

Other Second Moves for Black

In this section we take a look at 2...d6
(Game 24), 2...g6 (Game 25) and 2...e5
(Game 26). In Game 26 we also look at
miscellaneous other 2nd moves, including some that are quite respectable
but tend to transpose elsewhere.

Game 24
D. Howell – Gormally
Douglas 2014

1 e4 c5 2 c3 d6

This line is surprisingly popular,
not just in Internet blitz (where Najdorf and Dragon players 'pre-move'
2...d6) but in over-the-board play. The
game takes on Pirc/Modern character-
istics. White gets a perfect centre for
not much compensation, so this line
should be welcomed by c3 Sicilian
players.

Danny Gormally has played this
line several times, including escaping
from a worse position against me. David Howell (who has recently joined
the 2700-club) isn't so generous!

3 d4 ♘f6 4 ♗d3 *(D)*

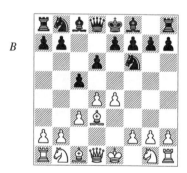

4...cxd4

Or:

a) 4...g6 gives White extra options
based on dxc5 (I myself obtained a
very nice position against Gormally in
this line, although I messed up and
drew), but the simplest approach is to
continue with 5 ♘f3 ♗g7 6 0-0 0-0 7

h3 when Black has nothing better than transposing to the game by taking on d4.

b) 4...♘c6 is playable, but falls short of equalizing in view of tactical points like 5 ♘f3 ♗g4 (5...e5 6 dxe5 is structurally pleasant for White) 6 d5!, when 6...♘e5? is bad due to 7 ♘xe5!, while after 6...♗xf3 7 ♕xf3 ♘e5, the disruptive check 8 ♗b5+ takes the wind out of Black's sails.

5 cxd4 g6 6 ♘f3 ♗g7 7 0-0 0-0 8 h3

Preventing ...♗g4. White has a perfect centre and it is up to Black to generate counterplay.

8...♘c6 9 ♘c3 e5 10 dxe5 dxe5 11 ♗c4

I like this active development of the bishop, although 11 ♗e3 is the most popular move.

11...h6

Or:

a) 11...a6, as in Zufić-Grbac, Poreč 2010, is best met by the simple 12 ♗e3 ±, when Black still needs to find a way to complete development (bearing in mind that ...b5 will weaken important squares on the queenside).

b) 11...♕c7 is well met by 12 ♗g5, and now:

b1) 12...♘d4 13 ♗xf6 ♗xf6 14 ♘d5 ♕d6 (14...♕d8 is more tenacious) 15 ♘xd4 exd4 16 f4! and White's kingside majority was menacing in Vysochin-Daulyte, Warsaw rapid 2008.

b2) 12...h6 13 ♗xf6 ♗xf6 14 ♘d5 ♕d8 15 ♕e2 ♗g7 16 ♖fd1 was more comfortable for White in Khairullin-Mamedov, Kirishi 2005.

c) The position after 11...♗e6 12 ♗xe6 fxe6 has been tried with both colours by Polish GM Krzysztof Jakubowski; he lost an instructive game to Howell. 13 ♗e3 ♕e7 (13...♘h5 14 ♕xd8 ♖axd8, as in Jakubowski-Czerwonski, Warsaw rapid 2006 is best met by 15 ♗c5! {so that the bishop won't be shut out by ...♘d4} 15...♖f7 16 ♘g5 ♖f6 17 ♖fd1 ± with a solid advantage) 14 ♕b3 ♘h5 15 ♖fd1 h6 16 ♖d3 (16 ♘b5! is even stronger) 16...♖ad8 (Black should have tried 16...♘f4 with good equalizing chances after 17 ♗xf4 ♖xf4 18 ♖ad1) was D.Howell-Jakubowski, Winterthur 2008 and now 17 ♖xd8 ♖xd8 18 ♖d1 would have left White with a very pleasant advantage.

12 ♗e3 *(D)*

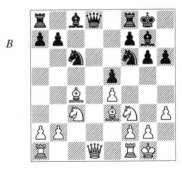

12...♕xd1

A very risky decision. It might look like Black is simplifying into a position with no weaknesses and a likely draw, but in fact he is increasing White's development advantage (since a rook now comes to d1 without loss of time). In addition, the black queen covered important squares like c7 and d6 – once it is exchanged, these squares are tempting targets for White's pieces (especially the c3-knight).

Other moves:

a) 12...♗d7 13 ♕d2 g5 14 ♖fd1 ♕c8 15 ♖ac1 ± Potkin-Ushenina, Abu Dhabi 2006.

b) Just how quickly things can go wrong for Black is illustrated by the game Rasulov-Umudova, Baku 2011, where White was already winning after 12...b6 13 ♕c1 ♔h7 14 ♖d1 ♕e7? 15 ♘d5 ♘xd5 16 ♗xd5 +−.

c) 12...♕e7 seems the most tenacious to me. After 13 ♕e2 b6 14 ♖ac1 ♗b7 15 ♖fd1 White had a pleasant edge in Wang Yiye-J.Vakhidov, Sharjah 2014 with the more active pieces in a symmetrical structure, but his advantage is certainly within manageable limits.

13 ♖fxd1

This position already looks really unpleasant for Black, who has serious queenside weaknesses and struggles to complete his development.

13...a6

To cover the b5-square.

14 a4

Gaining space on the queenside. Other moves:

a) 14 ♗b6 was played in Pavasović-Spoljar, Bizovac 2007, but this seems less logical to me since the bishop was already well placed on e3 and ...b5 isn't really a threat.

b) There is nothing wrong with the straightforward 14 ♖ac1. Black should probably acquiesce to an inferior position after 14...♗e6. Note that 14...b5?

15 ♗b3 just weakens more squares on the queenside and destabilizes the c6-knight.

We now return to 14 a4 *(D)*:

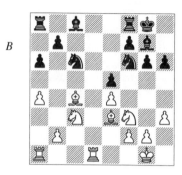

14...♖e8

14...♗e6 15 ♗xe6 fxe6 looks like a better attempt, as played in Ruchieva-Zozulia, Lvov 1999. Here I prefer White after 16 a5 ♖fd8 17 ♘d2, bringing the knight to the excellent c4-square.

15 ♖ac1 ♘a5

This just loses time, but it's hard to suggest good moves for Black here. 15...♗e6 16 ♗xe6 ♖xe6 (16...fxe6 is an inferior version of the note to Black's 14th move, since ♖ac1 is more useful than ...♖e8) 17 ♘d5 gives White strong pressure. The game might continue 17...♖d8 (17...♖b8 18 ♘xf6+ ♗xf6 19 ♖d7 is promising for White) 18 ♗b6 ♖c8 19 ♘xf6+ ♗xf6 20 ♖d7 with an excellent position.

16 ♗a2 ♗d7

16...♗e6 17 ♗xe6 ♖xe6 18 ♘d5 ♘xd5 19 ♖xd5 is probably the lesser evil.

17 ♖d6!

Taking control of important squares and preparing to double on the d-file.

17...♖ac8 18 ♘d5!

Howell conducts this phase of the game with enviable precision.

18...♘xd5

This loses. 18...♖xc1+ 19 ♗xc1 ♗e6 was the best attempt, but after 20 ♘xf6+ ♗xf6 21 ♗xe6 fxe6 22 ♗xh6 ± Black is a pawn down with a poor position.

19 ♖xd7! ♘xe3 20 ♗xf7+ ♔h7 21 ♖xc8 ♖xc8 22 fxe3 +–

White wins not because of his extra pawn (which is less than impressive on e3), but because of a direct attack on the black king.

22...g5 23 ♗e6!

Threatening 24 ♖xg7+, winning a piece.

23...♖c1+ 24 ♔h2 ♔g6 25 h4 gxh4 1-0

Black resigned rather than waiting for 26 ♘xh4+ ♔f6 (26...♔g5 27 ♖xg7+ ♔xh4 28 g3+ ♔h5 29 ♗g4# is a cute mate) 27 ♗d5 ♗h8 28 ♖d6+ ♔e7 29 ♘f5+ ♔e8 30 ♖xh6, making decisive material gains.

Game 25
Istratescu – Serafimov
Vaujany 2012

1 e4 c5 2 c3 g6

An ambitious continuation which is sometimes favoured by those who want to play for the win. However, White gains a stable advantage in the centre so I'm always happy to see this line played against me.

3 d4 cxd4 4 cxd4 d5

This is one of Black's ideas – rather than let White have an uncontested perfect centre, he claims a small share of central space.

5 e5

Gaining space. Black will aim to free his g7-bishop with ...f6 but, as we shall see, this gives White new opportunities.

The sharper 5 ♘c3 isn't completely convincing.

5...♘c6 6 ♘c3 *(D)*

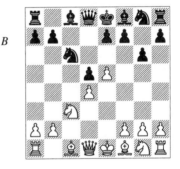

B

6...♗g7

Or:

a) 6...♘h6 7 ♗f4 ♗g7 8 ♕d2 ♘f5 9 ♘f3 e6 10 ♗b5 was comfortable for White in Laznička-Dubov, European Ch, Legnica 2013.

b) 6...a6 7 h3 h5 8 ♘f3 ♘h6 9 ♗d3 ♘f5 10 ♗e3 e6 11 ♗xf5!? gxf5 12 ♗g5 ♗e7 13 ♗xe7 ♕xe7 ± gave White a permanent advantage based on his extra space and the horrendous bishop on c8 in Tiviakov-Iliushin, Bornholm 2008.

c) 6...f6 7 exf6 (7 ♘f3 ♗g4 8 exf6 ♘xf6 9 ♗e2 ♗xf3 10 ♗xf3 was also slightly better for White in Pavaso-vić-Sax, Croatian Team Ch, Šibenik 2006) 7...exf6 (Black should probably play the more dynamic 7...♘xf6; for instance, 8 ♘f3 ♗g7 9 ♗e2 0-0 10 0-0 ♘e4 with balanced play in Mirallès-Bouchet, French Team Ch 2007) and now David Howell put on a model display of how to handle this structure: 8 g3 ♘ge7 9 ♗g2 ♗g7 10 ♘ge2 ♗e6 11 ♘f4 ♗f7 12 0-0 0-0 13 ♖e1 ♕d7 (D.Howell-Wantola, Leiden 2013) 14 ♗e3 followed by ♕a4 and ♖ad1 gives White a very pleasant advantage.

7 ♗b5

A straightforward continuation, preparing to compromise Black's structure and reduce the pressure on the centre by taking on c6.

The main alternative is the far more ambitious 7 h3 f6 8 f4 ♘h6 9 g4, but if this goes wrong for White it will go very badly wrong. Black can often aim to sacrifice material to destroy the white centre.

7...♘h6

Alternatively:

a) 7...f6 8 exf6 exf6 9 ♘ge2 ♗e6 10 ♘f4 ♗f7 11 0-0 ♘e7 12 ♗xc6+ bxc6 13 ♘a4 0-0 14 ♘c5 ♕c8 15 ♖e1 ♖e8 was pleasant for White in Pava-sović-Zelčić, Solin rapid 2002.

b) 7...♗d7 8 ♘f3 a6 was played in Bellini-Dragojlović, Padua 2011 and now I like 9 ♗e2, when the vulnerable d-pawn forces Black to lose more time.

8 h3

GM Misa Pap has used 8 ♘ge2 on several occasions with success, but I prefer developing the knight on f3,

where it has greater control of the centre. Of course 8 h3 is necessary first, to prevent Black from making a favourable exchange with ...♗g4.

8...0-0 9 ♘f3 *(D)*

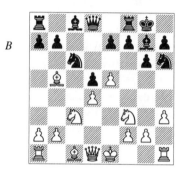

Black has tried a variety of moves here, but it seems difficult for him to generate meaningful counterplay.

9...♕b6

Or:

a) 9...♗f5 10 0-0 ♕b6 11 ♗e3 ♗e4 12 ♗xc6 (12 ♗d3!? looks like a promising alternative) 12...♗xf3 (12...bxc6 13 ♘xe4 dxe4 14 ♘d2 ♕xb2 15 ♘xe4 appears slightly better for White) 13 ♕d2 bxc6 14 ♗xh6 ♗xh6 15 ♕xh6 ♕xb2 16 ♕e3 ♗e4 17 ♖fc1 (Yudasin-Kacheishvili, Philadelphia 2009) and now 17...f5!? should equalize.

b) 9...♘a5 10 0-0 a6 11 ♗d3 f6 (after 11...♗f5 12 ♖e1 ♗xd3 13 ♕xd3 Black's pieces remained passive in Ni Hua-Ryjanova, Sydney 2015) was Lu Shanglei-Askarov, Albena 2015 and now I like 12 exf6 ♖xf6 13 ♗g5 ± with active play for White.

c) 9...♘f5 10 g4 ♘h6 has been tried by Guseinov, but it is hard to believe that the slight weakening of White's kingside is worth two tempi. After something like 11 0-0 f5 12 exf6 ♖xf6 13 ♗g5 White is to be preferred.

d) 9...f6 is one of the most logical moves in the position, immediately striking at the white centre. 10 0-0 fxe5 (10...♘f7 11 exf6 ♗xf6 12 ♖e1 was nice for White in A.David-Balokas, Anogia 2015) 11 dxe5 e6 12 ♖e1 ♘f5 13 ♗g5 ♕c7 14 ♖c1 ♕f7 15 ♗xc6 bxc6 16 ♘a4 (White has a bind on the dark squares) 16...h6 17 ♗f6!? ♗xf6 18 exf6 ♕xf6 19 ♖xc6 ♘h4 (Collins-Starostits, San Sebastian 2011) and now 20 ♖c3 retains a pleasant advantage.

10 0-0 ♗e6 11 ♖e1 ♖fe8 12 ♗f1 ♕d8 ±

Clearly Black's plan has been ineffective.

13 ♗f4 f6 14 ♘b5 fxe5 15 ♘xe5 ♘xe5 16 dxe5 a6 17 ♘d4 ♕d7 18 g4 +−

The knight on h6 is a miserable piece.

18...♖ac8 19 ♗g2 ♖ed8 20 ♕b3 ♖c4 21 ♖ad1 ♖xd4 22 ♖xd4 ♘f7 23 ♖ed1 1-0

Game 26
Nisipeanu – D. Bogdan
Romanian Ch, Curtea de Arges 2002

1 e4 c5 2 c3 *(D)*
2...e5

This continuation steers the game into a type of position more normally associated with the Ruy Lopez or the Italian Game. Black typically gets a

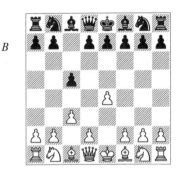

sound position, but a slightly passive one, and more importantly one which Sicilian players are not used to.

Here we shall review Black's remaining options on move 2:

a) 2...e6 is one of the most important sidelines, when after 3 d4 d5 White normally chooses between transposing to an Advance French with 4 e5, or 4 exd5 which transposes to our repertoire after 4...♕xd5 (see Game 19) or, after 4...exd5, leads to interesting positions where Black often defends an IQP after dxc5. However, within the context of our repertoire it makes most sense to play 4 ♘d2, when we have directly transposed into our line against the French.

b) 2...♘c6 is also a common sideline, but has little independent value, since after 3 d4, Black has nothing better than 3...cxd4 4 cxd4 d5 5 exd5 ♕xd5 6 ♘f3, transposing to lines we covered in Game 22.

c) 2...b6 has been played occasionally by strong players. Black doesn't offer a challenge in the centre, so White shouldn't be unhappy to see this; for instance, 3 d4 ♗b7 4 ♗d3 ♘f6 (4...cxd4

5 cxd4 ♘c6 aims to harass the bishop with ...♘b4, but after 6 d5 ♘b4 7 ♗e2 and a3 it is unclear what Black has achieved) 5 ♘d2 cxd4 6 cxd4 g6 7 ♘gf3 ♗g7 8 0-0 0-0 9 ♖e1 with a perfect centre and a nice game in J.Skoberne-Milenković, Nova Gorica 2011.

d) 2...♕a5 has been tried by Movsesian, amongst others. Black's idea is seen after 3 d4 cxd4, when 4 cxd4 is impossible because the pawn is pinned. I think the simplest is to develop the kingside before pushing d4; for instance, 3 ♘f3 e6 4 ♗c4 b5 5 ♗b3 ♗b7 6 ♗c2 a6 7 0-0 c4 8 d4 cxd3 9 ♕xd3 with an excellent game for White in Sveshnikov-Cvetković, European Seniors Ch, Plovdiv 2013.

3 ♘f3 ♘c6 4 ♗c4 ♕c7

Other moves:

a) 4...♗e7 is passive and well met by the immediate 5 d4 cxd4 6 cxd4 exd4 7 0-0 ♘f6. Here an interesting continuation in the style of our line in the Two Knights runs 8 e5 ♘e4 9 ♗d5 ♘c5 10 ♘xd4. If White consolidates he will be better with his extra space in the centre, so 10...♘xe5 is critical, but then 11 b4 ♘e6 12 ♘f5 looks dangerous for Black: 12...♗f6? (12...♗xb4?! 13 ♗b2 f6 14 ♘c3 0-0 15 ♘e4 gives White excellent compensation for the two pawns; 12...0-0 is more robust) 13 ♘d6+ ♔f8 14 ♘c3 with overwhelming compensation in M.Pap-M.Hess, Bad Wörishofen 2015.

b) 4...♘f6 allows White to execute his threat with 5 ♘g5. This is nothing fatal but I like White after 5...d5 6 exd5 ♘xd5 7 ♕h5 g6 8 ♕f3 ♕xg5 9 ♗xd5

♘d8 10 0-0 with an edge in Sevillano-Yankovsky, Monterey Park 2013.

5 0-0

5 ♘g5 ♘d8 6 f4 is the most popular, but this is not entirely clear and seems to be a lot of theory to learn for a minor sideline.

5...♘f6 6 d3

White sets up his pieces as in the Italian Game or the Ruy Lopez with d3. I think he has good chances for an edge here, in particular since Black has committed to ...♕c7 quite early and there is a tempting central outpost on d5.

6...♗e7 7 ♘bd2 0-0 8 ♖e1 d6 9 ♘f1 (D)

This position can be played with natural moves by White. There are basically two plans: a standard Ruy Lopez regrouping with h3 and ♘g3, aiming for play on the kingside; or play for the d5-square, with ♗g5 (and possibly ♗xf6) and ♘e3. The latter plan might be more promising here.

9...♖b8

Black has several reasonable moves, but none which stop White's plan:

a) 9...♗e6 10 ♗g5 ♖ad8 11 ♗xf6 ♗xf6 12 ♘e3 and White's control over d5 gave her the more pleasant game in Gaponenko-M.Muzychuk, Ukrainian Women's Ch, Odessa 2006.

b) 9...h6 prevents ♗g5 but weakens the kingside. 10 ♘e3 ♖e8 (10...♗e6 looks sounder, when 11 h3 ♖ad8 12 ♗d5 gives White chances of a small edge) was Spence-Karayiannis, Southend 2000 and now I like 11 ♘h4! followed by ♕f3 and ♘hf5 with strong kingside pressure (including the possibility of sacrificing on h6 at the right moment).

10 a4 a6 11 ♗g5 b5

Typical counterplay, gaining space on the queenside.

12 axb5 axb5 13 ♗a2 h6 14 ♗h4

14 ♗xf6 ♗xf6 15 ♘e3 ± is also logical, aiming for the d5 outpost.

14...♘h5 15 ♘e3 ♘f4

15...♗xh4 16 ♘xh4 ♘f6 is sounder, but I think White is more comfortable after 17 ♘hf5.

16 ♗g3! ♗e6?

This looks logical but fails for tactical reasons.

17 ♘d5! ♗xd5

Tolerating the knight was hardly better.

18 exd5 ♘a5

18...♘d8 is strongly met by 19 d4 ±.

19 b4! *(D)*

Black's queen's knight is often a problem piece in the Ruy Lopez, and

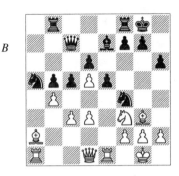

B

so it proves here. The knight is on a bad 'circuit' (a5, b7 and d8) and can't become active.

19...♘b7 20 d4! +−

White has executed his standard breaks in an ideal form, and Black has no defence.

20...cxd4 21 cxd4 ♘h5

This fails to a beautiful tactical shot, but there was nothing better.

22 ♘xe5! ♘xg3

22...dxe5 23 ♕xh5 is hopeless for Black.

23 ♘c6 ♘f5 24 ♗b1! ♗f6 25 ♗xf5

White is a pawn up with a dominant position. Rather than give drawing chances, the opposite-coloured bishops help White to build an attack. The strong Romanian GM went on to win smoothly.

25...♖be8 26 ♕d3 ♕b6 27 g3 ♖xe1+ 28 ♖xe1 ♘d8 29 ♖c1 g6 30 ♗d7 ♔g7 31 h4 h5 32 ♔g2 ♘b7 33 ♖a1 ♕c7 34 ♗h3 ♕b6 35 ♕d2 ♘d8 36 ♗d7 ♕b7 37 ♖a7 ♕b6 38 ♕a2 ♗xd4 39 ♘xd4 ♕xd4 40 ♕a1 1-0

4 Caro-Kann

1 e4 c6 2 c4

The Caro-Kann is a perennially popular opening for Black at all levels, and club players in particular have benefited from good recent repertoire books by Schandorff and Houska.

White has a couple of good options against the Caro-Kann that aim to steer play towards our preferred IQP positions. The most established of these is the Panov-Botvinnik Attack, 1 e4 c6 2 d4 d5 3 exd5 cxd5 4 c4 ♘f6 5 ♘c3. I have played this line regularly with decent results. However, I have decided not to recommend it for our repertoire, partly because of the range of positions to which it leads – while 5...e6 normally leads to standard IQP play, the other main defences, 5...♘c6 and 5...g6, tend to lead to different structures. In addition, 5...♘c6 has been very well studied and seems to lead to convincing equality for Black in all variations.

My proposed line is 1 e4 c6 2 c4 *(D)*.

Against Black's main reply, 2...d5 3 cxd5 cxd5 4 exd5 ♘f6, White can try to make Black's life awkward by interfering with the recapture on d5 through 5 ♕a4+ or 5 ♗b5+. These are reasonable options that worth exploring, but my recommendation is the simple 5 ♘c3

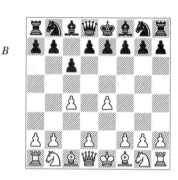

♘xd5 6 ♘f3, when White aims for standard IQP play.

Game 27
Zviagintsev – Yu Ruiyuan
Chinese Team Ch 2014

1 e4 c6 2 c4 d5

For 2...e5, which leads to completely different structures, see Game 29.

3 exd5

3 cxd5 may be a slightly more accurate move-order, for reasons which will be described in the next note.

3...♘f6

3 exd5 gives Black this additional option. Now taking on c6 would give Black a substantial lead in development, so White normally either transposes to the Panov-Botvinnik with 4 d4 or to our proposed repertoire with

4 ♘c3. Note, however, that in this move-order White loses the options of 5 ♕a4+ and 5 ♗b5+ (briefly discussed in the chapter introduction).

4 ♘c3 cxd5 5 cxd5 ♘xd5

5...g6 is examined in the notes to Game 28.

6 ♘f3 ♘c6 (D)

6...e6 leads to similar play, as discussed in Zviagintsev-Vasquez (Game 2) in the IQP introduction.

Lines with ...g6, namely 6...g6 and 6...♘xc3 7 bxc3 g6, are the subject of Game 28.

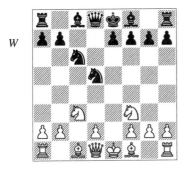

The text-move (6...♘c6) is Black's most common response. Now 7 d4 would transpose to the Panov-Botvinnik (when 7...♗g4 has been quite convincing for Black), but White has a good independent option.

7 ♗b5 e6

The point of White's move-order is that Black is now effectively forced to lock his light-squared bishop inside the pawn-chain: 7...♗g4? simply doesn't work after 8 ♕a4, when the pressure on c6 forces a concession. So we get to normal IQP positions.

8 0-0

By castling before advancing d4, White avoids annoying ...♗b4 options.

8...♗e7

Since the b5-bishop will normally drop back to d3 (after d4 has been played), Black can try to force the issue with 8...♘c7. Now 9 ♗d3 is obviously impossible, and other squares for the bishop are not as tempting. However, White can aim to exploit Black's loss of time and lag in development with 9 ♗xc6+ bxc6 10 ♕a4 ♗d7 11 ♘e5 ♗d6 12 d4. For example, in Hou Yifan-Gunina, Beijing blitz 2014, White was a pawn up after 12...0-0 13 ♘e4 ♗e7 14 ♗e3 ♘d5 15 ♖ac1 ♗e8 16 ♘xc6 ♕b6 17 ♘xe7+ ♘xe7 18 ♕a3 and went on to win.

9 d4 0-0 10 ♖e1 (D)

10...a6

Like in the previous note, Black wastes time encouraging White to exchange on c6. I don't see much wrong with dropping the bishop back to d3 but he can certainly capture on c6 under favourable circumstances, and the game gives us a chance to learn how to handle this structure since Zviagintsev plays brilliantly.

10...♗d7 can be met by 11 ♗d3. White has lost a tempo by spending two moves to get his bishop to d3, but Black is committed to a rather passive development with the bishop on d7 instead of b7. A different approach was used in Rapport-Laznička, Novy Bor (4) 2014: 11 ♗c4 ♗f6 12 ♘xd5 exd5 13 ♗xd5 ♗g4 14 ♗xc6 bxc6 15 ♗e3 ♖b8 16 b3 c5 17 ♗f4 ♖b4 18 ♗e5 and White had an edge.

11 ♗xc6 ♘xc3!?

I suppose this intermezzo was the point of Black's play. 11...bxc6 12 ♘e4 looks even worse for Black, since the knights have wonderful squares on c5 and e5 and the c6-pawn will be subject to attack on the half-open c-file.

12 bxc3 bxc6 13 ♘e5 (D)

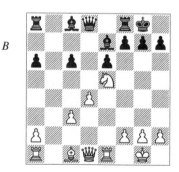

B

This position has been tested in a few games between strong players. I think White has quite a comfortable advantage, with a preferable structure, more space and more active pieces. Black has the bishop-pair but the light-squared bishop is extremely passive. It

should be noted that if White could exchange dark-squared bishops, his advantage would become much clearer.

13...♗d6

13...♗b7 both defends the c6-pawn and aims to make use of the light-squared bishop on the long diagonal. However, the bishop remains passive as long as the ...c5 break can be restrained. After 14 ♖b1 ♖a7 15 ♕g4 c5 (the most principled move, but Black is insufficiently developed to justify this) 16 ♗h6 ♗f6 17 dxc5 Black has to lose time regaining her pawn on c5. For example, after 17...♕d5 (17...♗a8 ± is more resilient) 18 ♗f4 ♗xe5 19 ♗xe5 f6 20 c4! White was already winning in Gustafsson-Zhukova, Dresden 2003.

We now return to 13...♗d6 (D):

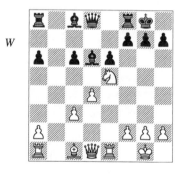

W

14 ♕h5

White can start with the positional 14 ♘c4 ♗c7 (14...♖b8 15 ♘xd6 ♕xd6 16 a4, threatening 17 ♗a3, looks preferable for White) 15 ♗a3 ♖e8 before playing 16 ♕h5, and perhaps this is a better option. 16...♖b8 (16...f6? allows 17 ♗d6!, exchanging dark-squared bishops with a big advantage in Schoorl-E.Hansen, Groningen 2012) 17 ♘e5 ♗xe5 18 ♕xe5 ♖b5 was Belikov-A.Sergeev, Alushta 2006 and now I like the simple 19 ♕e2, retaining White's pluses. His pieces are more active and his bishop seems more threatening in the long run.

Note that 14 ♘xc6? ♕c7 15 ♘e5 f6 ∓ is excellent for Black.

14...f6 15 ♘c4 ♗c7

15...♖b8 followed by 16...♖b5 is more active. The opposite-coloured bishop position resulting from an exchange on d6 looks quite unclear.

16 ♗a3 ♖f7 17 ♖ab1 *(D)*

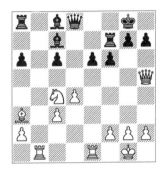

Now White has a similar pleasant edge to that achieved in the games referenced in the note to his 14th move.

17...♕d5

Black can make a bid for activity with 17...e5, but after 18 dxe5 fxe5 19 ♕e2! and 20 ♖bd1 White retains control and the black structure is quite weak.

18 ♕e2!

Of course White has no interest in either exchanging queens or improving Black's structure. The black king has few defenders since Black's queenside pieces are asleep.

18...a5 19 ♘b6 ♗xb6 20 ♖xb6 ±

White has a very favourable opposite-coloured bishop position, since Black struggles to develop his a8-rook or his c8-bishop. Zviagintsev has a large advantage and converts it into victory with energy and precision.

20...♖b7 21 ♖xb7 ♗xb7 22 ♕xe6+ ♕xe6 23 ♖xe6 ♖c8 24 ♖e7 ♗a6 25 ♗d6 ♗c4 26 a3 ♖d8 27 ♗f4 ♖d5 28 h4 ♖b5 29 ♖a7 ♗b3 30 ♗c7 a4 31 ♗d6 ♖d5 32 ♗e7 h5 33 ♖c7 ♔f7 34 ♗b4+ ♔g6 35 ♖xc6 ♖d8 36 f3 ♔f5 37 ♔f2 ♗c2 38 ♖c7 1-0

Game 28
Zviagintsev – Yakovenko
Khanty-Mansiisk rapid 2013

In this game we consider Black's options associated with ...g6.

1 e4 c6 2 c4 d5 3 exd5 cxd5 4 cxd5 ♘f6 5 ♘c3 ♘xd5

If Black wishes to fianchetto his king's bishop, he might consider doing so here with 5...g6. Now I like 6 ♗c4 ♘bd7 7 d3 ♗g7 8 ♘f3 0-0 9 0-0 ♘b6 10 ♕b3, as in Yakovenko-Siugirov, Russian Ch, Moscow 2009. Similar positions can arise from the Panov-Botvinnik Attack, but here White's set-up is more harmonious since his bishop can develop to c4 and be supported by d3. Clearly, if Black ever takes on c4, White will play dxc4, securing his extra d5-pawn.

6 ♘f3 ♘xc3

6...g6 is less common but has been tried by some strong GMs, including Kamsky. Here I like the computer-approved 7 ♕b3 ♘b6 8 ♗b5+ ♗d7 9 ♗xd7+!? (9 ♘e5 e6 10 ♘e4 ♗e7 leads to unclear play), with a pleasant position after 9...♘8xd7 (9...♕xd7 10 a4! aims to harass the b6-knight) 10 d4 ♗g7 11 0-0 0-0 12 ♖e1.

7 bxc3 g6 8 d4 *(D)*

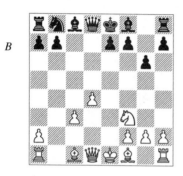

8...♗g7 9 ♗d3 0-0 10 0-0 ♘c6 11 ♖e1 ♗g4 12 h3

Immediately grabbing the bishop-pair. 12 ♗e4 keeps more tension, but 12...e5!? was a striking and logical novelty introduced by Carlsen to make an easy draw with Aronian: 13 dxe5 (13 d5 is White's critical try and led to success in Šolak-Prohaszka, Sarajevo 2011 but Black's play can be improved) 13...♕xd1 14 ♖xd1 ♗xe5 15 ♖b1 ♗xc3 16 ♖xb7 ♖ad8 17 ♖f1 ♘d4 18 ♗g5 ♖d7 19 ♖xd7 ½-½ Aronian-Carlsen, FIDE Knockout, Tripoli 2004.

12...♗xf3 13 ♕xf3 ♕a5

The most popular and active continuation. Otherwise:

a) 13...♕d7 14 ♗f4 ♖ac8 15 ♖ab1 e6 16 ♗e4 ♖fd8 17 h4 gave White the initiative on both sides of the board in Tarlev-Cioara, Romanian Team Ch, Mamaia 2012.

b) 13...e6 14 ♗a3 ♖e8 15 ♖ab1 ♕c7 (Neverov-V.Sergeev, Pardubice 2001) and now I like 16 h4, immediately starting play on the kingside.

14 ♗b2 *(D)*

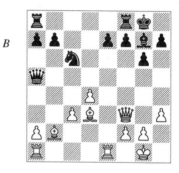

14...e6

Or:

a) After 14...♖ac8 15 ♗e4 e6 16 a4 ♖fd8, as in Gashimov-Wang Yue, Cappelle la Grande 2007, White retains an edge with 17 ♖ed1.

b) 14...♖ad8 was played in the game Nijboer-Korchnoi, Dutch Team Ch 1994/5. Black is aiming for ...e5. White's best response seems to be 15 a4 e5 16 ♗a3 ♖fe8 (16...♕xc3 17 ♗xf8 ♔xf8 doesn't look like full compensation for the exchange) 17 ♗c4 ±, when the opening of the position seems to favour the bishops.

c) 14...e5! was played against me by the strong GM Macieja. After 15 d5 ♘e7 16 d6 ♘c8 17 ♕xb7 ♘xd6

(Collins-Macieja, Freemont 2012) I should have settled for 18 ♕a6 ♕xa6 19 ♗xa6, with balanced chances.

15 h4

Going for standard play on the kingside. Instead, 15 ♖e2 ♖ac8 16 ♗e4 ♖fd8 ½-½ was Jaracz-V.Sergeev, Guben 2012, while 15 a4!? is a decent alternative, aiming for queenside play.

15...♖ac8 16 a4 ♖fd8

The position is balanced. Zviagintsev decides to complicate matters with an interesting pawn sacrifice.

17 h5!? ♕xh5 18 ♕xh5 gxh5 19 a5?! *(D)*

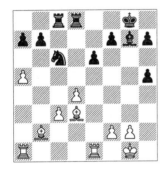

19...e5!

Black needs to generate play against the white centre.

20 a6

20 ♗f5 ♖c7 21 dxe5 ♘xe5 22 ♖ad1 is an interesting alternative.

20...bxa6 21 ♖xa6 exd4 22 cxd4 ♘xd4?!

In this rapidplay game, both players make some mistakes. 22...♘b4 23 ♖a3 ♘c2 24 ♗xc2 ♖xc2 would have given Black good chances in the endgame.

23 ♖e3 ♘e6 24 ♗xg7 ♔xg7 25 ♖xa7 ♖c3 26 ♖xe6 ♖cxd3 ½-½

Black's extra pawn is meaningless.

Game 29
Naiditsch – Dive
Istanbul Olympiad 2012

1 c4 c6 2 e4 e5

Other moves such as 2...e6 don't merit much consideration in my view, though they are played very occasionally. 2...e5 is more logical in that it challenges for the centre.

3 ♘f3 *(D)*

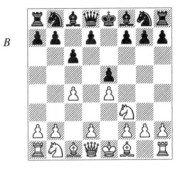

3...d6

Or:

a) Black can insert 3...♘f6 4 ♘c3, but attempts to get his dark-squared bishop outside the pawn-chain seem speculative. 4...♗b4 (4...♗c5? 5 ♘xe5 ♕e7 6 d4 ♗b4 7 f3 d5 8 cxd5 0-0 9 ♘d3 ♘xe4 10 fxe4 ♕xe4+ 11 ♕e2 ♕xd4 12 ♘xb4 ♕xb4 13 a3 +− and White consolidated his extra piece and won with careful play in Damljanović-Lajthajm, Serbian Ch, Subotica 2014) 5 ♘xe5 0-0 6 ♘d3 ♗xc3 7 dxc3

♘xe4 8 ♗e2 d5 9 cxd5 ♕xd5 10 0-0 ±
with the bishop-pair and a pleasant advantage in Melkumian-Pakleza, Reykjavik 2015.

b) 3...♕a5 can be met by many
moves, but Black is wasting so much
time that the gambit 4 ♗e2 ♘f6 5 0-0!
is already promising. 5...♘xe4 (after
5...♗e7 6 d4 d6 7 c5! 0-0, as in Iordachescu-Dobre, Romanian Team Ch,
Brasov 2011, 8 ♘bd2! would have
led to the collapse of Black's centre) 6
d4 d6 7 ♖e1 ♗e7 was Bu Xiangzhi-
L'Ami, Wijk aan Zee 2007 and now
the simple 8 ♘bd2 would have given
White excellent compensation.

4 d4 ♘d7
4...♗g4 5 ♗e2 ♗e7 6 ♘c3 is pleasant for White.

5 ♗d3
5 ♘c3 followed by ♗e2 leads to
King's Indian or Old Indian positions.
While these are obviously fine for
White (especially where Black has
committed to ...♘d7 systems), it seems
unnecessary to learn an entirely new
opening to deal with a sideline. Naiditsch's move is slightly more aggressive and leads to original positions.

**5...♘gf6 6 0-0 ♗e7 7 ♘c3 0-0 8
♖e1 ♖e8 9 h3 ♗f8**
Now Black might be considering
...exd4, so Naiditsch decides this is the
right moment to close the centre.

10 d5! a6 11 ♗e3 cxd5 12 cxd5 ±
This is a huge advantage for White,
who has an enormous advantage in
space in the centre and on the queen-side at no cost. Naiditsch had no difficulty pressing his advantage home on
the queenside.

**12...b5 13 b4 ♘b6 14 a4 ♘xa4 15
♘xa4 bxa4 16 ♖xa4 ♗d7 17 ♖a5
♕b8 18 ♕a1 ♗e7** *(D)*
18...♕xb4? 19 ♖b1 ends the game
immediately.

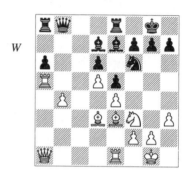

**19 ♘d2 ♗b5 20 ♗xb5 axb5 21
♖c1 ♘d7 22 ♖xa8 ♕xa8 23 ♕xa8
♖xa8 24 ♖c7 +−**
This is a nightmare King's Indian
for Black.

**24...♖d8 25 ♘b3 ♔f8 26 ♘a5 ♔e8
27 ♘c6 ♖a8 28 ♖b7 g6 29 ♖xb5
♖a1+ 30 ♔h2 f5 31 ♖a5 ♖b1 32
♘xe7 ♔xe7 33 ♗g5+ ♔e8 34 ♖a8+
♔f7 35 ♖d8 ♘b6 36 ♖xd6 ♖xb4 37
exf5 gxf5 38 ♖f6+ ♔g7 39 ♖xf5 ♘d7
40 ♗e7 ♖d4 41 d6 h6 42 g4 ♔g6 43
♔g2 ♖d3 44 h4 ♖d4 45 h5+ ♔g7 46
♔g3 ♖d3+ 47 ♖f3 ♖d4 48 ♖c3 ♔f7
49 ♖c7 ♔e6 50 g5 hxg5 51 h6 ♖d1 52
♔h2 e4 53 ♖xd7 1-0**

5 French

1 e4 e6

White has a range of options against the French, but many of the positions reached are quite unique (especially those from the Winawer, 1 e4 e6 2 d4 d5 3 ♘c3 ♗b4). French players often have more experience in these structures than their opponents do. Accordingly, it is particularly attractive to lure them into structures with which they are unfamiliar, which White can try to do with 2 d4 d5 3 ♘d2 (D) followed by ♘gf3, ♗d3 and c3, aiming to keep the pawn on e4 and meet ...cxd4 with cxd4.

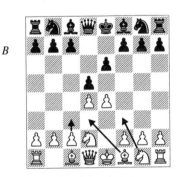

This option frequently gives rise to an IQP where Black has gained time over standard lines. This gain of time means that Black generally should be able to achieve a fully satisfactory game, but needs to be able to handle a new structure.

My coverage in this chapter has been firstly to cover the standard IQP lines, such as those reached after the following move-orders: 3...♘f6 4 ♗d3 c5 5 c3 ♘c6 6 ♘gf3 cxd4 7 cxd4 dxe4 8 ♘xe4; 3...c5 4 c3 ♘c6 5 ♘gf3 cxd4 6 cxd4 dxe4 7 ♘xe4; 3...♗e7 4 ♘gf3 c5 5 c3 ♘f6 6 ♗d3 ♘c6 7 0-0 cxd4 8 cxd4 dxe4 9 ♘xe4. In these lines, there isn't much theory and, as mentioned above, Black should, objectively, be fine. Accordingly, I have relied on the general knowledge gained about IQP positions in this and other chapters to equip you better than your opponents for the resulting middlegames.

I have devoted particular attention to attempts at early simplification which have been recommended in recent popular repertoire works. White actually needs to know some theory here to avoid being worse right out of the opening, but the simplified positions retain scope for the better player to win.

More specifically, the chapter is organized as follows: Games 30-32 examine the 'IQP' lines (following 3...♗e7, 3...♘f6 and 3...c5), while 3...dxe4 is the subject of Game 33, and we examine all other moves (most notably 3...♘c6) in Game 34. It is worth noting that against the variety of semi-waiting moves such as 3...a6 and 3...h6 that have become quite topical in recent years, the IQP system works rather well, as these little pawn moves do little to disrupt our development plan.

Game 30
Collins – Teeuwen
Kilkenny 2013

To start things off, let's look at a nice (if rather lightweight) game of mine. This was played in the legendary weekend tournament at Kilkenny. Over the years this event has attracted dozens of strong GMs including Michael Adams, Luke McShane, Ivan Cheparinov and Gawain Jones, who relish the chance to play entertaining chess in a highly informal setting.

This game was played in round 4, during a tournament which wasn't going especially well for me. Round 4 is played on Saturday night, the third round of that day, and I had White against a less experienced opponent. Rather than going for lines where he might be well prepared, I decided that the IQP system would be the perfect choice.

1 e4 e6 2 d4 d5 3 ♘d2 ♗e7

It can hardly be claimed that the IQP system leads to an advantage after this move, but the system becomes more attractive in my view since Black's options of early simplification with ...♗b4+ (such as we examine in Game 32) are ruled out. The lines after

3...♘f6 4 ♗d3 c5 5 c3 and 3...c5 4 c3 ♘f6 5 ♗d3 are covered in the next two games.

4 ♘gf3 ♘f6 5 ♗d3 c5 6 c3

White has set up his pieces in the standard fashion, refusing to release the tension on either the e4-pawn (with e5) or the d4-pawn (with dxc5).

6...♘c6 7 0-0 (D)

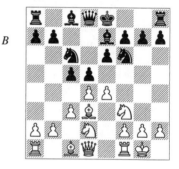

7...cxd4

Black finally decides to clarify the position in the centre. Continuing to wait would have resulted in some risk of confusing himself and ending up in a line for which he wasn't prepared. After 7...0-0, while White can stubbornly insist on maintaining the tension with something like 8 ♖e1 (or even 8 a3!?), he can also choose 8 e5, when after 8...♘d7 we have transposed into a variation of the Korchnoi Gambit, which begins with 1 e4 e6 2 d4 d5 3 ♘d2 ♘f6 4 e5 ♘fd7 5 ♗d3 c5 6 c3 ♘c6 7 ♘gf3 (instead of the standard 7 ♘e2). Black has several systems against this gambit (including accepting it with 7...cxd4 8 cxd4 ♕b6 9 0-0 ♘xd4), but the line with 7...♗e7

8 0-0 0-0 isn't one of the most popular systems (although it has been tried by French experts like Lputian and Shirov). If this isn't your opponent's preferred response to the Korchnoi Gambit, he is unlikely to want to allow it via this move-order either.

8 cxd4 dxe4

8...0-0 leads to similar considerations as outlined in the note to Black's 7th move. White can continue with 9 ♖e1 or 9 a3 (maybe more logical here than on the last move, since the b4-square is undefended and Black can't respond with ...c4), but the move that would probably put Black off castling is 9 e5.

9 ♘xe4 0-0 10 ♘c3 *(D)*

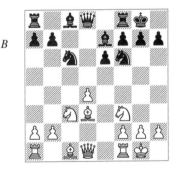

So we have a standard IQP position, but which lines can it be compared to?

White is actually a full tempo down compared to some well-established main lines (including ones from the Nimzo-Indian and the Semi-Tarrasch). For example, Sadler-Ortiz, Tromsø Olympiad 2014 went 1 d4 ♘f6 2 c4 e6 3 ♘c3 ♗b4 4 e3 0-0 5 ♗d3 d5 6 ♘f3 c5 7 0-0 dxc4 8 ♗xc4 ♘c6 9 ♗d3 cxd4 10 exd4 ♗e7, where we have reached the game position with White to move. Another example is Babula-Illescas, Istanbul Olympiad 2012: 1 d4 ♘f6 2 c4 e6 3 ♘f3 d5 4 ♘c3 c5 5 cxd5 ♘xd5 6 e3 ♘c6 7 ♗d3 ♗e7 8 0-0 0-0 9 ♖e1 ♘f6!? 10 a3 cxd4 11 exd4, and we have the text position with the extra a3 for White (which, as will appear, is a very useful move).

10...b6 *(D)*

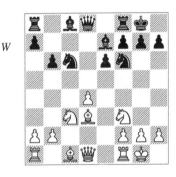

It should be noted that White sometimes obtains this position (with an 'extra' a3) from our chosen system, in particular where Black plays an early ...♗b4+ and later retreats to e7. As we have seen above, this manoeuvre is known from some lines of the Nimzo-Indian (and the Panov-Botvinnik Attack against the Caro-Kann), but it is hardly the most accurate here.

For instance: Sermek-Bukal, Croatian Team Ch, Pula 2001 went 1 e4 c5 2 ♘f3 e6 3 c3 ♘c6 4 d4 cxd4 5 cxd4 d5 6 ♘c3 dxe4 7 ♘xe4 ♗b4+ 8 ♘c3 ♘f6 9 ♗d3 0-0 10 0-0 ♗e7; A.Kornev-Gleizerov, Kaluga 2003 went 1 e4 e6 2 d4 d5 3 ♘d2 ♘f6 4 ♗d3 c5 5 c3 ♘c6 6 ♘gf3 cxd4 7 cxd4 dxe4 8 ♘xe4 ♗b4+ 9 ♘c3 0-0 10 0-0 ♗e7. A.Kislinsky-Fröwis, Moscow 2012 went 1 e4 e6 2 d4 d5 3 ♘d2 c5 4 c3 ♘c6 5 ♘gf3 cxd4 6 cxd4 dxe4 7 ♘xe4 ♗b4+ 8 ♘c3 ♘f6 9 ♗d3 0-0 10 0-0 ♗e7.

All of the black players in the three games given above were rated over 2400 (Gleizerov is a strong GM and a French specialist) and, frankly, I find the game from 2012 particularly surprising, since this line has been known for a while. However, it does demonstrate that it is possible for players to become confused when facing this system, especially since it gives rise to a structure that is highly unusual for the French.

Incidentally, the three quoted games gave rise to interesting and thematic attacking play, which we shall now examine. 11 a3 b6 12 ♖e1 ♗b7 13 ♗c2 *(D)* and then:

a) 13...♖c8 14 ♕d3 and here:

a1) The naïve 14...♖e8? runs into the absolutely standard 15 d5!. This motif (with the black rook on c8 or a8)

has been known for decades – the earliest and most famous example I know of is Petrosian-Balashov, USSR 1974. However, this doesn't stop experienced players from regularly falling for this idea (either in this exact position, or in similar ones); for instance, Karpov has fallen for it more than once.

a2) 14...g6 15 ♗h6 ♖e8 16 ♖ad1 ♘d5 17 h4 ♘xc3 18 bxc3 ♘a5 (the alternative 18...♕d5 is a good multipurpose move, directed against h5 and defending e6) 19 h5?! (19 ♗a4 is better, and at least avoids a disadvantage after 19...♗c6 20 ♗xc6 ♘xc6 21 h5) 19...♘c4? (Black falls for a simple shot; 19...♕d5 was necessary and good) 20 hxg6 hxg6 21 ♖xe6 ♗f6 (there's no time for 21...♘b2 since 22 ♖xg6+ will follow) 22 ♖xe8+ ♕xe8 23 ♖e1 ♕d7 (Kislinsky-Fröwis, Moscow 2012) and now 24 ♗b3 is best, with the better game since a3 is immune as g6 would hang.

b) 13...♘a5 14 ♗g5 h6 15 ♗f4 ♘c4 16 ♘e5 ♘d6?! 17 ♕d3 ♘f5 18 ♖ad1 (White has put all his pieces on good squares while Black has achieved nothing – in particular, he hasn't exchanged any minor pieces) 18...♘d5 19 ♘xd5 ♕xd5 (after 19...♗xd5? 20 g4 ♗g5 21 gxf5 White wins a piece, since 21...♗xf4 22 f6 g6 23 ♘xg6 is mate in a few moves) 20 ♕h3! ♘xd4? (Black should try to change the character of the game with 20...♖ad8 21 ♗e4 ♕xe4 22 ♖xe4 ♗xe4, although his compensation for the queen doesn't seem to be fully sufficient) 21 ♗xh6!

(a thematic shot, which works perfectly in this position) 21...♖fd8 (after 21...gxh6 22 ♕g4+ followed by 23 ♖xd4 White wins material) 22 ♖xd4! ♕xd4 and now 23 ♗g5 was enough for a large advantage in Kornev-Gleizerov, Kaluga 2003, but 23 ♕h5!! wins on the spot; for instance, 23...♖f8 24 ♗h7+ ♔h8 25 ♗e4 ♕xe4 26 ♖xe4 ♗xe4 27 ♗g5+ ♔g8 28 ♗xe7 and White wins.

We now return to the position after 10...b6 *(D)*:

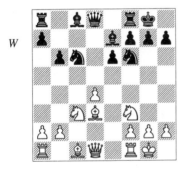

11 a3 ♗b7 12 ♗c2 ♕d7

Teeuwen's lack of experience in IQP structures begins to show. d7 is an unusual square for the black queen, as it is potentially exposed to ♘e5 (perhaps in combination with ♗b5) and, importantly, finds it difficult to vacate the central files. d6 would be a better square, when the queen can drop back to b8 once the a8-rook has been developed to c8 or d8.

13 ♕d3

Setting up the standard line-up on the b1-h7 diagonal.

13...♖ad8

13...a5! would be a more efficient version of the ...♗a6 idea that was used in the game. After 14 ♖d1 ♗a6 15 ♕e3 the game is balanced.

Interestingly, going back to move 12, 12...♗a6 13 ♖e1 has been used with success by some strong GMs as Black.

14 ♖d1 ♕c8

Already I was becoming optimistic.

15 ♗g5 ♗a6 16 ♕e3 *(D)*

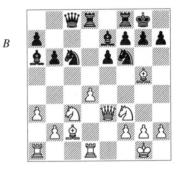

16...♘d5

16...h6 is critical, but Black is no longer able to equalize. After 17 ♗xf6! (the standard offer 17 ♗xh6??, which would lead to a winning attack after 17...gxh6?? 18 ♕xh6, here fails to the simple 17...♘g4 −+) 17...♗xf6 18 ♖ac1 it might seem as though Black has the bishop-pair and no weaknesses, but White's space advantage and more active pieces are more important here. White has strong pressure; for instance, 18...♗b7 19 ♘e4 ♗e7 20 b4 ♖d7 21 ♗b1 ♕e8 22 ♘g3 ♗d6 23 ♕d3 f5 (23...g6 24 ♘e4 is also promising for White) 24 ♖e1 and the pawn on e6 is weaker than the pawn on d4.

A neutral move such as 16...♖fe8 should be met simply with 17 ♖ac1, developing the last piece and retaining all the advantages of the white position.

17 ♘xd5 ♖xd5?

The symmetrical structure arising after 17...exd5 *(D)* favours the side with better-placed pieces, which tends to be White. Then:

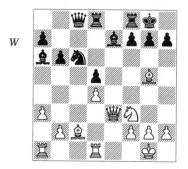

a) 18 ♖ac1 f6 (18...♗xg5 19 ♘xg5 g6 20 ♗a4 and Black is struggling to hold his weaknesses together) 19 ♗f4 ♖fe8 20 ♘h4 ♗d6 (20...g5? loses to 21 ♗f5!, based on the beautiful point 21...gxf4 22 ♕xf4 ♕b7 23 ♖xc6!! ♕xc6 24 ♕h6 followed by mate) 21 ♗f5 ♕c7 22 ♗xd6 ♕xd6 23 ♕c3 and Black should equalize with precise play.

b) 18 ♗xe7 ♖fe8 19 ♗xd8 ♖xe3 20 fxe3 ♕xd8 21 ♗d3 gives White good chances – the rooks will be able to penetrate on the c-file and it is hard for Black to generate an attack since his minor pieces are so far from the kingside.

18 ♗e4! ±

Black's scattered pieces are targets for White's attack, and White's initiative is already decisive.

18...♖d6

18...♗xg5 19 ♘xg5 forks d5 and h7, and so wins material.

19 ♖ac1 ♗xg5 *(D)*

This move walks into a nice version of the Greek Gift sacrifice, but there were no good options; for instance, after 19...f6 20 ♗f4 e5 21 dxe5 White wins a pawn while retaining much more active pieces.

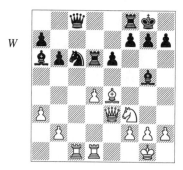

20 ♗xh7+!

Not especially difficult, but I'll permit myself an exclamation mark since it was the third game of the day! Instead, 20 ♘xg5? h6 gives White nothing special.

20...♔xh7 21 ♘xg5+ ♔g8

21...♔g6 22 ♕g3 ♔h6 23 ♕xd6, taking a rook and winning the knight on c6, is one of the tactical points.

22 ♕h3 ♖fd8 23 ♕h7+ ♔f8 24 ♕h8+ ♔e7 25 ♕xg7 ♖f8

There is more than one winning continuation here, but the line I chose is quite thematic.

26 d5! *(D)*

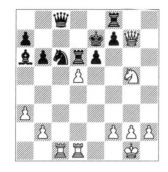

Blasting open the centre.

26...♕d8

The main line I calculated continued 26...♖xd5 27 ♖xd5 exd5 28 ♖e1+ ♔d7 (28...♔d6 29 ♘xf7+ ♖xf7 30 ♕xf7 and the three connected passed pawns, coupled with the continuing initiative against the black king, ensure an easy win despite nominal material equality) and now I had planned 29 ♘h7 followed by taking on f7, which wins, but apparently the elegant 29 ♘xf7! ♖d8 30 h4! is even simpler.

26...exd5 27 ♖e1+ ♔d7 28 ♘xf7 is very convincing.

27 ♘xe6!

Taking advantage of the pin on the f7-pawn, and winning the house.

27...♖xe6 28 dxe6 ♕c8 29 exf7 1-0

Game 31
Kislinsky – Svane
European Ch, Legnica 2013

1 e4 e6 2 d4 d5 3 ♘d2 ♘f6

3...c5 4 c3 ♘f6 5 ♗d3 transposes.

4 ♗d3 c5 5 c3 cxd4

If Black develops without making exchanges in the centre, then the play is likely to reach positions similar to those we saw in Game 30, with possible transpositions if he puts his bishop on e7.

6 cxd4 dxe4 7 ♘xe4 ♗d7 *(D)*

This solid and safe system has been recommended in several recent texts on the French. Black aims to put his bishop on c6 and his knight on d7, with a solid position.

While obvious, it is worth noting that Black can't aim to transpose to the next note by changing the move-order, since after 7...♘xe4 8 ♗xe4, 8...♗d7?? loses material. Note also that 8...♗b4+, seeking simplification, is the subject of Game 32.

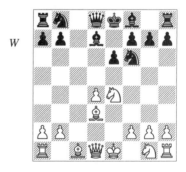

8 ♘c3!

Probably the best move, avoiding exchanges.

8 ♘f3?! allows 8...♘xe4 9 ♗xe4 ♗c6 with a solid position for Black from which White has scored appallingly; for instance, 10 ♕d3 ♗b4+ 11 ♗d2 ♗xe4 12 ♕xe4 ♗xd2+ 13 ♘xd2 ♘c6 14 ♘b3 0-0 and Black already

had the more pleasant position in Feuerstack-Vallejo Pons, Bundesliga 2012/13.

8...♗c6

8...♘c6 is less consistent and leaves White with a pleasant position after 9 ♘f3 (D):

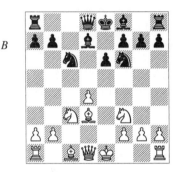

a) 9...♕b6 10 0-0!? is an interesting pawn sacrifice. White gets reasonable compensation after 10...♘xd4 (10...♘b4 11 ♗e2 ♗c6 12 ♘e5 ♖d8 13 ♗e3 was decent for White in Fougerit-Pons Carreras, Lisbon 2014) 11 ♘xd4 ♕xd4 12 ♘b5 ♕b6 13 ♗e3 followed by ♖c1.

b) 9...♗d6 was played against the godfather of this line, English GM Jim Plaskett. 10 0-0 0-0 11 ♖e1 ♘b4 12 ♗b1 ♕c7 13 ♗g5 ♘fd5? (13...♘bd5 is sounder) 14 a3 ♘xc3 15 bxc3 ♘d5 16 ♕d3 f5 17 c4 ♘f4 18 ♗xf4 ♗xf4 19 g3 ♗h6 20 ♗a2 followed by c5 gave White an outstanding position in Plaskett-D.Martinez, Roquetas de Mar 2010, but Black had played some very odd moves to get here!

9 ♘f3 ♘bd7 10 0-0 ♗e7 11 ♕e2 0-0

This is just a balanced position with no opening advantage for White. The main reason to aim for such a position is to take French players out of their comfort zone since such IQP positions arise relatively rarely in the French.

12 ♖d1

12 ♘e5 is another approach for White. 12...♘b6 (12...♘xe5 13 dxe5 ♘d5 looks fine for Black) 13 ♖d1 ♘bd5 14 ♗b1 ♖c8 15 ♕d3 ♘xc3 16 bxc3 ♗e4 17 ♕h3 ♕a5 18 ♗d2 ♖fd8 with unclear play in Trent-J.Silva, La Massana 2013.

12...♘d5 13 ♗e3 ♖c8 14 a3 ♕a5 15 ♘e4 ♘xe3 16 fxe3 (D)

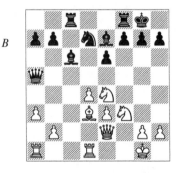

This is a structural change with unclear consequences. The d4-pawn is no longer weak and White gets a half-open f-file down which his rook can be active. In some cases the white centre might become mobile. However, Black has simplified the game, has won the bishop-pair and retains the superior structure, so it's not all bad from his perspective. I've traditionally scored well with these structures (both in the c3 Sicilian and, with reversed colours, the Tarrasch Defence) but suffered a painful defeat in Collins-Bern, Norwegian Team Ch 2014/15 so I would simply call these positions double-edged! This game is a good example of some of the key ideas.

16...♕b6 17 ♘c3 ♗xf3

Radically changing the position. Black could also hold the position with 17...♗d6, when White's best is probably to halve the bishop-pair with 18 ♗e4. The position is dynamically balanced.

18 gxf3

White could also consider 18 ♕xf3, since 18...♕xb2 19 ♘e4 is far from clear. However, Kislinsky's move is quite natural since it increases his central control.

18...♖cd8 *(D)*

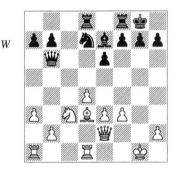

19 f4

I also like 19 ♔h1 followed by putting the rooks on c1 and g1, when all the white pieces have active roles.

19...f5!

Good positional judgement from the strong German junior. Black needs to fight for the centre.

20 ♖d2 ♘f6 21 ♖c1 ♘d5 22 ♕f3 ♘xc3

I'm not sure about this exchange, after which the e6-pawn becomes very weak. Simply 22...♖c8 looks reasonable.

23 ♖xc3 ♖c8 24 ♗c4 ♔h8 25 ♖dc2 ♖c6 26 h4?! *(D)*

26 ♗b3 ♖xc3 27 ♖xc3 looks excellent at first sight, but 27...g5!? gives Black active play down the g-file. The position is very unclear since there are opposite-coloured bishops and neither king is completely safe.

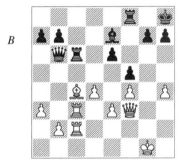

26...h6?

26...♗xh4 is critical. I haven't been able to find full compensation for White here, so perhaps his 26th move was just a bluff.

27 h5!

Now White has tied down the black kingside and, suddenly, Black has no active play.

27...♗f6 28 ♔f1

Kislinsky decides on a king march to the queenside, not an obvious decision since the black pieces are aiming in that direction.

28 ♕g2 looks good; for instance, 28...♖fc8 29 ♔h2 and White threatens 30 ♗xe6!.

28...♖fc8 29 ♕e2 a6 30 ♕d3 ♖6c7 31 ♔e1 ♕c6? 32 ♔d2?

32 ♗xe6! wins (a much easier move to play with a computer in front of you), since the checks lead nowhere: 32...♕h1+ (32...♗h4+ 33 ♔d2 ♕g2+ 34 ♕e2 +−) 33 ♕f1 ♕h4+ 34 ♔d2 ♖xc3 35 ♖xc3 ♖xc3 36 bxc3 ♕xh5 37 ♕g2 +− and Black loses material.

32...♕e8!

Targeting the h5-pawn.

33 ♗a2 ♖c6?

33...♖xc3 34 ♖xc3 ♖d8 ± is more tenacious.

34 ♖xc6 ♖xc6 35 ♖xc6 ♕xc6 36 ♕c4! *(D)*

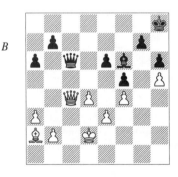

Normally pure opposite-coloured bishop endgames give excellent drawing chances one or even two pawns down, but here there are too many black pawns fixed on light squares (e6 would drop for a start). Therefore Black avoids the queen exchange, but the difference in queen and bishop activity begins to tell.

36...♕g2+ 37 ♔c3 ♕g1 38 ♕c8+ ♔h7 39 ♗xe6 ♕c1+ 40 ♔b3 ♕xc8 41 ♗xc8

Black found nothing better than to exchange queens anyway, but ended up in a very difficult endgame.

41...b6

41...g6 ± looks like a better try.

42 ♗xf5+ ♔g8 43 ♔c4 ♗h4 44 e4 ♔f8 45 ♗c8 a5 46 a4 ♗g3 47 f5 ♗f2 48 e5 ♗g3 49 ♔d5 ♗f2 50 ♔e4 ♔e7 51 ♗a6 ♗g1 52 ♔b5 ♗f2 53 d5 1-0

Game 32
M. White – Compton
Crawley 2012

In this game we examine the critical equalizing attempt with early simplification.

1 e4 e6 2 d4 d5 3 ♘d2 ♘f6 4 ♗d3 c5 5 c3 dxe4 6 ♘xe4 ♘xe4 7 ♗xe4 cxd4 8 cxd4 ♗b4+ 9 ♗d2 ♗xd2+ 10 ♕xd2 ♘d7 11 ♘e2 ♘f6 12 ♗f3 0-0 *(D)*

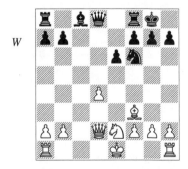

13 0-0

This is the most precise, leaving the c-file open for the white rooks.

I lost a very poor game after 13 ♘c3 ♖b8 (13...♕b6 14 0-0 ♖d8 is also very comfortable for Black, Zude-Eingorn, Bad Wiessee 2011) 14 ♕f4 ♗d7 15 ♕d6 ♗c6 16 ♕xd8 ♖fxd8 17 ♗xc6 bxc6 18 0-0-0 ♖b4 19 ♘e2 ♖db8 in Collins-S.Williams, Dublin 2012 when I fought my way back into the game only to make an horrendous blunder when playing on a 30-second increment in a trivially drawn rook endgame.

13...♕b6

13...♖b8 14 ♖ac1 b6 was Obrusnik-Sieciechowicz, Polish Team Ch, Poronin 2014. Now White's most consistent plan is 15 ♖c2 ♗b7 16 ♗xb7 ♖xb7 17 ♖fc1, when his control of the c-file compensates for his structural weakness.

14 ♖ac1 ♖d8 *(D)*

14...♗d7 15 ♖c3 ♕a5 16 ♕c2 ♖ac8 17 ♖c1 ♖xc3 18 ♘xc3 b5 19 a3 ♖c8 20 ♕d2 h6 21 h3 ♕b6 was agreed drawn after logical play by both sides in S.Pavlov-Fingerov, Kiev 2002.

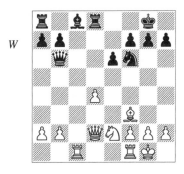

15 ♖c4
Or:

a) 15 ♖fd1 is a possible alternative; for instance, 15...♗d7 (15...e5 16 ♕e3 exd4 17 ♖xd4 leaves White slightly better mobilized with a completely open centre, which means Black is the one who has to equalize – though I am confident that he can) 16 ♖c5 (after 16 ♖c3 ♗a4 17 ♖dc1 e5 18 ♖a3 e4 19 ♖xa4 exf3 20 gxf3 ♘d5, Aagaard and Ntirlis correctly note that Black has good compensation for the pawn) 16...♖ac8 17 ♖dc1 ♗c6 18 b3 ♘d7 19 ♖5c3 ♘f6 with equality.

b) With 15 ♖c3 White is seeking to avoid Aagaard and Ntirlis's equalizing attempt in the next note, since 15...e5 16 ♖b3 ♕d6 17 ♗xb7 ♗xb7 18 ♖xb7 exd4 gives chances to both sides, though of course this means that White takes on some risk playing this way.

We now return to 15 ♖c4 *(D)*:

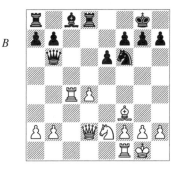

15...a5
Not a bad move, but also not the most purposeful in the position. Other moves:

a) 15...e5 is Aagaard and Ntirlis's suggestion in *Playing the French*. It is given by the authors as "a convincing route to equality", and I would have to agree. 16 ♘c3 ♖xd4 17 ♖xd4 ♕xd4 18 ♕xd4 exd4 19 ♖d1 ♗g4 20 ♖xd4 ♗xf3 21 gxf3 ♔f8 22 ♘e4 is level.

b) 15...♗d7, as in the game Rockmann-L.Engel, German Under-12 Ch, Magdeburg 2014, is best met by 16 ♖fc1 ♖ac8 17 ♖c5 with active play.

16 b3

16 ♖fc1 looks more consistent.

16...♗d7 17 ♖fc1 ♗b5 18 ♖c7

White should settle for 18 ♖c5 =.

18...♗c6!

Now the rook is trapped on c7.

19 ♕f4 e5 20 ♖7xc6!

The best chance. After 20 ♕xe5? ♗xf3 21 gxf3 ♖e8 Black wins a piece since 22 ♖e7 ♖xe7 23 ♕xe7 ♖e8 is the same tactic.

20...bxc6 21 dxe5 ♘d5 22 ♕f5 ♘b4 23 ♗e4 g6 24 ♕f6 ♘xa2 25 e6 ♘xc1?

25...♕c7! would have left White struggling to prove full compensation for his material deficit.

½-½

The white queen will deliver perpetual check from f7 and f6.

Game 33
A. David – Pelletier
Mitropa Cup, Zillertal 2015

1 e4 e6 2 d4 d5 3 ♘c3

Don't worry; I am not proposing that you broaden your repertoire by sometimes putting your knight on c3, as after Black's next move the play transposes back to lines relevant to our repertoire. 3 ♘d2 dxe4 4 ♘xe4 leads to

the same position, which is one of the main attractions of these systems for Black, since it isn't necessary to learn separate lines after 3 ♘c3 and 3 ♘d2.

3...dxe4 4 ♘xe4 *(D)*

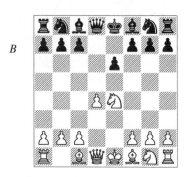

4...♘d7

This move, preparing to challenge White's knight by 5...♘gf6, characterizes the Rubinstein Variation. The immediate 4...♘f6?! is well met by 5 ♘xf6+, when Black does best to accept some structural damage with 5...gxf6 rather than lose more time after 5...♕xf6 6 ♘f3, threatening ♗g5 and ♗d3 to gain time on the queen.

The Rubinstein is generally thought to be somewhat passive for Black, and I think a good case can be made that White has good chances for an edge by simply developing his pieces (♘f3, ♗d3, 0-0 and so on). I also think it is a poor choice for most club players, since Black needs to know some theory here to avoid a prospectless position or a quick defeat. The most notable advocates of Black's position include GM Evgeny Bareev and, more recently, German GM Georg Meier.

4...♗d7, often called the Fort Knox Defence due to its solidity, is popular at club level but doesn't require much theoretical knowledge by White, who always gets a stable space advantage, often coupled with the bishop-pair. 5 ♘f3 ♗c6 6 ♗d3 ♘d7 7 0-0 ♘gf6 8 ♘g3 (avoiding a knight exchange, which would ease Black's defence) 8...♗e7 9 b3 h5 10 ♕e2 ♗xf3 11 ♕xf3 c6 gave White a pleasant game with more space and the bishop-pair in So-Gareev, USA Ch, St Louis 2015. Here I like the simple 12 h3, when Black's position looks rather dubious.

5 ♘f3 ♘gf6 6 ♗d3 (D)

6...c5

Top theoretician GM Parimarjan Negi notes "This is definitely the modern main line, despite not having been played as many times as 6...♘xe4 or 6...♗e7." Let's take a look at those two moves:

a) The slight delay inherent in 6...♗e7 means that White can consider some sharp plans; for instance, 7 ♕e2 ♘xe4 8 ♕xe4 ♘f6 9 ♕e2 0-0 10 ♗d2!? (10 0-0 is safe, with an edge) 10...b6 11 0-0-0 with dynamic play in Felgaer-An.Rodriguez, Montevideo Zonal 2013.

b) 6...♘xe4 is the most popular move, having been played in over 1000 games. After 7 ♗xe4 ♘f6 the modern trend, and the move most consistent with general opening principles, is to develop without loss of time by playing 8 ♗g5 (D).

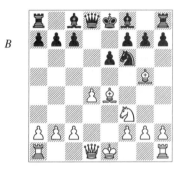

Then:

b1) 8...♗e7 is strongly met by 9 ♗xf6!:

b11) 9...♗xf6 10 ♕d3 followed by 0-0-0 is extremely dangerous for Black, who has no clear way to complete development. Kingside castling will have to be prefaced by ...g6 or ...h6, either of which will create a target for White's kingside pawn-storm. A recent example ran 10...c6 11 0-0-0 ♕a5 12 ♔b1 ♗d7 13 ♘e5 ♖d8 14 f4 h6 15 g4 and White went on to score a convincingly win against a GM rated some 200 points higher than him in Lombaers-Balog, Utrecht 2015.

b12) 9...gxf6 (relatively best) 10 0-0 c5 11 ♖e1 0-0?! 12 ♕e2 cxd4 13

♖ad1 ♕a5 14 ♘xd4 gave White an excellent game with superior development, a better structure and a safer king in Ganguly-C.Cruz, Spanish Team Ch, Linares 2014.

b2) Recently the bold 8...♕d6 has been tried by a couple of strong GMs, who rely on deep computer preparation to grab a pawn after 9 ♗d3 ♕b4+ 10 ♗d2 ♕xb2 11 0-0. Then:

b21) 11...♕a3 has twice been tried by IM Anna Zatonskih, but without success. 12 ♘e5 ♕d6 13 ♗f4 (improving on 13 ♗e3, as played in Kasparov-Anand, Kopavogur blitz 2000) 13...♕d8 14 ♕f3 ♗e7 15 ♗b5+ ♔f8 16 ♖ad1 with a strong initiative for the pawn in Sarić-Zatonskih, Bastia rapid 2013.

b22) After 11...♗e7 it is intuitively obvious that White has excellent compensation, with a big lead in development and prospects of gaining further time on the black queen. However, he is a pawn down so it seems prudent to have at least some idea of the plans here. The following recent game is a good example: 12 a4 ♕b6 13 ♗f4 ♕a5 14 ♘e5 0-0 15 ♘c4 ♕d5 16 ♗xc7 b6 17 ♘e3 ♕c6 18 ♗e5 ♗b7 19 c4, Rublevsky-Galkin, Rostov-na-Donu rapid 2014. White has regained his pawn and enjoys good prospects in a hanging-pawns position.

7 0-0

White's play makes a good impression. He has more space in the centre and has developed his pieces as rapidly as possible.

7...♘xe4 8 ♗xe4 ♘f6 9 ♗g5 (D)

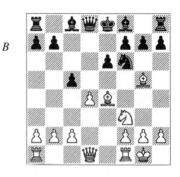

This is an important theoretical position. Pelletier tries an unusual move, but not one which changes the character of the position. To be completely honest, I'm not sure what attracts Black to this position – White scores heavily and, equally importantly, his play is quite natural since there are few sharp forcing lines.

9...♕c7

9...cxd4 10 ♘xd4 ♗e7 11 ♗f3 0-0 12 ♕d3 leaves the white pieces fabulously placed. A few examples:

a) 12...♕b6 was tried twice by strong GM Yuri Drozdovsky against super-GM Sergey Kariakin in a rapid match. 13 ♖ad1 ♖d8 14 ♗e3 ♕a5 15 ♕b5 ♕c7 16 ♕b3 (D) and now:

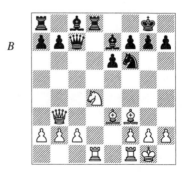

a1) 16...a6 was played in Kariakin-Drozdovsky, Odessa rapid (1) 2010. Then Kariakin's 17 ♘f5 was good enough for an advantage, but 17 ♘c6!! ± would have been extremely powerful. 17...bxc6 drops the exchange to 18 ♗b6, while after 17...♖xd1 18 ♘xe7+ ♕xe7 19 ♖xd1 Black can hardly survive his development deficit and the powerful bishop-pair.

a2) 16...♗d7 17 c4 e5 18 ♘b5 ♗xb5 19 cxb5 e4 20 b6 ♕e5 21 ♗e2, Kariakin-Drozdovsky, Odessa rapid (3) 2010. White has the initiative and the bishop-pair, and Black's defence seems difficult.

b) 12...♕c7 was Pelletier's old favourite, but he dropped it after two painful losses against strong GMs. 13 ♖fe1 ♖d8 14 ♖ad1 a6 15 ♗h4 *(D)* and now:

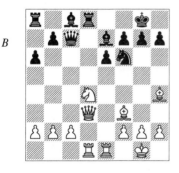

b1) 15...e5 16 ♕c3!? ♗d6 (after 16...♕xc3 17 bxc3 the pressure on the e5-pawn and Black's backward development are more important than the weakening of White's queenside) 17 ♘b3 ♕e7?! (for better or worse, Black should have swapped queens on c3)

18 ♘a5 left White much better in C.Balogh-Pelletier, European Team Ch, Warsaw 2013.

b2) 15...♗d6 (Pelletier's attempted improvement) 16 h3 h6 17 ♗xf6 gxf6 18 ♕e4 ♗f8 19 ♕h4 (it is notable that Meier recently allowed this position, but his opponent went for the less incisive 19 c3 and the game later ended in a draw in Blomqvist-G.Meier, Norrköping 2015; I'd be very interested in what Meier had in mind against 19 ♕h4 and I suspect we'll find out soon!) 19...♗g7 20 ♘e2! (starting a journey to the h5-square, from where the knight will menace the black kingside) 20...♗d7 21 ♘g3 ♗c6 22 ♗xc6 ♕xc6 23 c3 ♕b5 24 ♘h5 ♕g5 (Pelletier has defended well, bringing his queen to cover the important squares on the kingside, but he still has not equalized) 25 ♕g4! (excellent judgement: an exchange on g4 would be in White's favour, especially since the f6-pawn would be fixed and so the g7-bishop would remain passive) 25...f5 26 ♕f3 gave White the superior structure, better development and a safer king in Naiditsch-Pelletier, European Team Ch, Warsaw 2013.

10 ♕e2 *(D)*
10...♘xe4

Varying from the only other game to have reached this position, played over 100 years previously!

10...cxd4 11 ♘xd4 (White should prefer 11 ♗xf6 gxf6 12 ♘xd4 with some advantage; after the text-move, Black could have secured a reasonable game by taking on e4) 11...♗d7 12

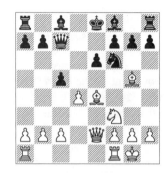

B

♖ad1 ♗e7 13 ♖fe1 0-0 14 ♕f3 ♘d5 15 ♗xe7 ♘xe7 16 ♗xb7 ♖ab8 was played in Marshall-Breyer, Bad Pistyan 1912, and now the best would have been 17 ♗e4 ± with a healthy extra pawn since 17...♖xb2?? drops a piece to 18 ♕a3.

11 ♕xe4 cxd4 12 ♖ad1

Perhaps 12 ♗f4 is stronger, when it is unclear how Black should proceed. 12...♕b6 (after 12...♕c6 13 ♕xc6+ bxc6 14 ♘xd4 White's superior structure arguably outweighs the bishop-pair) 13 ♖ad1 ♗e7 (13...♕xb2 14 ♘xd4 gives White a huge initiative for the pawn) 14 ♘xd4 0-0 15 b3 followed by doubling on the d-file.

12...f6 13 ♗h4

13 ♗c1 is also a good try for an edge.

13...♗c5 14 ♘xd4 ♗xd4

14...e5 is suggested as a better option by the computer.

15 ♖xd4 e5?

15...0-0 is superior, but after 16 ♖fd1 White controls the only open file and has an edge.

16 f4!

Winning material.

16...♗e6 17 fxe5 ♕xe5 18 ♕xe5 fxe5 19 ♖e4 ♖f8 20 ♖fe1 ♔d7 21 ♖xe5 *(D)* ±

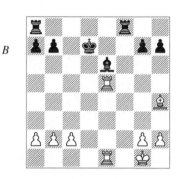

B

White is a pawn up, though Black has drawing chances due to the opposite-coloured bishops. David went on to win a good game.

21...♖ae8 22 ♖c5 ♖c8 23 ♖d1+ ♔e8 24 ♖xc8+ ♗xc8 25 ♖e1+ ♔f7 26 ♖e7+ ♔g6 27 ♖c7 ♗f5 28 ♖xb7 ♖f7 29 ♗e7 ♗xc2 30 ♖xa7 ♗d3 31 h3 ♖f1+ 32 ♔h2 ♖f2 33 ♗c5 ♖xb2 34 ♗d4 ♖d2 35 ♖xg7+ ♔f5 36 ♖xh7 ♗e4 37 ♖h5+ ♔f4 38 ♗e5+ ♔e3 39 ♖g5 ♖xa2 40 ♖g3+ 1-0

Game 34
Malakhov – Mu Ke
Chinese Team Ch 2014

1 e4 e6 2 d4 d5 3 ♘d2 *(D)*
3...♘c6

A number of other options are worth mentioning briefly:

a) 3...e5?! is an offbeat gambit idea which has been successfully used by French expert GM Emanuel Berg. White should proceed 4 dxe5 (and not

B

4 exd5, as Berg's opponent played) 4...dxe4 (4...♘c6 5 exd5 ♕xd5 6 ♘gf3 ♘xe5 7 ♕e2 looks a bit better for White) 5 ♕e2 followed by 6 ♘xe4.

b) 3...a6 is another popular sideline with some independent significance. However, here the IQP approach is stronger than after 3...♘f6, 3...c5 or 3...♗e7, since Black has spent a tempo on ...a6, which might not be useful. 4 ♘gf3 c5 5 c3 cxd4 (5...♘c6 6 ♗d3 cxd4 7 cxd4 dxe4 8 ♘xe4 ♗b4+ 9 ♘c3 ♘f6 10 0-0 0-0 reached a standard position for our repertoire, but with Black having already committed to ...a6, in Naroditsky-Rapport, Riga 2014) 6 cxd4 dxe4 7 ♘xe4 ♗b4+ (7...♗d7 8 ♗d3 ♘f6 9 ♘xf6+ gxf6 10 0-0 was slightly better for White in G.Jones-Nakamura, Italian Team Ch, Arvier 2012) 8 ♗d2 (8 ♘c3 ♘f6 9 ♗d3 0-0 10 0-0 is another possibility, as in Van Foreest-Zviagintsev, Moscow 2015) 8...♗xd2+ 9 ♕xd2 ♘f6 10 ♘xf6+ ♕xf6 11 ♗d3 ♘c6 12 0-0 ♗d7 13 ♖fe1 0-0 14 ♖e4 ♖fd8 15 ♖f4 ♕e7? (15...♕h6 is a better defence) 16 d5! (after original play, White demonstrates a thematic idea) 16...exd5 17

♖e1 ♗e6 18 ♖h4 h6 19 ♖xh6! ♕b4 20 ♕g5 ♕g4 21 ♗h7+ ♔f8 22 ♖hxe6 ♕xg5 23 ♘xg5 fxe6 24 ♘xe6+ ♔f7 25 ♘xd8+ ♖xd8 with an extra pawn for White in Naiditsch-Nikolić, Bundesliga 2013/14.

c) 3...h6 is a quirky sideline pioneered by Viacheslav Eingorn and occasionally used by Nigel Short. Again an IQP approach is legitimate, and probably more effective than against the main lines: 4 ♘gf3 c5 5 c3 ♘c6 (5...♘f6 6 ♗d3 cxd4 7 cxd4 dxe4 8 ♘xe4 ♘xe4 9 ♗xe4 ♗b4+ 10 ♗d2 ♗xd2+ 11 ♕xd2 gave White an edge in Bosković-Shulman, Dallas 2006 – he can build up on the queenside and in the centre, while ...h6 slightly weakens the light squares so a set-up with ♗c2 and ♕d3 might also be effective) 6 ♗d3 cxd4 7 cxd4 dxe4 8 ♘xe4 ♗b4+ 9 ♘c3 ♘f6 10 0-0 0-0 11 ♗c2 ♕a5 12 ♕d3 ♖d8 13 ♘e4 ♗e7? (13...♘d5 and 13...♘xe4 are far more robust defences) was Moiseenko-Anttila, Jyväskylä 2015 and now 14 ♘xf6+ ♗xf6 15 ♕h7+ ♔f8 16 ♗d2 followed by 17 ♗c3 would have given White a strong initiative.

4 ♘gf3 ♘f6 5 e5 ♘d7 6 ♗d3 *(D)*
6...f6

6...♘b4 7 ♗e2 c5 8 c3 ♘c6 leads to a theoretical position from the Korchnoi Gambit (namely that arising after 3...♘f6 4 e5 ♘fd7 5 ♘gf3 c5 6 c3 ♘c6), but with the extra move ♗e2 for White. While White invariably continues with the more active 7 ♗d3 in the Korchnoi Gambit, I find it impossible to believe that Black can equalize a

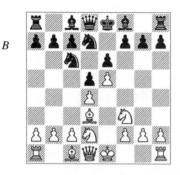

whole tempo down on established theory, especially where the extra tempo is a useful developing move. This position has been extensively tested by strong GMs and I shall give a few indications of how play might develop. 9 0-0 and then:

a) 9...g6 10 ♖e1 ♗g7 11 ♘f1 0-0 12 ♘g3 ♕b6 13 b3 cxd4 14 cxd4 f6 15 exf6 ♘xf6 16 ♗a3 ♖e8 was played in Navara-Firman, Bundesliga 2012/13, and now 17 ♖c1 seems slightly better for White.

b) 9...a5 10 a4 ♗e7 11 ♘b3 0-0 12 ♘xc5 ♘xc5 13 dxc5 ♗xc5 14 ♗d3 gives White good prospects.

c) 9...♕b6 10 ♘b3 c4 11 ♘bd2 and the white centre was rock solid in Vysochin-Y.Vovk, Lvov 2013.

d) 9...f6 10 exf6 ♘xf6 11 ♗d3!? cxd4 12 cxd4 ♗d6 is analogous to another theoretical position (with the knight on e2 instead of f3). The comparison seems in White's favour, since he can quickly occupy the e5 outpost; for instance, after 13 b3 0-0 14 ♗b2 ♗d7 15 ♘e5 ♕b6, as in Fedorchuk-Piorun, Wroclaw rapid 2014, I like 16 ♕e2 ♖ae8 17 ♘df3 with a bind.

7 exf6 ♕xf6 8 ♘f1 e5

The critical move, breaking out immediately.

After 8...♗d6, 9 ♘e3 prevents ...e5 and gives White a very promising position. A textbook demonstration of how to continue with White was given by Tarrasch expert GM Sergey Fedorchuk: 9...h6?! 10 c3 ♘e7 11 ♕e2 ♕f7 12 ♘g4 ♘f5 13 0-0 0-0 14 ♗d2 c5 15 ♖ae1 ♖e8 16 h3 ♖e7 17 ♘ge5 ♗xe5 18 ♘xe5 ♕f6 19 g4 ♘d6 20 f4 +− with a bind in Fedorchuk-Naumkin, Livigno 2011.

9 ♘e3 (D)

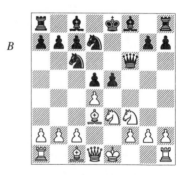

9...♘b6

9...♘xd4 is a tricky move. 10 ♘xd4 exd4 11 ♘xd5 ♕e5+ 12 ♕e2 seems to give White marginally better chances in a complex position:

a) 12...♕xe2+ 13 ♗xe2 ♗d6 14 ♗f4 ♘e5 (Black should settle for 14...♗xf4, but after 15 ♘xf4 Black is behind in development and will need to lose further time protecting his d4-pawn) 15 0-0-0 was excellent for White in M.Socko-Mkrtchian, Erfurt (women) 2014.

b) The computer move 12...♔d8! seems best, and now the untested 13 ♘f4 looks like a reasonable attempt for an edge.

10 dxe5 ♘xe5 11 ♘xe5 ♕xe5 12 0-0 ♗d6 13 f4 ♕f6

A forcing sequence has led to an interesting position. White has a kingside majority and hopes to generate some initiative on that side of the board. If Black can consolidate, his extra central pawn could prove important.

14 a4!

A typical device, gaining queenside space while harassing the knight on b6. Black has to stop this pawn with ...a5, after which White hopes that the weakening of the knight on b6 and the b5-square could be significant. On a very good day, there might even be a possibility of a rook-lift with ♖a3-g3/h3.

14...a5 (D)

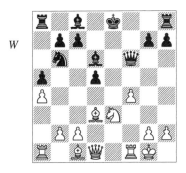

W

15 ♘g4!

Now White gains the bishop-pair, which should be an asset in a position with asymmetrical pawn-structures.

Fedorchuk had previously been successful with 15 ♕h5+ g6 16 ♕f3 0-0 17 f5 in Fedorchuk-Cornette, Salou 2011 but this is considerably more double-edged.

15...♗xg4 16 ♕xg4 0-0

16...♗c5+ 17 ♔h1 0-0 was tried in Godena-B.Kovačević, Padua 2013. White has a number of promising options but I like the game continuation: 18 ♗d2! ♕xb2? (a mistake, but otherwise White plays ♖ae1 or ♗c3, with a menacing kingside build-up) 19 ♕h3 g6 20 f5 gxf5 21 ♗xf5 and White's attack was already decisive.

17 ♗e3 ♖ae8 18 ♗xb6!

Trading in the advantage of the bishop-pair for an extra pawn.

18...cxb6 19 ♕h5 g6 20 ♕xd5+ ♔h8 21 g3 ♗c5+ 22 ♔h1 ♕xb2 23 ♕xb7 ♖e7 24 ♕d5 ♕d4 25 ♕xd4+ ♗xd4

Black has some drawing chances in the endgame due to the opposite-coloured bishops, but the presence of rooks makes his defensive task very difficult. Malakhov has one of the best techniques in the business and makes the position look like a forced win.

26 ♖ad1 ♗c5 27 ♔g2 ♔g7 28 h4 ♖f6 29 ♗b5 ♖fe6 30 ♖d5 ♖d6 31 ♖xd6 ♗xd6 32 ♖d1 ♗b4 33 ♖d5 ♖e6 34 ♗d3 ♖d6 35 ♖e5 ♔f7 36 h5 ♗c3 37 ♖g5 ♗f6 38 hxg6+ ♔g7 39 ♖b5 hxg6 40 ♔f3 ♗d8 41 ♖e5 ♗f6 42 ♖e8 g5 43 ♖b8 gxf4 44 ♖b7+ ♔f8 45 ♔xf4 ♗e7 46 ♔e5 ♖h6 47 g4 ♖f6 1-0

6 Pirc/Modern

The Pirc (1 e4 d6) and the Modern (1 e4 g6) are related openings where Black plays in a hypermodern spirit. White is allowed to occupy the centre, but Black hopes to break this centre down later in the game.

The Pirc and Modern have never been as popular as 1...c5, 1...e5, 1...e6 and 1...c6, and I don't anticipate either opening featuring heavily in the next world championship match. However, these openings have undergone a minor renaissance at top level, often being used in 'must win' games between elite players. At that level, preparation in the Sicilian or 1 e4 e5 is such that winning chances are hard to find with Black (especially against a well-prepared opponent who is happy with a draw), so this is almost the only remaining territory to obtain a fresh position.

White has a variety of responses against these lines, ranging from the extremely aggressive (systems based on f4, with or without ♗g5) to the moderately aggressive (systems with ♗e3, aiming to exchange dark-squared bishops with ♗h6 and/or castle queenside) to the positional (classical development with ♗e2, or systems based on g3).

My suggestion is based on the repertoire of strong GM (and c3 Sicilian expert) Sergei Tiviakov, who meets 1 e4 d6 2 d4 ♘f6 with 3 ♗d3, and responds to 1 e4 g6 2 d4 ♗g7 with 3 c3. You will note a strong resemblance between these lines and the system proposed against the 2...d6 variation of the c3 Sicilian. The main attractions of these systems are thematic consistency, ease of play (White occupies the centre in a straightforward fashion, and solidly protects his d4-pawn with c3), and the slight difference between these positions and what Pirc/Modern players typically get in the majority of their games.

An added bonus is that, by not meeting 1 e4 d6 2 d4 ♘f6 with 3 ♘c3, in addition to avoiding the 3 ♘c3 g6 main lines we avoid the sideline 3 ♘c3 c6 (which isn't bad) and the attempt to transpose to a Philidor after 3 ♘c3 e5 (i.e. 4 ♘f3 ♘bd7), which has become very popular.

This chapter features two main games. In Game 35 we examine lines specific to the Pirc move-order (mostly with Black avoiding ...g6), while Game 36 deals with the lines common to both openings.

Game 35
Handke – Broekmeulen
Barcelona 2011

1 e4 d6 2 d4 ♘f6 3 ♗d3 e5

3...g6 4 c3 will transpose to Game 36.

4 c3 *(D)*

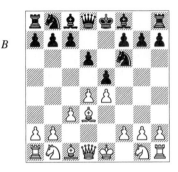

B

4...d5!?

This move is the critical attempt to exploit White's somewhat slow 3rd move. Other lines:

a) 4...♗e7 was played in a recent encounter between two strong GMs. Black's set-up is slightly passive, and after 5 ♘f3 ♘bd7 6 0-0 0-0 7 ♖e1 c6 8 a4 ♖e8 9 ♘bd2 White had a pleasant game in Svetushkin-Kovalenko, Moscow 2015. White is playing a Ruy Lopez (♘f1-g3 seems like a logical next step) while Black is struggling to find counterplay.

b) 4...♘bd7 5 ♘f3 g6 6 0-0 ♗g7 7 ♖e1 0-0 8 ♘bd2 ♖e8 9 ♘f1 b6 10 ♘g3 ♗b7 11 h3 exd4 12 cxd4 c5 13 d5 led to a white edge in Čabrilo-D.Popović, Belgrade blitz 2014. In these Benoni structures the bishop appears misplaced on b7, as it is restricted by the white centre.

c) 4...♘c6 has been the choice of some strong GMs. White replies 5 ♘f3 *(D)*, and then:

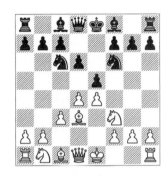

B

c1) 5...♗g4 loses some time with the bishop, so now 6 d5 is reasonable; for instance, 6...♘e7 7 h3 ♗d7 8 c4 ♘g6 9 ♘c3 (Black has scored very reasonably from this position but compared to a normal King's Indian I think White should be doing quite well) 9...♗e7 10 g3 (10 ♗e3 is also possible) 10...c6 11 h4 cxd5 12 cxd5 h6 13 ♔f1 0-0 14 h5 ♘h8 15 ♘h4 ± and Black was being squeezed in the game Iordachescu-Šolak, Turkish Team Ch, Konya 2012.

c2) 5...g6 6 0-0 ♗g7 7 ♘bd2 0-0 8 ♖e1 has been tested in over 150 games, many between strong GMs. I think White's strong centre gives him the easier play.

c3) 5...♗e7 6 ♘bd2 0-0 7 0-0 looks more pleasant for White. His centre is quite secure and the black knight on c6 is unstable. White shouldn't rush with d5 (which would give Black decent King's Indian counterplay after ...f5), but should just continue improving his position with ♖e1, h3, a4 and ♘f1-g3, while d5 might be a good idea some day.

5 dxe5 ♘xe4 6 ♘f3 *(D)*

Grabbing a pawn with 6 ♗xe4 dxe4 7 ♕a4+ is bad in view of 7...♗d7! 8 ♕xe4 ♗c6 with huge compensation after 9 ♕g4 h5 10 ♕h3 ♕d7! ∓.

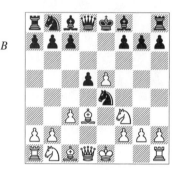

B

6...♘c6

Or:

a) 6...♘c5 7 ♗c2 ♗g4 8 ♗f4 ♗e7 9 ♘bd2 ♘c6 10 ♘b3 ♘e6 11 ♗g3 ♘g5 12 ♕d3 ♘xf3+ 13 gxf3 ♗h3 14 0-0-0 gave White good chances in Czakon-Lubczynski, Polish Team Ch 2015.

b) 6...♗e7 7 0-0 ♘c6 8 ♘bd2 ♘c5 9 ♗b5 leads to similar play as in our main game.

7 ♘bd2 ♘c5

White has a choice of bishop moves here, of which 8 ♗b1 is the most popular. I have chosen...

8 ♗b5

This scores well, has been used regularly by GMs, and is thematically consistent with the lines we examined after 1 e4 e5 2 ♘f3 ♘c6 3 ♗c4 ♘f6 4 d4 exd4 5 e5 d5.

8...♗d7

This is the most popular move and seems sensible, avoiding structural damage. Other moves:

a) 8...♗g4 9 h3 ♗h5 10 0-0 ♕d7 was played in Huss-Belotti, Swiss Ch, Grächen 1999. Now I like 11 ♘b3 a6 12 ♗e2 ♘e6 13 ♘fd4, when the white majority looks more mobile.

b) 8...a6 seems to compare favourably for White to our Two Knights lines. After 9 ♗xc6+ bxc6 10 0-0 a5 (otherwise b4 gives White good control of the dark squares) 11 ♖e1 ♗e7 12 ♘b3 the play is balanced. White can continue with themes from the Two Knights, trying to restrain the pawns on c7, c6 and d5.

c) 8...♗e7 9 ♘b3 0-0 (9...♘xb3 10 axb3 0-0 11 h3!?, stopping ...♗g4, was pleasant for White in A.Fedorov-V.Fedorov, Russia Cup, Moscow 1996) 10 ♗e3 ♘xb3 11 axb3 ♗g4 12 ♗xc6 bxc6 was Godena-Halkias, European Ch, Plovdiv 2012. Now, instead of the game's 13 b4 f6!, I suggest 13 h3 (D). Then:

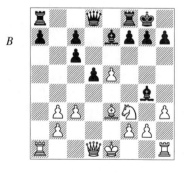

B

c1) 13...♗h5 14 b4 is an improved version of the game, since 14...f6 can be met by 15 g4!? (15 e6 is also interesting) 15...♗f7 16 0-0 with good chances.

c2) After 13...♗xf3 14 ♕xf3 f6 15 exf6 ♖xf6 16 ♕e2 perhaps White has an edge due to his superior structure and more active bishop, though Black's development is excellent.

9 0-0 *(D)*

I like this simple move, which has only been played in one game in my database. 9 ♕e2 has been extensively tested.

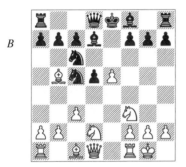

B

9...a6

Or:

a) The quiet 9...♗e7 is possible, but White has an easy game after 10 ♘b3.

b) 9...♘xe5 is critical. 10 ♘xe5 ♗xb5 11 ♖e1 ♗e7 12 a4! seems to give White excellent compensation; for instance:

b1) 12...♗d7 13 ♘b3 ♘xb3 14 ♕xb3 ♗c8 15 ♕b5+ c6 16 ♕e2 0-0! (giving back the material seems much more sensible than keeping the king in the centre with something such as 16...♕d6) 17 ♘xc6 bxc6 18 ♕xe7 with hopes of an endgame edge based on his superior structure.

b2) 12...♗xa4 13 ♖xa4 ♘xa4 14 ♕xa4+ leaves Black with nominal

material equality (rook and two pawns for two minor pieces), but in a complicated middlegame such as this I would prefer the pieces since White has good chances of generating strong threats against the black king.

b3) 12...♗c6 13 b4 (13 ♕e2 is also interesting) 13...♘e6 14 b5 ♗d7 15 ♘df3 ♗c8 16 ♖a2! 0-0 17 ♖d2, winning back the pawn. Black's bishop-pair compensates for the pressure and the game may be objectively roughly level after 17...♕e8 18 ♖xd5 a6. However, I think a human would find the white position easier to handle.

10 ♗xc6 ♗xc6 11 ♘b3 *(D)*

11 ♘d4 ± is also a good option for White.

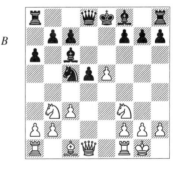

B

11...♗b5?

Clearly Black thought he was either forcing an exchange on c5 or gaining the bishop-pair after 12 ♖e1 ♘d3. While White retains some advantage after either of these options, he has something much stronger.

11...♗e7 is sounder. After 12 ♘fd4 ♕d7 13 ♘xc6 ♕xc6 14 ♘d4 ♕d7 15 ♕f3 White has a pleasant Two Knights position, with active pieces and a mobile kingside majority.

12 ♗g5! ♗e7?

This loses, but Black's position was already dire:

a) 12...♕c8 13 ♘xc5 ♗xf1 (after 13...♗xc5 14 ♕xd5 ♗b6 15 ♖fe1 White is a healthy pawn to the good, but this should probably be tried) 14 ♕xd5! with overwhelming compensation for the exchange; for instance, 14...c6 15 ♕d4 ♗e2 16 e6! ± and the black king will struggle to make it to safety without heavy material losses.

b) 12...♕d7 13 ♘xc5 ♗xc5 14 e6!! breaks open the position in White's favour. 14...♕d6 (14...fxe6 15 ♘e5 and 16 ♕h5+ is lethal) 15 exf7+ ♔xf7 16 ♗f4!! ♕xf4 17 ♕xd5+ ♔f6 18 ♖fe1! and Black is fighting for survival after 18...♗xf2+ 19 ♔xf2 ±.

13 ♘xc5 ♗xf1

13...♗xg5 14 ♘xb7 ♕c8 15 ♕xd5 is also winning for White.

14 ♘xb7 ♕c8 15 ♕xd5 ♗xg5 16 ♘xg5 0-0 17 ♕e4 1-0

An excellent crush, especially since Black (rated 2388) is hardly a weak player.

Game 36
Yakovenko – Rapport
Greek Team Ch, Achaia 2013

1 e4 g6 2 d4 ♗g7

2...♘f6 is the so-called North Sea Defence, made famous by Magnus Carlsen's loss with Black to Mickey Adams. Fortunately no extra knowledge is required here, since 3 ♗d3 d6

4 ♘f3 ♗g7 5 0-0 0-0 6 c3 transposes to the position after White's 6th move.

3 c3 d6 4 ♘f3 ♘f6 5 ♗d3 0-0 6 0-0 *(D)*

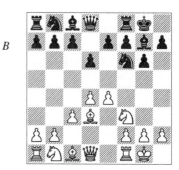

Black now has to find a way to challenge White's centre, a task which is far from simple. I really like having the pawn on c3, securely defending d4.

6...♘c6

This might look odd, but the idea is well known in the Pirc/Modern. Black provokes d5 at the cost of two tempi, in order to play against the white centre and provoke potential dark-squared weaknesses. Other moves:

a) 6...c5 will transpose to a line of the c3 Sicilian after 7 h3 cxd4 8 cxd4 (see Game 24).

b) In Tiviakov's latest game in this line (at the time of writing) his opponent opted for 6...♗g4 7 h3 ♗xf3 8 ♕xf3 ♘c6 9 ♗b5 ♘d7 10 ♗g5 a6 11 ♗a4 b5 12 ♗c2, but with the bishop-pair, a space advantage and a perfect centre, only White could be better in Tiviakov-Bajarani, Nakhchivan 2015.

7 d5

Black intended ...e5, so I like this move.

7...♘b8 8 c4

White now has a Classical King's Indian set-up with some extra tempi and his bishop on d3 (where it is arguably more active). One important point to note is that, unlike in the real Classical King's Indian, the centre hasn't been closed by ...e5. This means that Black's terrifying kingside attack is much harder to execute, since advances like ...f5, ...f4 and ...g5 are highly dubious when the opponent can play in the centre.

8...a5

A typical regrouping, preparing to bring the knight to c5 without fear of harassment by b4.

9 ♘c3 ♘a6 10 ♗e3 *(D)*

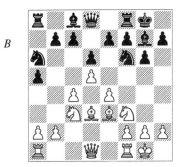

10...e5 11 dxe6!?

An important moment. Any other move would lead to a closed centre where Black can attack on the kingside. While White might be better there, Black obtains extremely dangerous King's Indian counterplay which an 1 e4 player may have no experience

of dealing with. Accordingly, taking *en passant* is my recommendation, when White relies on his space advantage and actively placed pieces.

11...♗xe6 12 h3 *(D)*

Controlling the g4-square and so restraining both ...♘g4 and ...♗g4. This position has been tested in two games between very strong GMs, and the provisional conclusion is that Black's defence is quite difficult.

12...♖e8

12...♘b4 led to similar play in Tiviakov-Rakhmanov, Minsk 2014: 13 ♘d4 ♘xd3 14 ♕xd3 ♘d7 15 ♕e2 ♖e8 16 ♖ad1 ♕e7 17 ♘db5! (this is an excellent square for the white knight in these structures once Black has played ...a5, since ...c6 is difficult to arrange so b5 is effectively an outpost; of course Black could have prevented this with ...c6 earlier, but this would have weakened the d6-pawn) 17...♖ac8 18 ♖fe1 ♘f6 19 b3 ♗d7 20 f3 (White's last two moves have solidified his structure; Black has no realistic prospects of achieving any breaks – ...a4, ...d5 or ...f5 – but White needs to demonstrate a way to improve his position) 20...h6 21 ♕f2 ♚h7 22 ♗d4 (now e5 is threatened, so Black tries to change the course of the game) 22...♗xb5 23 cxb5 c6 24 bxc6 bxc6 25 ♕d2 ±. Black's structure is full of weaknesses.

13 ♖c1 ♘b4 14 ♘d4 ♘xd3 15 ♕xd3 ♘d7 16 b3 ♘c5 17 ♕d2 ♗d7

Black could try to mix things up with 17...a4!?, intending 18 b4 ♗xc4 19 bxc5 dxc5 followed by ...♗xf1.

18 f3 ♘e6 19 ♘xe6 ♖xe6 (D)

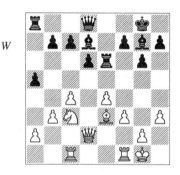

20 ♗d4!

'Halving' the bishop-pair by exchanging the more active piece on g7.

20...♗xd4+ 21 ♕xd4 ♗c6 22 ♘d5

This knight can't be tolerated indefinitely, but exchanging it will leave a chronic weakness on c7. Black might already be strategically lost, though the engines think he is only slightly worse.

22...♖c8 23 ♕d2!

Aiming to force ...b6, when ...c6 will be all but impossible to achieve after the exchange on d5.

23...b6 24 ♚h2 ♗xd5 25 cxd5 ♖e5 26 ♖c6 f5 (D)

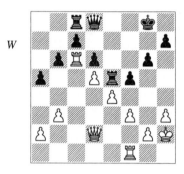

Rapport is an active player and correctly strives for counterplay.

27 exf5 ♖xf5 28 ♖fc1 ♖e5 29 ♖1c2 ♕d7 30 ♕c1! ♖xd5?

This loses on the spot, but 30...♖e7 31 ♖xb6 also looks horrible.

31 ♖xc7 ♖xc7 32 ♖xc7 ♕e6 33 ♕h6 ♖h5 34 ♕g7# (1-0)

7 Scandinavian

1 e4 d5 2 exd5 ♛xd5 3 ♘c3

The Scandinavian is an opening which remains reasonably popular at club level. Structurally, it can lead to positions that resemble the Rubinstein French or the Caro-Kann. However, it has the attraction of having considerably less theory than those openings. Certain lines have been rehabilitated, most notably 2 exd5 ♛xd5 3 ♘c3 ♛d6, which is the main defence of strong GM Sergei Tiviakov. It is also pleasant to be able to impose your will on the opponent from move 1!

White has a number of good responses to the Scandinavian, some of which involve more theory than others. My proposed solution was suggested to me by GM Kevin Spraggett based on some games he had seen and played. Rather than play for d4, when Black can try to base his counterplay around attacking or exchanging this pawn, White chooses a seemingly more modest formation with ♗c4 and d3. This can be followed up with some aggressive formations involving either ♛e2 and 0-0-0, or ♘ge2, 0-0 and a quick f4-f5 (which, of course, is not available when the knight is on f3). This system is gaining some traction amongst strong players and has the added advantage of being playable

against all of Black's main queen moves after 3 ♘c3.

I have also offered recommendations (in Game 39) against Black's option of 2...♘f6, which can lead to tricky gambit play.

Game 37
Efimenko – Kryvoruchko
Ukrainian Ch, Kiev 2013

1 e4 d5 2 exd5 ♛xd5 3 ♘c3 ♛a5

This is the traditional main line (and was even tried in the Kasparov-Anand world championship match in 1995), but recently attention has shifted to 3...♛d6, which we examine in Game 38 (together with a note on 3...♛d8).

4 ♗c4 *(D)*

4 d4 is the main move but, as explained in the chapter introduction, we have a different idea in mind.

4...♘f6 5 d3 c6 6 ♗d2 *(D)*

It is also possible to start with 6 ♕e2 but I prefer the text, a developing move which gains time on the black queen.

6...♕c7

It seems prudent to move the queen and this is the most popular option. Other approaches:

a) 6...♕d8 7 ♘f3 e6 8 ♕e2 ♗e7 9 d4 0-0 led to a shock defeat for White in Caruana-Valsecchi, Italian Ch, Martina Franca 2008, but this had nothing to do with the opening. Black has shut in his light-squared bishop (the development of which is one of the major aims of the Scandinavian), and would have a passive and poor position after the simple 10 0-0 ±.

b) 6...♗g4 was tried by French super-GM Laurent Fressinet, but after 7 f3 ♗h5 (7...♗d7 ± seems like the lesser evil) 8 ♘d5 ♕d8 9 ♘xf6+ gxf6 White had excellent play in D.Roos-Fressinet, Versailles (team event) 2006 and could have added to his initiative with 10 h4 (threatening to trap the bishop) 10...♗g6 11 h5 ♗f5 12 ♘e2 ±.

7 ♕e2 *(D)*

An example of the second plan mentioned in the chapter introduction goes as follows: 7 ♘ge2 ♗f5 8 0-0 e6 9 ♘g3 ♗g6 10 f4 ♗c5+ 11 ♔h1 0-0 12 ♘ce4 ♗e7?! (Black should prefer 12...♗xe4, although even there White has a very reasonable position) 13 f5 exf5 14 ♘xf5 ♗xf5 15 ♖xf5 with good attacking chances in Mokshanov-Yanchenko, Moscow 2015.

7...♗f5

A natural development but, as we shall see, the bishop can be a target here. Other moves:

a) 7...♘bd7 8 a3 ♘b6 9 ♗a2 ♗g4 10 ♘f3 e6 11 h3 ♗h5 12 g4 ♗g6 13 0-0-0 ♗d6 was Short-Ateka, Dar es Salaam 2013. Here I like 14 ♔b1 0-0-0 15 ♖he1 with a pleasant position.

b) 7...e6 is passive and locks in the bishop on c8. White can get a good game with normal play; for instance, 8 ♘f3 ♘bd7 9 d4 ♗d6 10 0-0 0-0 was Perunović-Ostojić, Serbian Team Ch, Valjevo 2012 and now I like the simple 11 ♖fe1, when Black is extremely passive, and suffering with less space without having exchanged any pieces.

8 h3 *(D)*

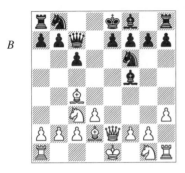

8...h5

Aiming to stop g4, but this comes at a positional cost. It is also notable that Black is way behind in development.

8...e6 9 g4 ♗g6 10 f4 ♗e7 11 ♘f3 ♘bd7 12 0-0-0 gives White a promising attacking position; for example, 12...♘b6?! 13 ♖de1 ♔f8 14 ♗b3 ♗d6 15 ♘e5 ♗xe5 was Short-D.Lioe, Calvia Olympiad 2004 and now 16 fxe5 ♘fd7 17 ♔b1 ± would have left the misplaced black king facing a vicious attack.

9 ♘f3 ♘bd7 10 0-0!?

White, with some justification, sees the weakening of the g5-square as a major positional concession, and seeks to shift the game back into quiet channels.

There is nothing wrong with the sharper continuation either: 10 0-0-0 ♗g6 (I would prefer to start immediate counterplay with 10...b5, although White still has the more promising

game) 11 ♘h4 ♗h7 (Beliakov-Bocharov, Sochi rapid 2015) and now 12 g4! ± is very dangerous for Black.

10...♘b6

10...e6 11 ♘d4 is good for White, who will gain the bishop-pair since any bishop retreat will be met by a strong sacrifice on e6.

11 ♗b3 ♘bd5 12 ♘xd5 ♘xd5 13 ♘d4

13 ♖fe1 0-0-0 14 ♕e5 gives White a serious advantage in the endgame.

13...♗d7 14 ♗xd5 cxd5 15 c4 *(D)*

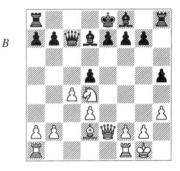

Efimenko has come up with a creative solution to open lines and discourage queenside castling.

15...dxc4 16 dxc4 e6 17 ♘b5 ♗xb5 18 cxb5 ♗d6 19 ♗c3 0-0 20 ♕xh5

Unsurprisingly, Black's h5-pawn has dropped off and White has secured a solid extra pawn. The game ultimately ended in a draw but this can hardly be counted as an opening success for Black.

20...♖fd8 21 ♖fd1 ♗f8 22 ♕e5 ♕e7 23 a4 ♖ac8 24 ♕e4 b6 25 g3 ♖d7 26 ♖xd7 ♕xd7 27 h4 ♖c5 28 ♕a8 f6 29 ♔g2 ♔f7 30 ♕e4 ♖d5 31

Xh1 &c5 32 h5 Xf5 33 f3 Wd5 34
Wxd5 Xxd5 35 h6 Xd8 (D)

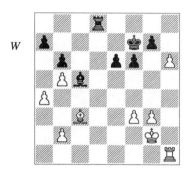

36 hxg7?!

36 h7!? looks strong, as White can
use the time Black must spend dealing
with the h-pawn to make inroads on
the queenside; e.g., 36...Xh8 37 f4
&g6 38 Xd1 and Xd7.

36...&xg7 37 f4 Xd3 38 g4?! &d4

Now Black has enough counterplay.

**39 Xh3 Xd1 40 Xh1 Xd3 41 Xh3
Xd1 42 b3 e5 43 fxe5 fxe5 44 &xd4
Xxd4 45 &g3 Xd3+ 46 &g2 Xd4 47
&g3 Xd3+ 48 &g2 ½-½**

Game 38
Pardo Simon – J. Ramirez
Montcada 2012

1 e4 d5 2 exd5 Wxd5 3 &c3 Wd6

As I mentioned in the chapter introduction, this is the modern main line.
Sergei Tiviakov plays it all the time,
and a number of other GMs regularly
rely on it. The recent book *Understanding the Scandinavian* by Sergey
Kasparov covers it in some detail, so

you may start to face it increasingly
often.

3...Wd8 (D), the solid but passive
'Banker' variation, obviously gives
White an easier time proving an ad-
vantage.

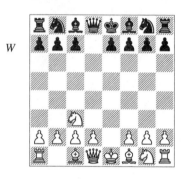

Here too, a system based on &c4
and d3 works well. 4 &c4 &f6 5 d3 c6
6 &ge2 &bd7 7 a3 (a useful precau-
tion, preserving the bishop from exchange in the case of ...b5 and ...&c5)
7...e6 8 0-0 &e7 9 &h1 &b6 10 &a2
&bd5. Now there are several ways to
continue but the standard approach is
quite possible, viz. 11 f4!?, and now:

a) 11...Wb6?! (this just gives White
time to kick the knight from d5) 12
&a4 Wd8 13 c4 &c7 14 &ac3 b5
(14...0-0 is more solid, but after 15
&e3 b6 16 &g3 &b7 17 We2 White
can continue with f5 and/or d4; Black
has no counterplay) 15 Wc2 &b7 16
&e3 0-0 17 Xad1 with a space advantage and the better chances for White
in Franke-Nautsch, Germany (team
event) 2005/6.

b) 11...0-0 is better, when White
can continue in aggressive fashion with

12 ♘g3 ♘xc3 (otherwise ♘ce4 would have been possible, with some initiative) 13 bxc3 ♗d6 14 ♕f3 with an unclear game in which White has some attacking chances.

We now return to 3...♕d6 *(D)*:

4 ♗c4 ♘f6

I have played with the move-order of this game, which actually began with 4...a6 5 d3 ♘f6.

5 d3 a6

By far the most popular move, and the best-scoring one.

6 a4!

I couldn't find anything convincing in the lines where Black is allowed to play ...b5 and ...♗b7, since his light-squared bishop is on a fantastic diagonal (and will threaten the white king in the event of kingside castling), while castling queenside is double-edged at best since Black has already started his pawn-storm on that wing.

Instead I like this time-out, restricting Black's queenside play. As we shall see in this game, White still hopes in some lines to use the plan with ♘ge2, 0-0 and f4.

6...♘c6

This is a very good square for the knight now that b4 has been weakened.

7 ♘ge2 ♗f5

Or:

a) 7...g6 8 0-0 ♗g7 9 h3 0-0 10 ♗f4 e5 11 ♗e3 ♘d4 and Black had no problems in Toma-Khurtsidze, European Women's Team Ch, Porto Carras 2011.

b) 7...e5 is the most popular move. 8 0-0 ♗e7 9 ♘g3 0-0 10 ♘ge4 ♘xe4 11 dxe4 was equal in Petzold-Mertens, 2nd Bundesliga 2011/12.

8 0-0 e6 9 ♘g3 ♗g6 *(D)*

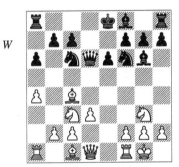

10 f4?!

But 10 ♘ge4 ♘xe4 11 ♘xe4 ♗xe4 12 dxe4 ♕e5 is viable for Black since after 13 ♕f3 ♗d6 14 g3 ♕c5 15 ♗d3 ♘e5 White is unable to keep the bishop-pair.

10...♕d4+

10...0-0-0 is better; for instance, 11 ♔h1 ♔b8 12 ♗e3 with very unclear play in which the computer prefers Black.

11 ♔h1 ♗c5

Again 11...0-0-0 was a more prudent course.

12 f5 &xf5 13 &xf5 exf5 14 &xf5 0-0-0

This is an interesting position. It looks rather dangerous to expose the white king by pushing the f-pawn, especially after castling on opposite sides. However, it seems that he is active enough to get a good position with this operation.

15 &g5! &e7

15...&e5 is interesting, but then 16 &xf6!? (16 &xf6 gxf6 17 &f1 is more sober) 16...gxf6 17 &xf6 &hf8 18 &f1! is a promising exchange sacrifice.

16 &f1 *(D)*

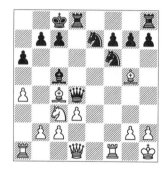

16...&g4?

16...&g6 ± is better.

17 &e4 f5 18 &e6+ &b8 19 &xf5 &xf5 20 &xf5 &xe4 21 dxe4 &xd1+ 22 &xd1 &f2+ 23 &xf2 &xf2

White is a pawn up with good winning chances.

24 g3 h6 25 &f4 &e8 26 &g2 g5 27 &xf2 gxf4 28 &f3 fxg3 29 hxg3 &f8+ 30 &e3 &g8 31 e5 &xg3+ 32

&f4 &g2 33 e6 &e2 34 &f5 c5 35 &f6 &f2+ 36 &g7 &e2 37 &f7 &f2+ 38 &e8 &c7 39 e7 &f6 40 &d7+ &c6 41 &d8 1-0

Game 39
G. Papp – Hangweyrer
Austrian Team Ch 2014/15

1 e4 d5 2 exd5 &f6 *(D)*

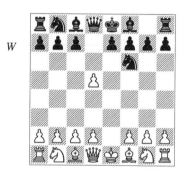

3 d4

White faces a major decision at move 3. Arguably the most consistent choice for our repertoire is 3 c4, after which 3...c6 4 &c3 cxd5 5 cxd5 transposes into my recommendation against the Caro-Kann. If you know your opponent goes 3...c6, and you like playing against the Caro-Kann, then this is a legitimate choice. The problem is that you have to be ready for 3 c4 e6!?, the Icelandic Gambit. Here Black gets a lot of compensation if White takes on e6. An alternative is to transpose into an Exchange French with 4 &f3 exd5 5 d4 (reaching a position which might be reached after 1 e4 e6 2 d4 d5 3 exd5 exd5 4 &f3 &f6 5 c4) – this leads to an IQP, but in a relatively comfortable version for Black.

My initial plan was to recommend 3 ♘f3 (when 3...♗g4?! 4 ♗b5+ leads to a pleasant white edge), but Graham Burgess noted that 3...♕xd5 leaves White unable to play systems based on ♘ge2 (which I have recommended against 2...♕xd5). That said, you may wish to investigate this option, since in the line 2 exd5 ♕xd5 3 ♘f3, Black normally chooses 3...♗g4, which generates more rapid counterplay (versus White's plan of d4 followed by c4) than does the move 3...♘f6 (to which he is already committed in our move-order here). For a detailed discussion of these points, see Sergey Kasparov's *Understanding the Scandinavian.*

Accordingly I have opted for 3 d4, which is the most popular move here.

3...♘xd5

This is the traditional and most popular move.

3...♗g4!? *(D)* is the Portuguese Gambit, which has been championed by Australian GM David Smerdon with excellent results. At the time of writing Smerdon has just released his magnum opus on this line (fittingly called *Smerdon's Scandinavian*) and the line might become more popular in practice.

Lines where White aims to hang on to the pawn with f3 and c4 seem to give Black rich compensation. I suggest playing less ambitiously with 4 ♗b5+, and now:

a) 4...c6?! 5 dxc6 gives White an extra pawn on more favourable terms

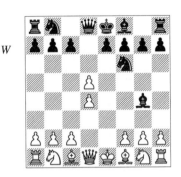

than in the main lines. 5...♕a5+ (after 5...♘xc6 6 ♘f3 e6 7 h3 ♗h5 8 0-0 ♗d6 9 c3 Black had zero compensation in Rombaldoni-Mevel, Cappelle la Grande 2014) 6 ♘c3 ♘xc6 7 ♘e2 0-0-0 8 ♗xc6 bxc6 (8...e5 9 ♕d3 bxc6 10 0-0 transposes) was Fressinet-J.Sanchez, Paris blitz 2009 and now I like 9 0-0 e5 10 ♕d3, when Black doesn't have a clear route to full compensation; for instance, 10...exd4 11 ♘xd4 ♕b6 (11...c5? 12 ♘c6!) 12 ♘ce2 and 12...♗xe2 is met by 13 ♕f5+ ♔b7 14 ♘xe2.

b) 4...♘bd7 is the most popular move and was Smerdon's choice when faced with this line. Here I think White is obviously slightly better after 5 ♗e2 ♗xe2 6 ♕xe2 ♘xd5 7 ♘f3, followed by 0-0, ♖e1 and c4, with a space advantage and excellent central control.

4 ♘f3 *(D)*

4...g6

Or:

a) 4...♗g4 fails to put any pressure on White's position. A recent example from a strong French GM: 5 ♗e2 ♘d7 (5...e6 can also be met by 0-0, h3 and c4) 6 c4 ♘5f6 7 ♕b3 ♖b8

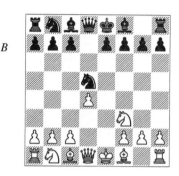

8 ♘c3 g6?! (a set-up with 8...e6 makes it easier for Black to keep his light-squared bishop) 9 h3 ♗xf3 10 ♗xf3 gave White more space and the bishop-pair in Mazé-Ov.Matras, Helsingør 2015.

b) 4...♗f5 is well met by the simple 5 ♗d3! ♗xd3 6 ♕xd3. White will castle, play ♖e1 and kick the knight with c4. Black has no central influence and no counterplay.

5 c4 ♘b6 6 a4

One of the ideas behind White's sixth move can be seen from an examination of the more common 6 ♘c3 ♗g7 7 c5 (White can also safeguard his centre with 7 h3 0-0 8 ♗e3) 7...♘d5 8 ♗c4 c6 9 ♕b3 0-0!. Now if White grabs the pawn with 10 ♘xd5 (10 0-0 is more common, after which Black plays 10...♘xc3 11 bxc3 b5 12 cxb6 axb6 with an edge for White) 10...cxd5 11 ♗xd5 ♘c6! Black has excellent compensation due, in part, to the threat of ...♘a5, exploiting the poor protection of the bishop on d5. For example, 12 0-0 ♘a5! 13 ♕a4 ♕xd5 14 ♕xa5 ♗g4 15 ♘e5 ♕xd4 16 ♘xg4 ♕xg4 17 ♕b5 ♕e4 18 ♗e3 ♖ad8 19 ♖fe1 ♕d5

20 h3 was agreed drawn in Pilavov-Akbaev, Dombay 2014. Black is certainly no worse in the final position and must have been very satisfied with such an easy draw against a 2600+ opponent.

6...a5

6...♗g7 has been played in a few games, but after 7 a5 ♘6d7 8 ♘c3 (D) Black's position looks appalling to me. He has no weaknesses, but this is largely because he has absolutely no space! Now:

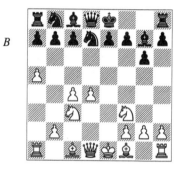

a) 8...c5 9 d5 0-0 10 ♗e3 ♘a6 11 ♗e2 ♘f6 12 0-0 favoured White in Palac-A.Muzychuk, Slovenian Team Ch, Murska Sobota 2007. Perhaps Black should have transferred her f6-knight to d6, but I still prefer White in view of his massive space advantage. In the game she went for a quick ...e6, but opening the position favoured the better-developed white forces.

b) 8...0-0 9 ♗e2 ♘c6 10 d5 ♘b4 11 0-0 and White's extra space guaranteed him the more comfortable game in Swiercz-B.Savchenko, European Ch, Budva 2009.

7 c5 ♘d5 8 ♗c4 ♗g7 9 ♘c3 *(D)*

White can start with 9 ♕b3 but, as will appear from the next note, the exchange on c3 is not to be feared.

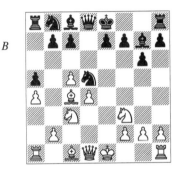

9...c6

Or:

a) 9...♘xc3 10 bxc3 ± is a very favourable transformation for White. His bishop on c4 rules the a2-g8 diagonal, his centre has been strengthened and the half-open b-file is a good avenue for attack; in particular, Black will have to deal with the b7 weakness.

b) 9...♘b4 10 0-0 0-0 11 h3 b6 was played in Ni Hua-A.Muzychuk, Wijk aan Zee 2010. Then I like 12 ♕e2 ♗a6 13 ♖d1 ± with a very active position.

10 ♕b3 0-0 11 ♘xd5!

As in the position without the inclusion of a4 a5, White can castle here, with reasonable chances. However, I think it is more critical to take the pawn.

11...cxd5 12 ♗xd5 ♘c6 13 ♗e3 e6

13...e5 is an ambitious idea, but it doesn't work. After 14 ♘xe5 ♘xe5 15 dxe5 ♗xe5 (O.Ruiz-Kleinplatz, Montreal 2014), the simplest reply is 16 ♖d1 ♕e8 17 0-0 ±. White is overwhelmingly active and b7 is chronically weak.

14 ♗xc6

Now Black gets reasonable compensation, in part due to the ability to find work for the light-squared bishop on the a6-f1 diagonal.

I would suggest instead 14 ♗c4! ♘xd4 15 ♘xd4 ♗xd4 16 ♖d1 e5 17 0-0. Black will probably lose the pawn back shortly; for instance, 17...♗f5 18 ♗d5!.

14...bxc6 15 0-0 ♗a6 16 ♖fe1 ♖b8 17 ♕c2 *(D)*

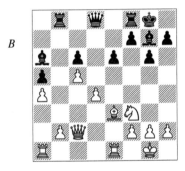

17...♕d5

It can be seen that Black's construction is tough to crack, though I would still take White. However, from a theoretical viewpoint White's alternative on move 14 looks stronger.

18 ♗f4 ♖b3 19 ♗e5 f6 20 ♗d6 ♖a8 21 ♖e3 ♖b4 22 ♖ae1 ♗c8 23 ♗c7 ♕a2 24 ♕e4 ♗d7 ½-½

8 Alekhine

1 e4 ♘f6

The Alekhine Defence is an opening which has never achieved mainstream status, but remains a viable option for players looking for an unbalanced game. For many years the leading regular exponent of the Alekhine Defence was GM Alex Baburin, my team-mate on the Irish Olympiad team, and I have learned a lot from him about this opening (often by failing to obtain any advantage in my white games against Alex!). The system I am recommending is one which Alex has often viewed as particularly annoying for Black to face:

2 e5 ♘d5 3 d4 d6 4 c4 ♘b6 5 exd6
(D)

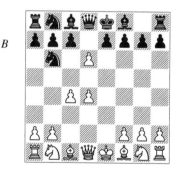

B

Avoiding the main line based on 4 ♘f3 (when White has good chances for an edge, but Black can choose

from several reasonable systems) and the Four Pawns Attack with 5 f4 (which is an ambitious try to blast Black off the board, but one with a lot of theory and serious risk for White if things go wrong).

Instead White forces Black to make a serious decision early in the opening: to play for gradual equality after 5...exd6, or to unbalance the play (with significant risk) by choosing 5...cxd6. We shall examine them in that order in the next two games.

Game 40
Duda – Bortnyk
Wroclaw rapid 2014

1 e4 ♘f6

Developing the other knight with 1...♘c6 is also tried sometimes. I suggest the simple 2 ♘f3 *(D)*.

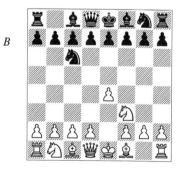

B

Then we shall transpose to 1...e5 lines if Black plays 2...e5. His other continuations give White easy play:

a) 2...d5 3 exd5 ♕xd5 4 ♘c3 is a Scandinavian where Black has committed to an early ...♘c6.

b) 2...d6 3 d4 ♘f6 4 ♘c3 ♗g4 5 ♗e3 gives White a perfect centre at no cost.

c) 2...♘f6 3 e5 ♘d5 4 d4 d6 5 c4 ♘b6 transposes to an Alekhine line where 6 e6!? is a sharp pawn sacrifice. The calmer 6 exd6 exd6 7 d5 ♘e5 gives White a choice between 8 ♘xe5 dxe5 9 ♗d3, with space and kingside chances, and 8 ♘d4!? intending f4.

2 e5 ♘d5 3 d4 d6 4 c4 ♘b6 5 exd6 exd6 *(D)*

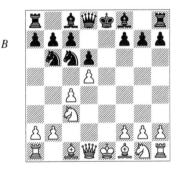

The most solid continuation. Black aims to complete his development with ...♗e7, ...0-0 and ...♘c6. He hopes to find a useful square for his light-squared bishop. In some positions the break ...d5 can give Black counterplay. The pawn-structure is now symmetrical but White has considerably more space. The system of development I am proposing aims to put White's pieces on useful squares but is also directed against Black's light-squared bishop, in particular by avoiding a pin by ♘f3 ♗g4.

6 ♘c3 ♗e7

Black can try to avoid the set-up in the main game by attacking d4 with 6...♘c6 (thanks to Alekhine expert Graham Burgess for bringing this to my attention!). Then 7 ♗e3 is a quiet continuation. White aims for ♗d3 and ♘ge2 (like in our main game), but there is a key difference: Black will often be able to free his game with ...♘b4, exchanging the bishop, with chances of equality. Therefore I recommend the critical 7 d5 *(D)*, and now:

a) Houdini is initially enthusiastic about the untested 7...♕e7+, but soon realizes that 8 ♗e2 ♘e5 9 f4! is strong for White, based on the following variations:

a1) 9...♘exc4? 10 ♔f2! ± leaves Black's position on the brink of collapse. White threatens ♗xc4 followed by ♕a4+, but otherwise intends the simple ♘f3 and ♖e1. For example,

10...c6 (after 10...♘a5 11 b4 ♘ac4 12 ♘f3 +− there is no good response to ♖e1) 11 ♘f3 ♔d8 12 ♖e1 ♘a5 13 ♔g1!! +− with overwhelming compensation.

a2) 9...♘g4 10 ♕d4 (preventing ...♘e3) 10...c5 11 dxc6 bxc6 12 ♘f3 c5 13 ♕e4 ± with an edge for White.

b) 7...♘e5 8 f4 ♘ed7 (8...♘g4 9 ♘f3 g6 10 h3 favoured White in Bagi-Gažik, Slovakian Team Ch 2012/13; 8...♘g6 9 ♘f3 ♗e7 10 ♗d3 with a space advantage) 9 ♘f3 ♗e7 has been played in several games, but I like the untested suggestion of GM Niclas Huschenbeth: 10 ♗d3!?. His analysis continues 10...0-0 11 0-0 ♘c5 12 ♗e3 ♘xd3 13 ♕xd3 g6 14 ♘d4 with an edge − White's space advantage outweighs Black's bishop-pair, which is rather passive at the moment.

7 ♗d3 ♘c6 8 ♘ge2 (D)

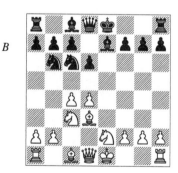

B

8...♗g4

This move is more popular than 8...0-0, which will normally transpose after 9 0-0. A nice example of White's general strategy here is Drenchev-L.Popov, Bulgarian Team Ch, Sunny Beach 2014, which continued 9 b3 ♖e8 10 0-0 ♗f6 11 ♗e3 ♗g4 12 ♕d2 ♗xe2. This avoids 13 f3 (which would most likely transpose to our main game) but still allows White a nice position after 13 ♘xe2 d5 14 c5 ♘d7 15 b4 ♘f8 16 b5 ♘e7. I find it hard to understand the appeal of such a position for Black – White has a massive space advantage and the bishop-pair for no compensation. Any reasonable continuation here looks promising, but Drenchev was obviously in the mood for blood: 17 g4!? ♘eg6 18 f4 and Black was gradually pushed off the board.

9 f3

Taking away the option of an exchange on e2 although, as Drenchev-L.Popov in the previous note illustrates, this exchange is not always in Black's favour.

9...♗h5 10 0-0 0-0 11 b3! (D)

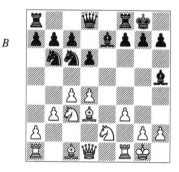

B

An important move, protecting both the c4-pawn and the c4-square (otherwise ...d5, c5 ♘c4 might be an option for Black). Black's position is playable but he lacks space and counterplay.

11...♗f6

11...♗g6 12 ♗xg6 hxg6 13 ♗e3 is similar to the game.

11...♖e8 can lead to different play. 12 ♗e3 *(D)* and then:

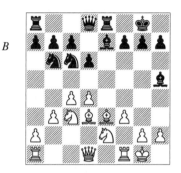

a) 12...♗g6 13 ♗xg6 hxg6 14 d5 ♘e5 15 ♗d4 with a space advantage and more active pieces in Goh Wei Ming-Datu, Olongapo City 2010.

b) 12...♗h4 13 ♕d2 ♕e7 was tried in An.Rodriguez-Szmetan, Santiago 1999 and now I like 14 ♗f2, when White retains his positional trumps.

c) 12...♘b4 13 ♗b1 doesn't inconvenience White; for instance, 13...c6 14 ♕d2 d5 15 c5 ♘d7 16 a3 ♘a6 17 ♘f4 and Black had achieved little in D.Schuh-Kirkebo, Maastricht 2010.

d) 12...♗g5 (Bortnyk's subsequent attempt to improve over our main game) 13 ♗f2 d5 (13...♗e3?? loses material to 14 ♗xe3 ♖xe3 15 ♗e4 +− and the rook is trapped, as in Günnigmann-Haselhorst, Senden 2009) 14 c5 ♘c8 15 g4 ♗g6 16 f4 ♗xd3 17 ♕xd3 ♗h4 was Predke-Bortnyk, Moscow 2015 and now 18 ♕f3 would have retained control for White.

12 ♗e3 ♖e8 13 ♕d2 *(D)*

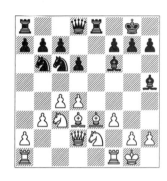

13...d5

13...♗g6 14 ♗e4!? (14 ♗xg6 hxg6 15 d5 is also pleasant for White) 14...a5 (White intends to meet ...♗xe4 with fxe4, when the f7-pawn will be weak) 15 ♘f4 ♗g5 16 ♖ae1 left White with a good game thanks to his space advantage, Arizmendi-Philippe, La Massana 2010.

14 c5 ♘c8 15 ♖ad1

White has a stable space advantage and the easier play in my view. Duda (one of the top juniors in the world) gives a good demonstration of White's trumps.

15...♗g6 16 ♗xg6 hxg6 17 g4 *(D)*

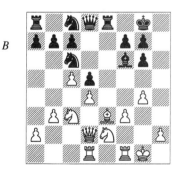

An interesting decision, gaining further space and taking control of the f5-square (anticipating ...♘8e7). Black correctly looks to the queenside for counterplay but subsequently goes wrong.

17...b6! 18 ♔g2 ♕d7 19 ♗f2 ♘d8

This might have been a good moment for Black to try to change the character of the position with 19...bxc5 20 dxc5 ♘8e7. His pieces remain a little passive but he has more counterplay here than in the game.

20 ♘f4 ♗g5? *(D)*

An understandable tactical error in a rapid game. 20...♘e7 is sounder, when White can continue his kingside expansion with 21 h4.

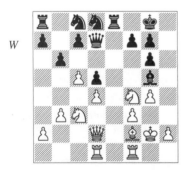

W

21 ♘cxd5!

2600-rated juniors aren't normally afraid of calculating sharp lines, and here Duda sees that he can grab a pawn and live to tell the tale.

21...c6 22 h4! ♗xh4

Black had to try 22...♗h6, but White is a pawn up for insufficient compensation after 23 ♘c3 ♗xf4 24 ♕xf4 ♘e6 25 ♕d2.

23 ♗xh4 +−

The attack down the h-file should be decisive, though Duda doesn't execute it with his characteristic precision (again, understandable in a rapid game).

23...cxd5 24 ♗xd8 ♖xd8 25 ♖h1 ♘e7 26 ♖h2 ♖ac8 27 ♖dh1?! f6 28 b4?

This gives Black a reprieve, though White ultimately goes on to win (presumably in a massive time-scramble).

The computer gives a complex win beginning with 28 ♖h7, but for our purposes we can cut our analysis short here.

28...bxc5 29 dxc5 g5 30 ♘h5 ♘g6 31 ♕d3 ♕f7 32 ♔f2 ♖e8? 33 ♘g3 ♘h4 34 ♘f5 d4 35 ♘xh4 ♕xa2+ 36 ♔g3 gxh4+ 37 ♖xh4 ♔f7 38 ♖h7 ♕d5? 39 ♖xg7+ ♔xg7 40 ♖h7+ ♔f8 41 ♕g6 ♖e3 42 ♕g7+ ♔e8 43 ♖h8+ 1-0

Game 41
Inarkiev – Brunner
European Clubs Cup, Eilat 2012

1 e4 ♘f6 2 e5 ♘d5 3 d4 d6 4 c4 ♘b6 5 exd6 cxd6 *(D)*

Until recent years this was clearly the most popular way to recapture. Black keeps options of counterplay (in particular, with a well-timed ...e5 break) but also takes on more risk than in the previous variation – for instance, after ...e5, dxe5 dxe5, White has a dangerous queenside majority and an outpost on d5.

6 ♘f3

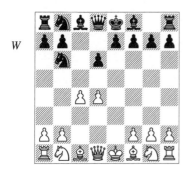

The main line here begins with ♘c3 and ♗e3, leading to complex positions with a lot more theory than I would like. However, I have seen a couple of strong GMs recently opting for quiet development of the kingside, and getting promising positions. This was an old favourite of Karpov and is worth investigation on that basis alone!

White can also start with 6 h3 if he is worried about the pin – this was the move-order used in Romanov-Shomoev (note to Black's 13th move).

6...g6 7 h3 ♗g7 8 ♗e2 0-0 9 0-0 ♗f5 10 ♘c3 ♘c6 11 ♗g5 *(D)*

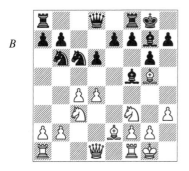

The last few moves have not required much explanation – both sides

have rapidly developed their pieces to the best squares. With the text-move White puts his bishop on a good square while targeting e7 and preventing the ...e5 break.

11...h6

Otherwise ♕d2 could follow, with prospects of ♗h6 and a kingside attack. Note how far Black's knights are from the defence of their king.

12 ♗e3 *(D)*

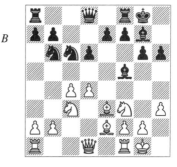

If Black now plays passively, White will build up his position with natural moves like ♕d2, ♖c1 and ♖e1, with excellent chances based on his imposing space advantage. Accordingly Black should break in the centre.

12...d5

The best move. Black's other standard pawn-break, 12...e5, is poor here on account of 13 d5 ♘e7 14 a4 ± with very promising play on the queenside for White.

13 b3 dxc4

Slower play with 13...e6 allows White to consolidate by means of 14 ♖c1; his space advantage must count for something. The following game (between two strong GMs) is an interesting example: 14...♗e4?! (14...g5 is a computer suggestion but I like White after 15 ♖e1; it is hard to see how Black can get meaningful counterplay when White has a space advantage and well-placed pieces) 15 ♘e5!? (changing the structure and emphasizing the insecure position of the bishop on e4) 15...♘xe5 16 dxe5 ♗xe5 17 ♘xe4 dxe4 18 ♗xh6 ± (White has the bishop-pair and a mobile queenside majority; his technique is impressive from here) 18...♖e8 19 ♕xd8 ♖exd8 20 ♖fd1 (of course the d-file, being the only open file in the position, is of paramount importance) 20...♘d7 21 ♗e3 b6 22 b4! (getting the pawn-majority rolling, with the support of two strong bishops) 22...f5 23 g3! (this is the major difference between the majorities: because of Black's doubled pawn – coupled with his less active pieces – it is harder to mobilize the kingside pawns) 23...♘f6 24 a4 ♔f7 25 a5 ♗c7 (25...bxa5 26 bxa5 would open lines on the queenside and expose the weakness on a7) 26 ♖xd8 ♗xd8 27 a6!? (there was nothing wrong with 27 ♖a1, but this is also a standard method: now Black must be constantly on the lookout for ♗xb6 followed by promoting the a-pawn) 27...♗e7 28 ♖b1 ♘d7 29 h4! (further reducing the effectiveness of Black's kingside majority) 29...♖c8 30 ♔f1 ♔e8? (this allows a well-masked tactical shot, but Black's position was unpleasant in any event) 31 c5! bxc5 (at first sight it seems better to return the king to f7, but 31...♔f7

32 ♗b5 is also instantly hopeless for Black) 32 ♗b5! +– (the pin will cost Black material) 32...e5 33 bxc5 f4 34 gxf4 exf4 35 ♖d1 1-0 E.Romanov-Shomoev, Vladivostok 2012.

14 bxc4 *(D)*

14...e5

The most dynamic approach, immediately trying to break up the hanging pawns. Black can also try plans based on getting his knight to c4, which always leads to counterplay, but I slightly prefer White in the resulting positions:

a) 14...♘a5 15 c5 ♘bc4 16 ♗f4 g5 17 ♗g3 ♕d7 18 ♖e1 b6 was played in Karpov-Neckař, World Junior Ch, Stockholm 1969, and now 19 ♖c1 would have given White a pleasant edge.

b) 14...♖c8 15 ♖c1 ♘a5 16 c5 ♘bc4 17 ♗f4 g5 18 ♗g3 *(D)* and now:

b1) 18...b6 led to quick equality after 19 ♗xc4 in Karpov-A.Petrosian, USSR Team Ch, Rostov-na-Donu 1971, but 19 ♘b5! is critical; for instance, 19...♕d7 20 ♘c7! e5 21 ♗xc4 ♘xc4 22 ♖xc4 ♖xc7 23 ♘xe5 with an

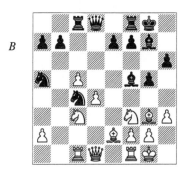

B

extra pawn, though Black has some compensation, including the bishop-pair.

b2) 18...♕d7 was played in Karpov-Vaganian, USSR Under-18 Ch playoff, Leningrad 1969. Here I like simple development with 19 ♖e1 ±.

15 ♘xe5

The untested 15 d5 might be better; for instance, 15...♘a5 16 c5 ♘bc4 (16...e4 17 ♘d4 ♘xd5 18 ♘xd5 ♕xd5 19 ♘xf5 ♕xf5 20 ♖b1 gives White excellent compensation for the pawn) 17 ♖c1 with an unclear game in which White's chances seem to be preferable.

15...♘xe5 16 dxe5 *(D)*

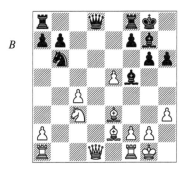

B

16...♕xd1?!

16...♗xe5, as in M.Sun-Bleau, Trois Rivières 2013 is probably a stronger move, leading to a better version of the game after 17 ♕xd8 (17 ♕b3 ♕h4 gives Black strong counterplay, with ...♗xh3 in the air) 17...♖fxd8 18 ♖ac1. If anything Black is to be preferred here, so White's alternative at move 15 is worth close consideration.

17 ♖fxd1 ♗xe5 18 ♖ac1 ♖fd8! *(D)*

Giving up a pawn for counterplay seems to be the best practical approach. 18...♔g7 19 c5 ± gives White a very strong initiative.

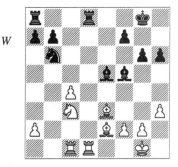

W

19 ♗xh6 ♖xd1+ 20 ♘xd1 ♖d8 ±

Black certainly has some compensation here, but in the game White manages to unravel. We have already seen enough for our purposes, especially in view of the proposed improvement on move 15.

21 ♔f1 ♘a4 22 c5 ♗e6 23 a3 ♗d4 24 c6 bxc6 25 ♖xc6 ♘b6 26 ♗e3 ♗xe3 27 ♘xe3 ♖d4 28 ♖c3 f5 29 ♖c6 ♗f7 30 ♗b5 ♔g7 31 ♖c7 f4 32 ♗e8 fxe3 33 ♖xf7+ ♔h6 34 fxe3 ♖e4 35 ♗c6 ♖e6 36 ♗f3 a5 37 ♔f2 ♖d6 38 ♖c7 ♘d7 39 ♖a7 1-0

Index of Variations

Numbers refer to pages.

1 e4
Now:
A: 1...d5
B: 1...c6
C: 1...e6
D: 1...e5
E: 1...c5

Other moves:
a) 1...♘c6 2 ♘f3 *150*
b) 1...♘f6 2 e5 ♘d5 3 d4 d6 4 c4
♘b6 5 exd6 (Chapter 8):
b1) 5...cxd6 *154*
b2) 5...exd6 *151*
c) 1...d6 2 d4 ♘f6 3 ♗d3 (Chapter 6):
c1) 3...g6 4 c3 ♗g7 5 ♘f3 *138*
c2) 3...e5 *134*
d) 1...g6 2 d4 (Chapter 6):
d1) 2...♘f6 3 ♗d3 *138*
d2) 2...♗g7 3 c3 *138*

A)

1...d5 2 exd5
(Chapter 7)
2...♕xd5
2...♘f6 *146*
3 ♘c3
Now:
3...♕d8 *144*
3...♕a5 *141*
3...♕d6 *144*

B)

1...c6 2 c4
(Chapter 4)
2...d5
2...e5 *113*
3 cxd5 cxd5 4 exd5 ♘f6 5 ♘c3
♘xd5
5...g6 *111*
6 ♘f3
Now:
6...e6 *11*
6...g6 *112*
6...♘xc3 7 bxc3 g6 *112*
6...♘c6 *109*

C)

1...e6 2 d4 d5 3 ♘d2
(Chapter 5)
3...c5
3...e5?! *130*
3...♘f6 4 ♗d3 c5 5 c3 – *see 3...c5 4*
c3 ♘f6 5 ♗d3
3...a6 *131*
3...h6 *131*
3...♗e7 *116*
3...♘c6 *130*
3...dxe4 4 ♘xe4 *126*
4 c3 ♘f6 5 ♗d3 cxd4 6 cxd4 dxe4 7
♘xe4
Now:
7...♗d7 *121*
7...♘xe4 8 ♗xe4 ♗b4+ *124*

You can read nearly 100 Gambit books on your tablet or phone, and you don't need a set or board – you can see all the positions and play all the moves just by tapping on the screen. It's like a chess book that has magically come to life.

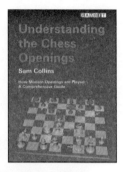

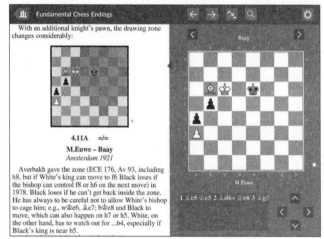